About the Author

John Phillips is a senior lecturer at the National University of
Singapore, where he lectures on Critical Theory, Literary Modern-
ism and Modern Culture. He was educated at the Universities of
North London and Sussex (where he did doctoral work). He has
edited a collection of essays on Melanie Klein (*Reading Melanie
Klein*, Routledge, 1998) and is the author of numerous articles on
Critical Theory, Modernity, Modernism and Postmodernism.

Contested Knowledge
A guide to critical theory

John Phillips

Zed Books Ltd
LONDON • NEW YORK

Contested Knowledge: A guide to critical theory was first published by
Zed Books, 7 Cynthia Street, London N1 9JF, UK and Room 400,
175 Fifth Avenue, New York, NY 10010, USA in 2000.

Distributed in the USA exclusively by St Martin's Press, Inc.,
175 Fifth Avenue, New York, NY 10010, USA

Cover designed by Andrew Corbett
Set in Monotype Ehrhardt and Univers by Ewan Smith, London
Printed and bound in the United Kingdom by Bookcraft, Midsomer
Norton.

A catalogue record for this book is available from the British Library.
US CIP data has been applied for from the Library of Congress.

ISBN 1 85649 872 2 cased
ISBN 1 85649 873 5 limp

Contents

How to Use This Book

This book is a guide to contemporary Critical Theory. To understand current writers the new reader must be aware of the arguments and issues that inform and provoke their thinking. Some of the problems and questions informing the most modern ideas reach across centuries and so will seem at first to be ancient and even a little alien (though that may be even more true of the most recent thought). The aim of this book is to outline some of the most pressing problems for contemporary thought by relating arguments from some of the most powerful of sources. It is divided into chapters, each of which may be read independently of the others, but which add up to a general introduction to the field. It is not a history of ideas and although earlier sections deal with ancient Greek philosophers, and later ones explore selected aspects of late twentieth-century thought, the earlier material is no less advanced than the later. If it is necessary to grasp some aspects of traditional philosophy in order to understand recent writers, it is these later writers who inform our readings of the earlier ones. For those who know the field, my discussions of Plato, Aristotle and Descartes may feel more recent than my discussions of Derrida and of psychoanalysis. Indeed, the book may be read with the chapters in different orders. So the discussions of authors, periods and topics are each time made from the point of view of their relevance to current concerns in Critical Theory. The main text provides arguments with examples and should be read in tandem with the primary texts that I discuss and with reference to current debates. The Bibliography gives an indication of where to continue more detailed research into specific areas. Because the arguments are the most important aspects of Critical Thought, I have selected a very particular path through the field. I could have chosen others. Of the more recent material I have chosen to focus on specific aspects in detail, particularly on deconstruction and the work of Jacques Derrida as well as certain aspects of psychoanalytic theory. This has allowed me to present what I believe to be the most critical aspects of current thought (or theory) and, in that sense, deconstruction acts as a kind of paradigm or example (though nothing so simple as an example will have been possible). This book is intended to foster an informed critical attitude to contemporary problems and, rather than simply provide the reader with a level of knowledge, aims to encourage readers to participate actively in the critical process.

■ 1 Introduction to Critical Theory ■

I Critical

> Our age is the age of criticism, to which everything must be subjected. The
> sacredness of religion, and the authority of legislation, are by many re-
> garded as grounds of exemption from the examination of this tribunal.
> But, if they own they are exempted, they become the subjects of just
> suspicion, and cannot lay claim to sincere respect, which reason accords
> only to that which has stood the test of a free and public examination.
> (Immanuel Kant, *The Critique of Pure Reason*)

This book is about a certain kind of writing that has emerged in recent years
with the force of an independent discipline, without ever taking on the status
that an independent discipline normally achieves. You may have heard of
some of the names involved, certainly the key historical references, such as
Marx, Nietzsche and Freud, perhaps even the more recent upstarts, like
Kristeva, Foucault and Derrida. On the other hand, you may not have heard
of these and you may have only a shadowy knowledge of what arguments
and influences they represent. You may have heard of certain developments
such as structuralism, deconstruction, postmodernism, and you probably have
a fairly good awareness of some of the issues that hide behind those words,
having seen many discussions and portrayals in books, films and on radio and
television.

You may, on the contrary, know quite a lot about Critical Theory, whether
or not you are or ever have been a student of the Humanities or Social
Sciences. This book does not presuppose any special knowledge of the subject,
just as the writer can have no special knowledge of his reader. For those with
little or no knowledge of Critical Theory, this book is designed as an introduction to and a guide through what is an intrinsically complex field dealing
with intrinsically complex issues. For those who have some knowledge, even
a lot of knowledge, about the field, the book will appear in the form of an
argument. In either case, it aims to provide something like a framework for

1

a field that in its most essential moments is concerned with questioning and adjusting frameworks.

In that case the book can best be described as a *critical* guide to Critical Theory. It emphasizes what is *critical* about the knowledge it presents. I will go on to explore these two key words, 'critical' and 'frameworks', in this Introduction. There are many books, for both general and specifically academic markets, that might easily be described as non-critical. What this means is that they present knowledge that does not require any complicated questions about its status or role as knowledge. Books that tell you how to develop certain skills and that provide an appropriate level of awareness require little more than clear presentations of methods and facts. For instance, successful organic gardening would require an awareness of the appropriate techniques and materials necessary for practising good gardening. And it would depend to an extent on knowing how to cultivate an ecosystem in tune with the seasons, how to produce fertilizers from natural waste and knowing about the cyclic nature of the soil's fertility. This knowledge can be given without a lot of philosophizing about the ethical preference for organic gardening over gardening that makes use of chemical pesticides. There are in fact many books on organic gardening that do present critical grounds for practising organic cultivation. The erosion of the global ecosystem, the massive escalation of the production of non-reusable waste, global warming and the consumption of the human spirit by vast systems of commodity capitalism are grounds enough, some feel, for turning away from modern techniques and developing a more ecology-friendly attitude to the Earth. Yet you wouldn't need to make those points if you were writing a manual on organic gardening. Think of your market (the publisher suggests); give them the skills and the knowledge they need, but don't bother them with distracting philosophizing. So with or without the critical awareness, the books on organic gardening can sit happily alongside the books on other types of gardening in your local bookshop or library. By the same token, your local supermarket will stock, alongside tomatoes labelled according to type, region and colour, a strain or two of organic tomato (generically asymmetric and a little unevenly coloured). The supermarket sells products that represent a mode of production that is essentially antithetical to the actual supermarket itself. But that does not threaten the supermarket. Committed vegetarians have their own section not far away from the meat.

This book is not about growing tomatoes. But I could have attempted to lay it out as if it was. I could have presented an overview of the names and the thought associated with them, a history of ideas within which ideas are produced and disseminated. I could have given short accounts with handy examples of the methods, variously, of structuralism, deconstruction, psycho-analytic theory, hermeneutics, stylistics and so on. While you will find this kind of knowledge embedded in the following pages, that is not the main concern of this book. The guiding concerns of this book are what certain German philosophers would once have called the 'grounding concepts' (*Grundebegriffe*). And rather than provide a framework through which you may understand the multiplicity of critical forces out there, I have drawn out a framework from what is consistently *critical* in what all these thinkers and writers do. *Contested Knowledge,* in other words, does not aim simply to provide knowledge and awareness of Critical Theory; rather, it is intended to draw attention to what *provokes* Critical Theory. You will not find an exposition of every important contemporary thinker in the field; rather, you will find a series of expositions of the basic problems that concern us when engaging both with the tradition out of which Critical Theory emerges and with contemporary thinkers too.

A *critical* preface to Critical Theory would be expected to examine the meaning of its terms in their intellectual context, just as a book on organic gardening would be expected to explain what is meant by 'organic' in the context of gardening. The word 'critical' involves a complex web of ideas so it is appropriate that we begin with an exposition of the term. Ordinary uses do not provide much of a clue. If I were to observe that the British electorate was critical of Harold Wilson's Cabinet during the 1960s, I'd be using the ordinary sense of the word 'critical', meaning 'inclined to criticize severely and unfavourably'. In fact, critics get a bad name for the way they are often too critical (in the ordinary sense) of artists, writers or film-producers. The word 'critic' comes from the Greek *kritikos,* which denotes the ability, or even licence, to discern or to judge. A critic is someone who expresses a reasoned opinion on any matter, especially involving a judgement of its value, truth, righteousness, beauty or technique. So in 1711 the poet Alexander Pope, in his *An Essay on Criticism,* was able to admonish the many critics of the time for their failure to take responsibility in their task:

> 'Tis hard to say, if greater Want of Skill
> Appear in *Writing* or in *Judging* ill;
> But, of the two, less dang'rous is th' Offence,
> To tire our *Patience,* than mis-lead our *Sense*:
> Some few in *that,* but Numbers err in *this,*
> Ten Censure wrong for one who Writes amiss;
> A *Fool* might once *himself* alone expose,
> Now *One* in *Verse* makes many more in *Prose.*

The opening lines point out that while it is difficult to say whether bad writing is worse than bad criticism, there is little doubt that bad criticism is more dangerous because it misleads us, whereas bad poetry is only going to irritate us. Furthermore, there are many more bad critics than there are bad poets. The *Essay* raises questions about responsibility in judgement and attempts to answer them with some prescriptions about the grounds for judging properly and responsibly:

> First follow NATURE, and your judgment frame
> By her just Standard, which is still the same:
> *Unerring Nature*, still divinely bright,
> One *clear*, *unchang'd*, and *Universal* Light,
> Life, Force, and Beauty, must to all impart,
> At once the *Source*, and *End*, and *Test* of *Art*.

Nature, which is another extremely complicated word, especially here – so don't take anything for granted – is to be understood as having the following attributes: it is just; it is unchanging; it is incapable of error; it is divine; it is bright; it is transparent; it is universal. It is from this Nature that art springs (its source) and gets its purpose (its end), so it is by Nature that the critic must judge it. The *Essay* presents a condensed version, as we will discover in chapters that follow, of the 'good' in Greek philosophy and the 'truth' in Christian theology. As such, the *predicates* of nature (the qualities Pope attributes to it) add up to a *metaphysics* in the grandest sense, given that it is hypothesized as being the source for all the best things in our experience of the world.

Pope's metaphysical notion of Nature asserts that the source (or the condition) of art remains invisible. We know it is there only because of its effects (beautiful pictures and poems, in analogy perhaps with beautiful natural phenomena such as mountains, lakes, flowers and trees). The real worry here is the plethora of bad critics (in analogy with an unjust world). The trouble is that taste, or good judgement, requires a certain art itself – it is not self-evident or simply given. So the art of criticism requires a developed sensibility that goes beyond mechanical means (as Pope goes on to argue in his poetic *Essay*). So against the everyday notion of criticism (an act of harsh judgement) the more refined notion is considerably more complex, involving serious questions about the nearly always unstable criteria for analysing, evaluating and appreciating works of art. Art thus signals a problem concerning unconditioned origins. The problem calls on, or provokes, theory (if not an all-out metaphysics).

In the most basic sense, then, Critical Theory would offer some principles upon which criticism might responsibly proceed. Pope's *Essay* can thus be regarded as a form of Critical Theory, with his particular reading of the concept of Nature playing a decisive role. Notice that it has to be a decision because Nature, in his conception, remains apart, withdrawn, from the 'effects' we come across as evidence for its existence. There are beautiful works, thus their source in a transcendent wellspring called art-in-general can be securely inferred. We ought to be able to see already that the responsibility of

Metaphysics

The prefix *meta-* (meaning 'on' or 'about') when added to the word *physics* denotes a realm of determination or conditioning. If I pay my taxes on time my behaviour may be determined by a number of things. They would include the laws laid down by my government as well as my desire to obey the laws, which may perhaps also be conditioned by my belief that the taxes will be used for the benefit of my society (i.e. paying nurses, removing my rubbish and so on). Each of these conditions itself has a number of conditions that can be said to determine it, such as my government's desire to stay in power or the smell and discomfort that is caused when the council workers or nurses go on strike for better pay. All of the conditions above can be grasped as effects in the conditioned world. There is nothing there that we would say was *unconditioned*. They therefore come within the realm of observable and explicable phenomena, and can be examined within one of the disciplines set up to examine these things, such as physics (and the 'natural' sciences), individual ethics and politics. *Metaphysics*, traditionally and since the Greeks, who invented the word, sets out to examine what lies beyond, above and upon, the observable conditions in the world. The key notion is *the unconditioned*, which applies to supposedly timeless abstract concepts like virtue, truth, good and, the metaphysical concept *par excellence*, Deus or God. The twist here, as we shall repeatedly discover, is that because the highest concept, the first condition, denotes a power that lies beyond and above the observable world of conditioned beings, it must remain unobserved and, thus, mysterious. The notion of an unconditioned first cause maps over on to most notions of a singular god. We could choose to ignore it (after all, I know why I pay my council tax, don't I?) but we will find that there needs an explanation for the existence of theological thinking too. Much of Critical Theory proceeds from this problem.

judgement can rely on nothing but its own resources – responsibility and judgement – in order to arrive at the decisions that constitute criticism. When standing in the National Gallery gazing at the work of one of the respected great masters, such as John Constable's *The Hay-Wain*, on what grounds can we make an appreciation of it? The fact that it is housed in a major institution for displaying great artworks perhaps says something about its greatness. But does that fact alone determine our experience of its grandeur? It might do. Then our decisions are already to a large extent made for us, by historical art institutions and established criticism. Does the professional curator's judgement, then, guarantee all our tastes? Art history has proven that anybody's judgement may be called in to question, no matter how much institutional authority they have been granted. Yet, on the other hand, we do find that we like, even love, without clear criteria, certain artistic forms – though not necessarily generally accepted ones. What is it about Megadeath's latest album? What is that *je ne sais quoi* that makes us love them so much we beat

---

Man

Up until the mid-1960s the generic name for the human race was always 'Man'. Two developments in critical thinking have called this name into question and so it is rarely used now. A famous international conference in Paris, France, titled 'The Ends of Man' featured a number of thinkers who are considered to be instrumental in contemporary Critical Theory, including Michel Foucault and Jacques Derrida. In drawing attention, in various ways, to the historical perspective in the use of a supposedly general term, thinkers like these have loosened its generality and it is now seen as an historical index of attitudes. The title of the conference plays on the word 'end', which can mean to finish, even to die out as in 'come to an end'. Or, as a noun, an end can be a purpose. So the reasons for learning (the *ends* of learning) can be variously considered by students as (1) a qualification, (2) increased knowledge and (3) better ability to respond to complex situations. Most students would not assume that the end of learning (that is, its reason) was at the same time the end of learning (that is, bringing learning to a full stop so that no more learning goes on). But the history of modernity does seem to involve a paradoxical formulation such that the end of man is the end of man. Man's purpose is to finish himself off. The most radical voices

our heads against the PA system until our ears bleed? Where does our appreci-ation come from? At what point can we say that our individual judgements constitute responsible *criticism*?

The word 'criticism' comes from a Greek word (as do so many of the words we use), *krinein*, meaning 'to decide'. And it does look as if the work of criticism requires some form of decision. If I think Constable's *Hay-Wain* is a magnificent work of art, I have made a decision. Or I might have done. The curator, of course, might have already made it for me, so in this case I don't *have* to decide. Everyone knows it is great. It is in the National Gallery, not to mention adorning the walls of countless semi-detached living rooms and chocolate boxes, endlessly and cheaply reproduced for sale in markets and department stores. When people say, 'I don't know much about art but I know what I like,' they often turn out to have the same taste as millions of others. How do you decide to like something? One answer would be to say that beauty, in its most refined sense, is something objective, inherent in

suggest that he has practically succeeded. Good old man (whoever *he* is). The other development, perhaps easier to focus, has been the various critiques understood collectively as feminism. The critique of *man* follows both a linguistic and ideological path. Language and ideology can be seen as mutually supporting systems, such that the language we use more or less supports the most fundamental attitudes we adopt when interpreting our experience of the world. Feminism involves a powerful critique of what we call *patriarchy*, in which a system of social relations that privileges the masculine as opposed to the feminine is supported by habitual patterns of language use (e.g. the generic use of Man for the human race). However, the critique turns out to be yet more powerful, for in dissolving the comfortable reliance upon a universal term to cover a universal being it puts into suspense, by extension, the concept of the *human* and all the meta-physical qualities that are attached to it as its predicates. Metaphysical notions like truth, goodness and nature have often been associated with the special domain isolated as the human (e.g. in the phrase 'human nature'). Much Critical Theory involves breaking down deeply held assumptions associated with an uncritical *humanism*, which was especially prevalent throughout the nineteenth and the first half of the twentieth centuries.

beautiful objects like trees and artworks. This would be an attempt at a metaphysical explanation. Metaphysics requires a range of abstract concepts that cannot ever be experienced *as such*, but must somehow be deduced from the evidence of experience. So because there are beautiful things there must be the eternal quality that informs things with greater or lesser amounts of beauty. However, against this, as the phrase 'beauty is in the eye of the beholder' suggests, people have noticed that there is little agreement, certainly nothing of a universal kind, about what beauty is.

Perhaps what we like or what we find beautiful says more about us than the thing perceived. Another way of saying this is that beauty is *subjective*. It is a wonderfully reassuring thought for those who come to being in what we now call the modern world, or *modernity*. Modernity, as I will explain in Chapter 2, roughly outlines a broad historical process and a set of fundamental attitudes that help to structure specific kinds of interpretations of the world. Most decisively (there's that word again), modernity involves a tension, sometimes even a contradiction, whereby the emphasis on *observation* and scientific models of research is compensated for by the relegation of subjective experience to the realm of *aesthetics*. The contradiction roughly marks out the separation of experience into objective and subjective realms. So science is objective and aesthetic experience is subjective. Why is this separation reassuring? Historically, science tends to discredit explanations derived from religions and mythologies, with a corresponding de-centring of the place of mankind in the universe. If it was once thought that man on earth was the single most important creation of an eternal and infinite god, scientific knowledge provides strong evidence against this belief. The lack of grounds for criticism, then, or at least the apparent lack of universal grounds for judging aesthetic experience, provides some compensation for the objectification of the world in the subjectification of the person. A person can now be thought of as an independent, free-thinking individual, unique in himself (and later herself) and distinguished from others. Modernity thus implies the individuation of the members of the collective called *Man*.

So the human *subject* turns out to be yet another metaphysical repository for values that we have inherited historically, as modern subjects. And the *subjectivity* of the subject is finally guaranteed only by freedom of decision, and thus exemplified in aesthetic judgement. However, so long as this subjectivity remains bounded within fields of aesthetic experience, the hope remains that other dimensions can be brought under the governance of the ever more powerful resource called *objective judgement*. The physical sciences are modernity's great paradigms for the power of objectivity. But the ideals of objectivity have never been fully realized in the fields that deal with actions and relations (ethics and politics). It seems that wherever objective criteria are not available a decision of some kind is called for. Decisions must be made, whether in the field of ethics or in politics. Should I visit my parents for Christmas and make the family happy or should I stay at home and work, thus pleasing my university? Should we tax the rich, thus incurring their wrath, or should we continue to tax the poor, maintaining our wealth and continuing their wretched state? The easiest decisions are the ones that meet with least resistance. What this normally means is that they are not decisions at all but forms of acquiescence to established norms and expectations. If only I could use the certainty I have about the beauty of the new Megadeath CD to help me decide what to do for Christmas (hey! does anyone know if they are playing at Christmas?). Critical evaluation, because it is so much a question of taste, offers perhaps some hope that an equivalent mode of judgement might be used in domains other than the aesthetic. But why do we need this hope? The answer rests with yet another derivation from this powerful Greek word, *krinein*, that is *crisis*.

Crisis It is still fairly common to observe that we (whoever that is supposed to be) live in a time of great social and cultural change. The observation is undoubtedly correct but there are few moments in the long evolution of the human race when anxieties about rapid change have not been voiced. We would thus take most interest in the nature of the specific changes and what they mean for the future. Phrases of the kind 'the present crisis' indicate that something has gone badly wrong. After 1933, with the rise of Adolf Hitler and the National Socialist party in Germany, politicians and journalists throughout Europe and America regularly used the phrase 'the present crisis'. Everyone knew what it meant. Everyone feared for the future; many referred to 'this dark time', or 'in these dark days'. Their fears were justified of course – beyond their worst imaginings – but it seems that conditions of crisis are nearly always at the point of threatening any community with an uncertain and fearful future. Memories of those 'dark days' still live, vicariously in the generation born after the so-called Second World War but actually for those that lived through it and live on with specific memories of the time, as its survivors. The name 'Hitler' often gets used as a kind of moral touchstone in debates and arguments about ethics, power and politics. And names like Auschwitz, Nagasaki and Dresden have the power, like so much of the past, to haunt us with dark premonitions of the future. The point here is that a crisis doesn't just come to us like a rent, a great rip, in the otherwise solid fabric of the present, but it dogs us like some tenacious ghostly embodiment of someone long dead but who refuses to go away. There seems never to have been a time without crisis or at least the threat of crisis. It is worth noticing, then, that even without the negative connotations attached to the term when we think of Hitler and National Socialism, crisis is almost always associated with rapid social and cultural change. Distressing events may happen such that names can then be given to what may actually be more like a permanent principle of existence. In fact, the rise of National Socialism, according to a most complex history, can be partly attributed to a certain way of identifying and responding to the so-called National Crisis that Germany faced in the early 1930s, which manifested in widespread social and economic disaster. Hitler's party was able to exploit a number of scapegoats as a way of claiming certain causes – most notoriously, and with horrifying consequences, Judaism and Jewish business interests, but also communism and what at the time was called 'degenerate' culture, which included, by no coincidence, the works of the radical avant-garde.

So rather than see the rise and popularity of National Socialism as itself the embodiment of a crisis, it may be more accurate to see it is a response to crisis generally. In the early years of the Third Reich many Germans were filled with optimism for a future imagined in contrast to a wretched recent past. In so far as crisis refers to a situation that causes anxiety, it may be that there is no situation without at least a little cause for anxiety, though people are perhaps happier when they don't have to think too much about things that make them anxious. So anything that promises to remove a cause of anxiety may in certain circumstances achieve success and popularity. That is one reason why self-help books are so popular.

There are many kinds of crisis in the sense I'm teasing out here. I don't just mean major kinds that seem to affect whole swathes of the globe's population (exaggerated in fictions like *Star Wars* as the universe oppressed by an evil empire). The Asian economic downturn, the great depression, global warming, can each be thought of as a major crisis. We must also consider the apparently more minor kinds, personal crises, which each of us has to face from time to time. Among the earliest of these may be that first moment when a hungry baby finds the mother absent, when hunger is met by the absence of a sustenance that had never before been an issue. The trauma and panic accompanied by this discomfort are perhaps echoed by later incidents where expectations are dashed, needs not supplied and desires not fulfilled. Society often codifies, even naturalizes, our anxieties by naming them and giving them likely stages of onset, such as personality crisis or mid-life crisis.

It is clear that coping strategies, both in individuals and groups, are extremely cunning and complex, but nearly always involve an adjustment to what we might call *frameworks*. Frameworks are constituted by habits of thought and action, the ways, and indeed the styles, we adopt in order to be confident and more or less secure in our relation to the world and to others. However, these frameworks in fact constitute what we see as the world and the way we see 'others' too. So there is nothing, strictly speaking, in our experience that is accessible outside these frameworks. Crisis tends to threaten whatever frameworks prevail at any time, frameworks that are erected to deal with crisis in the first place. When someone or something appears outside the frameworks of expectation and experience, the frameworks may be altered to accommodate their ghostly or uncanny form. There are those who are unwilling to change, of course. The adjective 'conservative' describes this attitude, in which security and a certain level of consolation are guaranteed only to the extent that negative judgements can be made about change, about difference and about other ways of interpreting things. Negative judgements ('I don't think much of these new-fangled computers' or 'They don't write songs as well as they used to') can sometimes conceal conservative coping strategies. However, the enthusiastic embracing of 'the new' can also often be seen as a coping strategy on the part of the dedicated follower of fashion. In this case, negative judgements are directed towards tradition, towards the past as a way of affirming the modern. For this attitude, just as rigid a framework is in operation as for the conservative one. Both attempt to hold on to the transient fixity of a present. And neither is able to adjust to the situations that constantly arise, that instantiate the trace of a past as it progresses into an unpredictable future. A critical perspective would be one capable of making room for the new while acknowledging its debts to a history and a past whose ghosts refuse to depart. The new thus appears as a changed version of the old, a little like history, with some of the changes being surprising if not downright shocking.

Critique One common complaint made today is that there is a crisis in knowledge. But it seems that, whenever *knowledge* attempts to establish itself in the field of human experience, it faces crisis. The key source for today's use of the term Critical Theory is the work of the German eighteenth-century philosopher Immanuel Kant. Kant uses the word 'critical' to describe his mature philosophy. The three main texts that make up the critical philosophy answer broadly to three pressing questions. The first is the question of what we can know (epistemology) and is treated by *The Critique of Pure Reason* (*The First Critique*). *The Second Critique* makes up the so-called practical philosophy, dealing with questions of morality and ethics (what should we do?). *The Third Critique*, embodied by the extraordinary *Critique of Judgement*, was intended by Kant to bring his 'entire undertaking to a close'. If the first critique deals with knowledge (what can be known as necessarily the case – the necessary laws of nature) and the second critique deals with the freedom of human action, the *Critique of Judgement* was supposed to reconcile the two otherwise opposed realms (nature and freedom). Tellingly, the third critique is focused on questions of pleasure and judgements of taste contrasted to the kinds of judgements that can be called objective. It would be impossible to overestimate the importance of the third critique for the critical tradition since Kant, though this is not the place to explore it.

The quotation that begins this chapter comes from the preface to the *First Critique*. Let's have another look:

> Our age is the age of criticism, to which everything must be subjected. The sacredness of religion, and the authority of legislation, are by many regarded as grounds of exemption from the examination of this tribunal. But, if they own they are exempted, they become the subjects of just suspicion, and cannot lay claim to sincere respect, which reason accords only to that which has stood the test of a free and public examination.

Criticism *puts* all grounds for knowledge into crisis. Even religious authority and state law must be tried in the law courts of reason. Readers of Kant quickly note how important the metaphor of law, and legality, is for him. Accordingly, the word 'reason' is to be understood as a kind of law. In this sense it is not unlike the concept of 'nature' as we found it used in Alexander Pope's poetic *Essay on Criticism* (and it is not by chance that Pope was one of Kant's favourite poets). Notice how he puts it: by submitting to the tribunal, even state law and religious authority can win their right to sincere respect and may then be free of suspicion. It is a positive action – as long as these authorities pass the test. The gesture is designed as an attempt to save traditional authority but will also put the notion of authority into the gravest danger.

Kant's preface evokes the *warlike* state that knowledge finds itself in. He tells a story full of violence about the battle for the right to legislate over the relationship between experience and knowledge. At the centre of the battle-field, he says, is a queen named *Metaphysics*:

> In the beginning, under the administration of the *dogmatists*, her rule was *despotic*. Yet because her legislation still retained traces of ancient barbarism, this rule gradually degenerated through internal wars into complete *anarchy*; and the skeptics, a kind of nomads who abhor all permanent cultivation of the soil, shattered civil unity from time to time. But since there were only a few of them, they could not prevent the dogmatists from continuously attempting to rebuild, though never according to a plan unanimously accepted among themselves. (Kant 1998: 100)

There is much at stake for Kant in this graphic account of the history of philosophy. The antagonism and the lack of legal authority for knowledge suggest both a crisis and the promise of its resolution. The story is now a canonical history of ideas. It tells of a century-long battle between rationalists such as Christian Wolff and empiricists such as John Locke. For Kant, neither had been able to defend metaphysics from the nomadic (homeless) terror of David Hume's scepticism. The critical philosophy of Immanuel Kant thus steps in to clear the domain. In short, there are two main claims about know-ledge in struggle with each other. Very simply, but we'll come back to this point in other chapters, knowledge is either determined empirically, that is, through experience, or it is determined rationally, by virtue of human faculties of understanding and through logic. The rationalist view is what Kant calls 'dogmatism', and it refers us to the fact that the metaphysical assumptions of rationalism had never been tested and were, therefore, vulnerable to sceptical attack. The strong, sceptical, position of David Hume refutes any knowledge that is not precisely grounded in experience, including logic. So Kant's project is one that should save metaphysics from powerful sceptical attack. The critical project, in other words, sets out to establish irrefutable grounds for philosophy by subjecting all its existing grounds to the most rigorous and painstaking questioning. But, unlike the sceptical tendency, the critical project aims to establish the grounds it is questioning.

The main issue rests on the status of *Reason*, given that the aim of estab-lishing a critical tribunal implies a position of judgement that remains free of suspicion. For this reason *The Critique of Pure Reason* must establish the grounds of reason through reason alone, and we see reason turning back on itself in a pattern that comes to inform the critical attitude since Kant. However, Kant has been criticized for insufficiently putting this self-critical approach into operation. We thus find some of the most powerful influences on critical theory supporting what is truly critical in Kant's philosophy while expressing scepticism regarding the residually dogmatic aspects. Most famously, G. W. F. Hegel shows that there is no available position from which something like reason can criticize itself. Later on, Karl Marx followed Hegel in his dialectical thinking, but criticized him too for idealizing his own concept, *Geist* (or spirit) without sufficient self-criticism. In Marx's own phrase, it is necessary to extract the 'rational kernel' from the 'mystical shell' of Hegel's philosophy. Perhaps somewhat surprisingly, several brands of Marxist, or Marxian, thought often fail to maintain a critical attitude to the writings of Marx, who, as it has been argued, also falls prey to certain lapses that can yield to dogmatic ideas. Friedrich Nietzsche too, whose influence on critical thought is difficult to overestimate, was highly sceptical of Kant's attempt to establish the tribunal of reason. And during the twentieth century, critique became synonymous with a constant critical vigilance such that thought should never be allowed to ossify into dogmatic presentations of ideas, as if fixed in place for all time.

Critical Theory   The phrase 'Critical Theory' was adopted most famously by a group of philosophers now known as the Frankfurt School, and is associated particularly with two major twentieth-century thinkers, Walter Benjamin and Theodor Adorno. Writing from the 1920s, their work represents a vital contribution to the field. Benjamin (who died by his own hand at the border of France and Spain while fleeing from the Nazis) leaves a large number of extraordinary texts that are often difficult to categorize. Adorno emigrated from Germany to the United States and with his colleague Max Horkheimer contributed significantly to the theorization of modernity, technology and mass culture. Most importantly, his critical rethinking of the notion of the aesthetic (and thus the place of the artwork) since Kant has become increasingly more relevant.

Postmodernism and Critical Theory   A number of contemporary thinkers have contributed to the problem of knowledge – what guarantees its truth, its rightness, its importance, and so on. Two in particular have been influential, the French philosopher Jean-François Lyotard and the sociologist

---

Four Stages of Simulation

1. The image reflects reality (a naturalist painting such as Constable's *The Hay-Wain*).

2. The image 'masks and perverts a basic reality'. The post-impressionist paintings of the nineteenth century draw attention to the *way* of seeing as a *style* rather than to the objectivity of representation. The way of seeing masks what is seen by perverting it.

3. The image 'masks the absence of a basic reality'. This stage probably corresponds to the modernist period in art, where faith in the possibility of any actual objective reality falls to an all-time low. The image seems not to represent at all, rather it *produces* what it makes visible, like the paintings of Paul Klee or Pablo Picasso.

4. The image (in its manifestation in postmodernity) 'bears no relation to any reality whatsoever'. Watch a TV ad. Is there anything that could honestly be called a 'basic reality' represented there?

of knowledge Jean Baudrillard. Lyotard's 1983 book *The Postmodern Condition* argues that ideas about civilization, human progress and the ideals of liberation are rooted in assumptions that take the form of what he calls *Grand Narratives*. A narrative is a story, like a fairy tale or popular myth. In the western world, assumptions about the progress and virtual completion of the human race through technology and civilization are no longer credible. Totalitarian regimes that attempt universal control and the extermination of all outsiders (most markedly the Holocaust of the Nazi regime under Hitler) can be compared with regimes in knowledge that aspire to universal truth. Such systems tend to manifest impulses like the annexation, containment, expulsion or extermination of any knowledge that lies outside or contests the norm. Thus, the allegorical evocation of mystery and death we find in literature and art, especially in the avant-garde, can be contained in an enclosure called 'the aesthetic' where it is valued for its strange beauty in a way that does not threaten the bland and complacent promise of technological knowledge. 'Let us wage war on totality,' writes Lyotard, in a famous battle cry of postmodern theory, echoing, of all people, Winston Churchill, standing alone against appeasement and the Nazis.

The work of Jean Baudrillard focuses on the role of the image in the mass media and he joins others in seeing at the end of the twentieth century a culmination of the logic of capitalism in consumer society. He suggests that in the past humanity was able to make a sure distinction between a 'real world' and its forms of representation in books, paintings and other signs. But now signs have become detached from their function of representing a world and have instead *become* the postmodern world of floating images and *simulacra*, that is, copies with no originals.

Baudrillard's arguments have contributed to the way we understand the status of a certain notion of reality or the real in contemporary life (i.e. it is a mythical object that has disappeared). But it may be that he is in danger of letting us fall into a mythical notion of the past. Human experience was always a construction and a function of institutions organized in complex ways. Certainly the mass media constitute a profound (and profoundly new) way of organizing experience. But it seems that ways of organizing were always governed to an extent by modes of signification, interpretation and institutionalization. The following section is intended to explore these modes in a preliminary way.

II Representations

Books and Life

> Some say you can learn a lot from books
> Thrill ride to second-hand living
> Life is just as deadly as it looks
> But fiction is more forgiving
>
> (Richard Thompson)

The lyrics above repeat a distinction that has become so commonplace over centuries that it seems fundamental. But the distinction between books and actual life takes such an extraordinary range of different forms that just thinking about it too much can make us dizzy. The distinction changes each time we consider one of the many different kinds of book. History books relate to life in ways differing from those of fairy tales or works of fiction. The Bible and the Koran relate to life rather differently too. A biography would be at least subtly if not markedly different from an autobiography, especially if they each relate the 'same' life. The workshop manual for my Citroën Avantage relates to life in an entirely different way again.

Perhaps it is a little worrying that these distinctions also imply differences in meaning for the word 'life'. The life of a man or woman who is the subject of a biography or autobiography is not exactly what is meant by life as recorded in history books. The relation between my workshop manual and my car is one of book to life too but does that mean my car lives? Why not? When I finally junk it for the obligatory £25 scrap value, I'll probably tell my friends that it died. I am using a metaphor, of course. The difference between fiction, which is often dense with metaphors, and real life implies a rather different meaning of the word life as well – though none of these meanings is unrelated. It is possible to speak of life generally, the life of nations, villages, communities as well as animal and plant life or the life of the planets in the universe, and to speak of a particular life, the life of a man or a woman like Napoleon, George Bush or Madonna. Perhaps, a little oddly, it is easier to talk of a particular life when it is over, when its subject is dead. With a living person the life is felt to be unfinished, it is yet to be fully determined. The same might be assumed for history too – it is surely easier to write a history once the period in question is over and done with. The implicit association of death with writing seems almost as fundamental as the distinction between books and life. Despite this, as far as history, biography and autobiography especially are concerned, the eyewitness account is valued above second- or third-hand accounts, as being that much 'truer' to life. The value, of course, remains idealistic, for the eyewitness is well known to be chronically vulnerable to lapses of memory, mistakes, misperceptions, skewed perspectives, projections and unnoticed assumptions and presuppositions. So we always require a more objective and thus removed commentator to sift through the welter of conflicting evidences. That's life.

If our perspectives on life are as unstable as they so often seem to be, then a similar condition holds for our varying perspectives on books. When I read the Bible I read a very different text to the one that is read by the Jehovah's Witnesses who knock on my door at 11.00 on a Friday morning (just in time for coffee) to tell me 'the good news'. For them the Bible is the revealed truth; for me it is a complex, often contradictory, text with a peculiar historical status. So a book relates to life in different ways depending upon who reads it, as much as anything else. That is, *between* the book and the life lies a complex if only ever partially perceptible realm in which a number of structuring principles and conditions combine to organize our experiences and actions generally. These principles and conditions include memories, histories, desires, other books that have had an influence (of whatever kind), as well as, most importantly, the variety of institutions that govern both readings and lives. By *institution* we should understand, family, school, church, university, workplace, village, town, city, nation, and also the genres we put books into, the expectations we bring to them, the functions we assume they play and the ways in which we assume they relate to life. That is, a kind of book, whether theology, history, fairy tale, poetry, biography, fiction or philosophy (and there are many missing from the list) is thought to serve some function for the people who read it. It might be entertainment, edification, identification, consolation or instruction. Whatever, this function concerns the ways in which the book in question relates to life. The function is often that of teaching; the book is supposed to provide the reader with some knowledge or understanding that he or she did not have before, about history if it is a history book or about someone's life if it is a biography, or about how to fix that darned carburettor if my car won't start in the morning. The Bible, if you are a Christian child, contains knowledge of the one God and tells you how to act. Because this knowledge is only obscurely accessible from the text itself, a whole industry of (sometimes conflicting) commentaries exists to tell you how to understand it. In each case, a single notion explicitly or implicitly governs the sense of value we generally have regarding the book in question. That notion is called *truth*.

Truth   The institutions we discussed above also govern the meaning of the word truth. The Latin *adaequatio* captures the notion rather well. It means a making equal, an adjusting or adapting. It is this notion of truth – adapting or adjusting something to make it equal to something else – that comes to dominate western notions. You can see how this works with history and biography. Is the account adequate to the life? That is the key criterion. If there were a false account of the Citroën Avantage carburettor in my workshop manual I'd never get to work in the morning. With the Bible, on the other hand, things are rather tricky. If the account is measured against something existing we are all at sea. Many (like my Friday morning visitors) none the less assume that some truth is there behind the text. But let's have another look at the word 'truth'. Where does it come from and what else might it mean?

When you define a word as important and as powerful as 'truth' it is never enough simply to look it up in a dictionary. It is often helpful to look for its etymology. An etymology is the history of a linguistic form (i.e. a word) which can be shown by tracing its development since its earliest recorded occurrence in the language where it is found, or by tracing its transmission from one language to another, by analysing it into its component parts, by identifying its cognates in other languages, or by tracing it and its cognates to a common ancestral form in an ancestral language. By applying this deep form of analysis, we are already departing from the 'making equal' notion of truth, which would have had to assume that the true meaning of a word is what it is equal to. Rather, in this way, we are likely to open the meaning of a word to a wider range of possibilities.

The word 'truth' seems to have developed from the Middle English *trewthe*, which is a development of the Old English *treowth*. *Treowth* meant something like 'fidelity' and it is clearly akin to the Old English *treowe*, which meant faithful. Because the word meant fidelity and was used to describe a character – i.e. someone who could be trusted to remain constant in their loyalty and, by extension, someone who was sincere – it also comes to mean what we understand by it today, that is, the state of 'being the case'. The words 'fact' and 'actuality' refer us to the body of real things and events. These things and events that make up what we call actuality (or, more colloquially, 'life') become the measure of truth in its new sense – does your account fit the facts? If so, then it is true. This kind of truth, in so far as it can be tested, would be considered as *empirical* truth, the truth of experience. Truth, however, with a capital T would be a *transcendent* fundamental or spiritual reality. A reality that is transcendent cannot be tested by experience (rather obviously) so it becomes rather difficult to provide proof of it in the sense that is demanded by *adaequatio* (making equal). However, it is not difficult to see that if *adaequatio* is just 'truth' then you don't need to prove *The* Truth, which gets another name: God. God, then, by association with Truth, is the name for that which allows us to make things equal (like books to life); though this 'making equal' is going to get very complicated.

If we go back to the etymology briefly we find some further links (this is like following a 'clew' in an old mystery). The Old English *treowe* (faithful) is directly linked to the Old High German *gitriuwida,* also faithful, the Old Irish *derb*, meaning sure, and very probably to the Sanskrit *daruna,* which means hard, from *daru* for wood. What is certain is that the words *true* and *tree* share their early etymologies. So if to be true is to be steadfast, loyal, honest, even *just* in certain contexts, and rather centrally to be consistent (as in 'he's true to character'), then this is probably on the analogy with the deep roots and the firm trunk of those tall woody arboreal plants called trees. How true is true to tree?

Our answer to that would concern the kinds of meanings that the words true and truth are used in place of when translating from Greek and Latin. We've already looked at *adaequatio,* 'to make equal', but we also find that 'truth' can be used in relation to the odd word *allegoria,* allegory, that is, a figurative representation of a thought or of an abstract truth (literally 'to mean something other than what is said'). An allegory uses symbolism or imagery in a way that consistently, or cumulatively, carries what is symbolized through from beginning to end in a speech, or a poem or story. The notion of constancy or consistency is helpful here, of course, but I'm not sure the *adaequatio* aspect is sufficient to account for truth in the allegorical sense. The word *verum,* on the other hand, which means true in the sense of real, actual, genuine and is therefore opposed to *falsus,* false, seems closer to our sense of *adaequatio.* However, *verum* is also conventionally opposed to *fictus,* which means feigned, false or counterfeit and is derived from *fingo,* meaning to mould, imagine, compose, suppose, form, shape, invent, contrive. Not only is it impossible to imagine a fictional truth (as in 'that story seems very true to life') or figurative representation without this *fingo,* but also the very possibility of adapting something like a narrative or an account or adjusting it so that it is 'made equal' to the facts would disappear too. There would be no *adaequatio* without the possibility of *fingo.* There would be no truth without the possibility of fiction.

My conclusion to that little diversion into etymology implies that the meaning of the word truth (and the institutions that govern it) hides the fact that it is based upon a notion (*fingo,* the figure of the counterfeiter) that is radically excluded from the meaning. The meaning of the word truth, in its hidden historical dimension, is a lie (on its own terms). This doesn't, of course, mean that ordinary senses of the word 'true' are no longer usable for people like me. On the contrary, if my workshop manual is not adequate in its representation of the carburettor in my Citroën then I won't get to work this morning and I'll be serving coffee again to the Jehovah's Witnesses, while they attempt to convert me from my stubborn atheism. Rather, I now understand that the very possibility of constructing a workshop manual in the first place – apparently stripped of all fictional or figurative aspects as an ideal historian might aspire to do with his or her account of history – is the possibility of fiction.

If we now return to the lyrics with which we began this section, we find some characteristics attached to our opposed categories, *books* and *life*. To 'learn a lot from books' is qualified by the line, 'Thrill ride to second-hand living'. Books are, thus, life at one remove, a second-hand as opposed to first-hand life. If I read the life of Napoleon or Madonna, I live their lives second hand in some simulated form. If I read about the Battle of the Somme I couldn't say I was actually there at the battle. In the same way, if I read about some fictional character, Raymond Chandler's Philip Marlowe as he pursues the answer to some mystery set in the mean streets of 1920s Los Angeles, I am living a life second hand, but it is a second-hand life that was never lived first hand. There is something *intrinsically* second hand about books, whether they emulate a first-hand life or just evoke a fictional one. Fiction, we learn in the fourth line of the quotation, is 'more forgiving' than 'life', which is described (with characteristic relish) as 'deadly'. There's no doubt about this, of course, life is, at its most basic and essential level, deadly. The truest (most consistent) aspect of life is that it comes to an end, usually unpredictably. It is unforgiving in that sense. It is also unforgiving in another sense; in the sense that it never gives up on throwing unexpected contingencies under our feet – I mean, how was I to know that the carburettor would fail this morning, and now this knock on the door? – life consistently excludes our attempts to calculate it. Fiction, on the other hand, can be remarkably comforting in its well-formed and consoling patterns, its tidy oppositions and structural consistency. We judge our allegorical reading not by its *adaequatio* to actual life, which let's face it can be a mess, but by its internal consistency. Fiction can give us the sense that there are laws and rules to the game, while in actual life events and organizations seem arbitrary and often unfair. Like fiction, history, philosophy, theology and other types of book that attempt to address the absence of system and order in life do so by supplying one where it is *actually* lacking. Even discourses that adhere to the narrowest (strictest and thus most true) criteria of *adaequatio*, the empirical sciences, do so at the cost of considerable exclusion. An empirical science must deal only with what is possible and actual and must do so in a way that produces maximal predictability. These criteria provide a very powerful resource in the development of knowledge but the cost has been a vast blindness to the conditions that make such resources possible. Until scientific theory can cope with a wider and less stable notion of truth, until knowledge can build unpredictability into its under-standing of existence and knowledge, it will remain blind to its own conditions. The only way forward is one that can engage seriously with what has always been regarded as the *second-hand* nature of *books* (regarded as a particular example of representation generally) in relation to *life*. It is easy to see that life too tends to be governed to a very large extent by structures – governments, families, schools and other institutions that are more often characterized by their own internal consistency – rules ('the rules of this house'), laws and just the ordinary etiquette of conventional habits (leading people to say things like 'it just doesn't seem right' when they are transgressed), than by anything outside them that might be considered as, say, *natural*.

I have already pointed out that *between* the book and the life we may explore a complex if only ever partially perceptible realm in which a number of structuring principles and conditions combine to organize our experiences and actions generally. These structuring principles and conditions take the form neither of an unfolding life yet to be represented in a memory or an account, nor of a finished book, words on a page or set in stone. That is because they *are* the principles upon which we understand our lives and books. But as soon as those principles are brought into the open – that is, com-municated or written down in some form or another – the communication or writing is already a second-hand version, to be interpreted and thus subject to the rules of interpretation, whatever they happen to be (and *adaequatio* is not much help here). It seems always necessary to have passed through some second-hand structure (whether thought of as fiction or fact, *fingo* or *verum*) in order to arrive at either the book or the life. The structure or possibility of memory must precede the life to be remembered. Otherwise we'd remember nothing. What that means is that the life appears to us only within the structures of representation, which make further representations possible. Furthermore, we cannot reduce these structures of representation to the historical institutions that so seem to govern them – the family, school, church, state, nation – for they too are governed just as much by the unpredictable life that they seem set in place to manipulate and tame.

In Between   The chapters that follow chart arguments that have in recent years attempted to engage with what I have called this *in between* realm which structures our experience both of books and life. The history of philosophical thought has always attempted to locate its first principles in some more stable realm, a transcendent one very often, where truths remain unchanging and eternal. There have been numerous attempts to outline the rules and the law of such a realm, in metaphysics, logic, mathematics and theology, to name a few. It was not until very recently that thinkers turned to the medium – the *between* of the two poles of human experience, life and representation – to locate what was formerly regarded as being beyond experience, that is, the truth of life and representation. However, this turn to mediation as the fundamental ground could not have taken place without a systematic re-reading of the tradition, a re-reading that refuses to extricate the logic of philosophical thought from its historical evolution. The consequences of this refusal include radical rethinking about both logic and history. What we find is not development, as such, but repetition. The classical notion of truth is repeatedly broken into two opposing parts – truth and its representation – which can thus be measured only according to the making equal or *adaequatio* of representation with that which is represented: the original life, or *presence*. However, representation will not be so tamed, as we shall discover in the chapters that follow. Instability, always excessive to *adaequatio*, consistently makes trouble for the equation. This is especially the case where whatever is supposed to be represented has departed the coop (a god or a benevolent monarch). Sometimes the departed thing (*res* or 'something' in Latin) has never in living memory been present yet a representation must none the less be made. Somehow the structure of representation can do this (witness any number of mythologies in world history); but not without an unstable excess that is always and unavoidably 'more than' just re-presentation. The 'more than' can always be regarded as superfluous, yet it is the superfluous aspects that make representation possible in the first place (or second place if we are strict). So representation (already in opposition to truth, which governs the relation between representations and things or books and life) has to be divided into two again. There is representation governed by truth (*adaequatio*) and representation excessive to truth (or *fingo*). The Greeks, for instance, used two important words that characterize the repetition of this distinction between truth and representation. They opposed *logos* to *mythos*. The first is a kind of discourse or account and is consistently connected to notions of truth, not to mention logic, which gets its name from the *logos* along with all the sciences that take the *logos* as their suffix: for example, geology, sociology, psychology. The second means 'plot' or 'story' and is consistently associated with the fictions that take their name from *mythos*, the myths or stories that speak the truth only by allegory.

One of the most famous statements in world literature is found originally in Greek. The first sentence of St John's Gospel is as follows: 'In the beginning was the Word, and the Word was with God, and the Word was God.' The Greek sentence runs like this:

εν αρχη ην ο λογος και ο λογος ην προς τον θεον και θεος ην ο λογος

In the beginning (*arche*) was the word (*logos*). We still do not know how to interpret this. *Logos* is a very complicated word itself and does not mean 'word' in any simple sense. The Latin translates *logos* as *verbum*, which is supposedly divided between 'word' and 'idea'. The idea remains the same (presumably) while different forms of the word are used *(logos, verbum,* word, idea) to denote it. If not, then translation would be impossible, but it is possible so something must remain the same. The sense that 'something remains the same' supports the argument (and 2000-odd years of Christian teaching maintains this) that 'the word' means the truth, in the transcendent sense, and that this transcendent truth is God. However, the distinction implicit in the word (*verbum*) between word and idea repeats the form of the distinction we started with – that between book and life or representation and actuality – and it does so on the basis of an implicit notion of *adaequatio*. The implicit notion is made explicit in that St John's Gospel (as with each of the other three) is an account of a concrete event, the crucifixion and resurrection of the Son of God (a kind of biographical history). But this is a fragile point because St John is writing 150 years after the event is supposed to have happened and, as an apparently Gnostic and allegorical writer (see the Revelations for the really wild stuff), may not be writing in as historical a style as some have believed. If the word must be 'made equal' to the idea, then the trouble here is that we have no idea. All we have is the word, and that might mean anything (other than making equal, which would just be a tautology, making 'making equal' equal to itself). If by 'word' (*logos*) we chose instead to understand the *structure* of signification (rather than the thing signified) then we would make better sense of the otherwise enigmatic statement, 'In the beginning was the word'. Before everything else was the ability to represent – *representability*. Word is divided between the visible or audible word and 'something signified'. The 'something' now must rather obviously be left open, at least to a certain extent, or we would never be able to use any words at all in any of the ways we always actually do: to mean particular things in particular circumstances. The price we pay for meaning is that we must be governed to a large extent by the powerful institutions that regulate it. These do not just govern particular meanings but rather they govern the frameworks of meaning. In fact, because they don't govern particular meanings very tightly we have a relative independence with respect to them, which allows me, for instance, to debate the meaning of St John with the Jehovah's Witnesses.

Critical Theory is consistently marked by attempts, which are very often contradictory, to draw attention to the frameworks of both meaning and action. Why are these attempts so contradictory? Well you might ask this, impatiently, and quite right too; why should things be so undetermined? The point is this: in keeping what is undetermined in focus (though never literally 'in sight') we bring the more determined structures into view. One of the most influential attempts to do this belongs with the German philosopher Martin Heidegger, who, between the late 1920s and into the 1970s brought a singular way of questioning to bear on the intellectual world. His method was to concentrate almost exclusively on the word 'being'.

To Be A being is something that exists, something that *is*. The word is a noun produced from a verb that says nothing more of something than that it just *is* (the verb 'to be'). The very least that we can say about anything at all is that it *is*. And that is not yet saying very much, if anything. But we must assume at least that before we can say anything else about it. So 'beings' denote things that *are*. And, thus, it can be said that beings have a relation to their being. This last term is both absurdly trivial and extremely peculiar. It divides a being between what it is particularly, i.e. this being here – or, to use a concrete example, that tree outside my window – and what it is generally, i.e. one of the many beings – or back to the example, one of the very many trees. A particular being belongs to being generally. The translation of Heidegger's first published work, *Sein und Zeit* (*Being and Time*), introduced the English-speaking world to the notion *Being* with a big B. All German nouns are spelled with a capital letter, but in order to distinguish the word 'being', in the various senses that Heidegger is chasing after, from the verb or noun senses we ordinarily use, the earliest translators kept the capital B for Being in English. So in the English translations beings are related to their Being, which designates the so-called ontological level. Ontology (*ontos*–being–*logos*) provides an account of the basic grounds of existence (actuality or life in our traditional terminology) as opposed to epistemology, which is supposed to provide an account of knowledge. Do you see how the distinction between Knowledge and Being compares with the distinction between books and life? Heidegger's earliest aim was to prepare the grounds for what he called a 'fundamental ontology', which would dig beneath mere knowledge of beings, what he called *ontic* knowledge, to the very grounds of both knowledge and beings – their respective Being. His readings of western thought reveal a repeated pattern of thinking that grounds Being in a transcendent realm through what he calls *Ontotheology*, manifested by all Christian philosophy (all western philosophies after about the first century). Christian and Greek philosophies tend to assume that Being resides, in its most essential state, in a realm that transcends Man's 'fallen' state (finitude, unpredictability, partiality, anxiety, sin and death). This *Other* realm would (we pray) be eternal, infinite and complete, and if anyone could ever get to it they would know everything and be all-powerful; they would reside outside the constraints of time and space. Heidegger's earliest publications cause this implicit interpretation of Being to begin to shake. And for the first time the implicit reservations about 'the way things are' become aspects of life that can be affirmed. The 'fallen' state of beings perhaps best characterizes the realm of Being itself, whatever that is.

In an unexamined sense, Being refers to the most general, the highest of superordinates. A superordinate relates a being to its type and puts beings in hierarchies, for instance as follows:

> Tweety
> Canaries
> Birds
> Creatures
> Beings
> Being

Compare the list to a similar hierarchy, one from a fiction this time, James Joyce's *A Portrait of the Artist as a Young Man*, which includes a section near the beginning in which his protagonist, Stephen Dedalus, begins to daydream during a boring geography class:

> He turned to the flyleaf of the geography and read what he had written there: himself, his name and where he was.
>
> > *Stephen Dedalus*
> > *Class of Elements*
> > *Clongowes Wood College*
> > *Sallins*
> > *County Kildare*
> > *Ireland*
> > *Europe*
> > *The World*
> > *The Universe*

That was his writing: and Fleming one night for a cod [joke] had written on the opposite page:

Stephen Dedalus is my name,
Ireland is my nation.
Clongowes is my dwellingplace
And heaven my expectation.

He read the verses backwards but then they were not poetry. Then he read the flyleaf from the bottom to the top till he came to his own name. That was he: and he read down the page again.

The hierarchy of superordinates seems to provide a consistent and reversible line between the young Stephen and the universe, in which he is thus securely placed. His identity is considered in terms of location. Notice that the hierarchy is one of spatial surroundings. Stephen is placed within a class, which is itself within a school, and so on until the world, and presumably the round Earth, is placed within a more general universe that surrounds it. The conception evokes a pre-Copernican universe (Copernicus is the astrologer whose name most clearly evokes the famous discovery that the Earth circled the Sun, thus dislodging 'Man' from the centre of his universe and inaugurating modern science). So Joyce represents the child's world picture as corresponding to the medieval one. However, against this comforting hierarchy of centralizing and embedded locations Stephen faces, on the opposite page, Fleming's 'joke' – a narrative which, owing both to the peculiar language of poetry and the temporal progress of narrative, is not reversible. The narrative is no less medieval than the hierarchy, of course, in so far as his destination is regarded as being beyond death and outside of locality; in this case, outside of nation. The finite and temporary condition of 'Man' is thus supposed to have its destiny beyond the finite in the fabulous yonder called 'Heaven'. But the question of what lies beyond seems to trouble the boy in Joyce's book:

What was after the universe? Nothing. But was there anything round the universe to show where it stopped before the nothing place began? It could not be a wall; but there could be a thin thin line there all round everything. It was very big to think about everything and everywhere. Only God could do that. He tried to think what a big thought that must be; but he could only think of God. God was God's name just as his name was Stephen.

He thus begins with the thought of 'nothing' beyond the outer limits of the universe. However, as you'll agree I'm certain, it is virtually impossible to think of nothing; you always ends up thinking a minimal frontier. As minimal as you make it there won't be just nothing, there'll be at least a 'thin thin line.' And on the other side of the thin thin line not nothing but a name – the name of God. The difference between nothing and God at this stage in Stephen's fictional development is this 'thin thin line'. The thin thin line also seems to separate Stephen from God, in the form of an analogy. Just as Stephen's name is Stephen, God's name is God. The analogy either proves the existence of God or denies any essential existence to Stephen, as if Stephen was nothing but naming and placing. This analogy will become decisive for us too, for the analogy between Stephen and God corresponds to the analogy between truth as *adaequatio* and truth as the transcendent truth of the word, between empirical truth and transcendental truth.

'Is' and 'Ing' If we return to Heidegger's meditations on Being (which he began almost contemporaneously with Joyce's fiction) we find a similar 'thin thin line' separating beings from their Being. Being is just the most general of superordinates, more general than the universe (in the register of space) and bounded only to the extent that there remains something rather than nothing. However, we quickly find that Being doesn't mean anything, at least nothing simply or consistently. If I say, 'the canary is yellow', the *is* doesn't mean the same thing as it does for 'it is raining', or even 'the weather is foul'. In each case something appears to me – the canary and its yellow colour, or this rain and what is foul about it – which I decide on the basis of my sensations of coldness and discomfort. Even the sentences 'the weather is foul' and 'I am cold,' which seem to be making the same point, can be subjected to pedantic distinctions. In point of fact the 'is' in each case means something different. In the first case the 'is' belongs neither to the foulness of the weather nor to the weather itself but links the two. This is what is meant by the word 'copula' in grammar. A copula (as the verb 'to be' is) links a subject to a predicate (the canary is yellow). For this reason the apparent richness of meaning that the verb 'to be' has is nothing more than a function of the fact that the word is utterly and essentially empty of meaning. It simultaneously has more meanings than we would ever be able to add up and no meaning at all. And the second case shows that the copula cannot be reduced to a subjective viewpoint, as if the weather is foul just because I think it is. My daft friend beside me treating the world to a vigorous rendition of 'Singing in the Rain' clearly thinks the weather is fine. Rather, the 'is' in 'I am cold' (the 'am') also belongs neither to me nor to the coldness but links the two on this occasion. The 'is' therefore belongs neither to any objects nor to any subjects but provides subjects and objects with a potentially infinite richness of meaning by having no specific meaning at all.

Heidegger privileges the word Being, especially in his earlier writings, but the principle, as it turns out, pervades all our meaning making. An example from yet another contemporaneous work can illustrate how. A contemporary of both Joyce and Heidegger, Walter Conrad Arensberg's radical experiments with language and structure reveal ways in which emptiness of meaning none the less contributes essentially to meaning making. His poem 'Ing' shows how the element that, for instance, links the verb 'to mean' to the substantial noun 'meaning', means nothing in itself:

ING

Ing? Is it possible to mean ing?
Suppose
     for the termination in *g*
          a disoriented
          series
     of the simple fractures
          in sleep.
          Soporific
     has accordingly a value for soap
          so present
          to sew pieces
               And *p* says: Peace is.
And suppose the *i*
     to be big in ing
     as Beginning.
               Then Ing is to ing
as aloud
     accompanied by times
and the meaning is a possibility
          of ralsis

Playful poetry of this kind can at first glance appear trivial and even irritating in its failure to address the apparently big questions of man, exist-ence, knowledge and truth. Yet the poem does as much as Heidegger's hefty questioning concerning the truth of being to draw our attention to the inevit-able emptiness and simultaneous productivity of our systems of signification. There would be no meaning if it wasn't for the funning and punning of language. Notice the ways in which the poem exploits little accidental qualities ('suppose the *i* to be big in ing as Beginning') and parodies the style of philosophical logic (suppose [...] then [...]). A traditional view would assume that the poem is exploiting what many refer to as the 'material' or 'formal' aspects of language, in preference to the meaningful aspects of it. Yet this charge cannot stand, for what the poem shows is that you cannot separate the two entirely. The distinction is itself a formal one, designed to simplify the difference between language and meaning. What the poem shows is that we pass through a strange middle world each time we communicate, but without noticing it. The middle world provides our frameworks of meaning, allowing meaning to emerge by withdrawing from our notice. The middle world is the locus, however, of our understanding and our interpretation, so this is the realm on which we bring criticism to bear in Critical Theory.

III Theory

The Empirical and the Transcendental

THEORY: an explanation or system of anything: an exposition of the abstract principles of a science or art: speculation as opposed to practice. [Gr. *Theorema, -atos*, spectacle, speculation, theorem, theoria, view, theory – *theoreein*, to be a spectator, to view.]

SCIENCE: knowledge: knowledge ascertained by observation and experiment, critically tested, systematized and brought under general principles: a department or branch of such knowledge or study. [L. S*cienta – sciens, -entis*, pr.p. of *scire*, to know.]

Theory, especially in its modern form as science, has always been opposed to experience. I intend to substantially weaken that opposition.

It is inevitable that we pass through some implicit or explicit theoretical understanding or interpretation when participating in critical discourse. Sometimes this understanding or interpretation is a matter of convention, usage, expectation or otherwise anticipating structure. At other times this understanding or interpretation is rooted more specifically in traditional theoretical discourse. Whatever the case, there is nothing we come to without from the beginning adding something extra to the bare fact of our experience. For this reason the notion of the bare fact, without anything added, is impossible. If it were possible it would be called 'the empirical'. Empirical experience concerns the experience of the here and now – our experience of presently existing things like these chairs and tables and these other people. Empirical experience puts us in a place and a time that exists independently of our experience of it. So it is the kind of experience that we ought to be able to be confident about. However, as the history of philosophy shows, no one has ever been able to isolate the empirical in a way that could be considered truly objective. The closest we have come to this ideal is through modern science, whose methods of judgement and testing (empiricism) demand that our theories be made explicit and explicitly testable according to the palpable existence of the things in question (rocks for the geologist, for instance). However, these methods are always based upon certain clearly defined axioms and postulates, which rest upon certain less well-defined or understood assumptions and interpretations. Opposed to 'the empirical' is 'the transcendental'. The transcendental refers to any form or pattern of being or thinking which stands outside and exists independently of the empirical, but which conditions and determines it. Mathematics is the best example but, as Heidegger has pointed out, the mathematical simply means that which is 'already known'. In 'The Age of the World Picture' he writes:

> *Ta mathema* means for the Greeks that which man knows in his observation of whatever is and in his intercourse with things: the corporeality of bodies, the vegetable character of plants, the animality of animals, the humanness of man. Alongside these, belonging also to that which is already known, i.e., to the mathematical, are numbers [...] Only because numbers represent, as it were, the most striking of always-already-knowns, and thus offer the most familiar instance of the mathematical, is 'mathematical' promptly reserved as a name for the numerical. (Heidegger 1977: 118–19)

It seems that there is no knowledge as such that does not pass through something 'always already known'. The relationship between experience and the always already known falls into the traditional and pervasive distinction between what we may refer to as the empirical and the transcendental. Modern Critical Theory gets going by finding problems with this distinction. There are some things, apparently, which cannot be reduced to this difference (like 'difference' itself, as we shall discover). The literary text (and by extension whatever it is we mean by 'textuality') is particularly resistant to the kinds of thinking based upon this distinction. To get to the empirical we have to pass through perception – in its crudest form, through the senses – and to get to the transcendental we must pass through the intelligible (understanding and then to reason itself, ratiocination, logic and the lofty mathematical and then on, it is supposed, to the spiritual realm, which is, of course, fundamentally opposed to the crude material one). But we never achieve either the empirical or the transcendental in any pure way. Instead, it seems, human experience is stuck somewhere between. This somewhere between is defined and delimited by the standard notion of a text.

What Theory is and Why It is Necessary   The most basic problem for theory is the need to formulate concepts that can stand over against objects, as traditional science does. A scientific theory might, for instance, provide an explanation, a system and a set of principles which would explain, describe and predict processes in the natural world. In the arts and social sciences, however, theories need to be formulated that can explain, describe and predict processes involving persons, events and historical situations. Traditionally this need has been met in diverse ways by separate disciplines: sociology, psychology, anthropology, history in the social sciences; and music, literary studies, art history and linguistics in the arts. Since their respective developments during the eighteenth and nineteenth centuries, and until recently, these disciplines have been more or less content to pursue their own individual paths towards the aim of scientific objectivity in an academic atmosphere of mutual distance and respect. Yet even within any one of these diverse disciplines controversial debates constantly arise and are seldom resolved to the satisfaction of a consensus. In other words, the integrity of all autonomous academic disciplines in the arts and social sciences has always been on the verge of crisis.

Over the last quarter of the twentieth century theoretical issues played an increasingly significant role for such disciplines, reflected in the fact that 'theory' has come to define specific and often central strands for most kinds of course. Not only does 'theory' now seem to describe a field within which new disciplines such as Critical Theory, Cultural Studies, Film Theory, Literary Theory, Social Theory, Feminism, Postcolonial Theory and Media Studies all in many senses meet; but it also describes a development within which, to a large extent, otherwise diverse disciplines have begun to interact.

However, the recent history of theoretical developments has not been one of organic growth, mutual tolerance and support. Theories abound that contest and explain each other, each from its own particular point of view or chosen ground. Herein lies a paradox. If theory develops through contestation and debate, each perspective contesting others while making specific claims to objectivity or truth, then what or who can ultimately provide sound objective principles for academic work in these disciplines? Even to say that there are no such principles is implicitly to lay down such a ground, and that too requires theoretical explanation.

The answer to this problem lies with the root of theory itself. The very word carries residual historical associations that we need to understand as having been transformed by the more influential recent work. It will be useful to discuss this transformation here because it embodies the process or pattern by which traditional modes of thinking generally have undergone transformations in contemporary theory. Our aim is, on the one hand, to reveal how contemporary theory develops through the constant transformation of both traditional and common-sense ways of thinking and, on the other hand, to show that the possibilities for this kind of transformation have been implicit in philosophical and theoretical texts throughout western history.

We must first return to the common and traditional senses of the word 'theory' itself. What does it mean traditionally, and what does it mean in everyday language? Traditionally, a science or an art can be thought of as the application of certain principles that may be abstracted in explanation, exposition or as a system. So a theory is an explanation or a system of anything, an exposition of the abstract principles of a science or an art. Theory is the speculative, abstract aspect in contrast to the actual practice of that science or art. A poet would make use of what is called 'prosody' as a theory of poetry, including rules for rhyming, metre, assonance, dissonance and so on. The actual practice in this case, and this will be instructive, may well involve creatively breaking some of those rules. In science, just think of Isaac Newton's theory of gravity or Albert Einstein's theory of relativity ($E = MC^2$), both abstract systems that account for all known possibilities in their field (the movement of bodies in space). Sigmund Freud's theory of repression and the unconscious, as well as Charles Darwin's theory of evolution, follow this pattern, but with some subtle differences. For now we note merely that traditionally theory is coupled either with a practice (for which it supplies a set of rules), or with a situation (for which it supplies an explanation). In any given discipline theory in fact usually plays both these roles. Theory always involves either working with methods that provide the means to formulate explanations, or working with explanations that provide the means to understand objects. It is unlikely that any discipline could do without some sort of theory.

If we now investigate the conventional concept of theory further, we find that it is in fact a modification of a wider-ranging concept. This modification has occurred through long-term historical trends and across languages. We need to return to the language of the ancient Greeks to see how and why this modification, which has many parallels, has taken place. We do this not to find the 'real' meaning of the word theory – the real meaning of a word is not simply what it used to mean – but it can help to show the kind of trends in thought that occur over long stretches of history. In ancient Greek, *theoria* means 'way of seeing' or 'setting in view'; and this root provides not only our own current sense of the word theory but also the notion of the theatre, the place where dramas or events (like plays or operations) can be viewed; theory indicates the role of an audience too. The root, at base, involves the sense of seeing, and this sense is precisely what is carried over into the meaning of the word theory. Theory is fundamentally a way of seeing things or of setting things in view. When someone begins a sentence with the phrase 'in my view …' we may expect, however humble, contradictory or crude, at least the trace of a theory ('In my view the Communist Party would do a better job than New Labour' indicates at least a basic political theory; '*Friends* is funnier than *Bilko*' suggests the vestiges of a theory of comedy). So in the broadest sense we each use theory all the time, or at least while we are awake, certainly while we think, speak or write, for it is in thinking, speaking and writing that theory is unavoidably expressed.

So the conventional meaning of the word 'theory' can be seen as a modification of a more general meaning, a modification designed perhaps to avoid the pitfalls of everyday language with its imprecision and lack of systematic foundation. Here, however, we face a paradox. For we begin to see that no theory, however systematic we try to make it, can escape its own foundations in the shifting, often quite vague sphere of everyday understanding and common sense. Theory in the sciences and arts is each time a powerful modification of everyday understanding, infected with a common sense and informed by a historical background.

Now this is only rarely a problem for the various well-founded arts or scientific disciplines. Each discipline is informed by a tradition of customs and practices supported by theories and methodologies that are ideally suited to their purpose. If, for instance, theories of human motivation help managers manipulate the behaviour of their workforce so that it is more efficient and productive, so much the better if the theories are in tune with the common-sense thinking of most managers. But every now and then a crisis occurs where basic assumptions and principles may need questioning and perhaps setting up afresh. Contributions to the development of a given discipline are generally made within existing rules and any changes are painlessly gradual. Without rules we could hardly function at all, so we put up with nagging problems with the odd basic principle. But a crisis in any given discipline involves a re-examination of first principles and basic grounds. A striking and famous historical example would be the so-called Copernican revolution in which it was discovered, to the shock of the scientific world, that the planets circled in orbit around the Sun rather than around the Earth. Not only was this discovery 'counter-intuitive' in that it went against the common sense but it went against the most entrenched teaching of the Church whose authority at the time was of course all powerful. In this case a theoretical discovery not only contradicted the rules but actually broke the law. The kind of 'de-centring' that occurred over the following hundred years or so is typical of the adjustments that need to be made during a crisis. Now try to imagine a discipline that is constantly in crisis, continually questioning its own basic premises. Critical Theory often seems to be in this state: continually in crisis, without faith in any founding frame of theoretical reference, constantly questioning its own or others' basic principles. But this is only the way it seems. Critical Theory seems to be in crisis only because of its basic field of analysis, which is the rhetorical, historical and cultural background from which all theories must have at some time emerged. It is this background of intimate, residually historical, culturally focused ideas, feelings and opinions that make up a confused yet apparently coherent everyday understanding that contemporary theory turns its attention to. Theory, in other words, is turned around and applied to its own grounds in both traditional and everyday understanding. Thus we tend to find a more or less consistently applied self-reflexivity accompanying most influential forms of critical theory, because in the first place the only concepts available are those we use in traditional and everyday practice.

So we should now be able to see the difference, on the one hand, between traditional and conventional concepts of theory, and new meanings of the term, on the other. The new sense involves a practice that concerns itself with the very grounds of theory generally, the limits of any theory. So, you might ask, why do we still call it theory? But what else could we call it? We are from the beginning limited to what we can say by concepts derived from the evolutionary patterns of rhetoric, so we must use the terms available, even if it means extending and transforming them as we have with 'theory'. And that is the basic method of contemporary theory. As we look back over the history of the term we find that there has always been this tension between a 'theoretical' (systematic, abstract) point of view and a 'pre-theoretical' (everyday, common-sense) one. By investigating the nature of the so-called pre-theoretical background, contemporary theory radicalizes the very notion of theory itself, undoing the grounded certainty of traditional theoretical positions. In other words, today we find the same patterns at work in both theoretical and pre-theoretical domains of thought, a tension that describes the intractable mutual relationship between the two.

Object and Concept   Traditionally, all objects that are set-into-view by a science are set down under 'concepts'. A concept is a 'general notion', a notion that can account for a range of examples. Thus, theory is nothing without concepts. The concepts of a theory are designed to account for the range of objects that fall under its domain. In the 'natural' or 'physical' sciences, for instance, we find that a concept like 'oscillation' can account for a range of motions: the vibrations of a stringed instrument when struck or bowed, the swinging of a pendulum, the movement of a needle on a lie detector, the body's shivering when exposed to cold. The concept 'oscillation' accounts for an abstract relationship between each of these motions and thus pays no attention to the particular, idiosyncratic aspects of our examples of it. Thus oscillation is simply 'swinging to and fro; vibration' and we need make no reference to the cello, violin or guitar, no reference to the lie detector and no reference to a body.

Analogy We should also be able to see that each of these examples falls under a single concept by analogy. There can be few more decisive concepts in theory than analogy, for analogy is the very concept that describes the process of making concepts. Think about the ways in which the concept of oscillation gets used to describe, by analogy, types of text, like theoretical texts, as well as fictional and mass media texts. A critic may say that the arguments of Walter Benjamin oscillate between the historical and the mystical; or we might argue that the narrative in George Eliot's *Daniel Deronda* oscillates uneasily between her two plot lines; or that the popular British TV series *Crocodile Shoes* oscillates between representations of the North and the South of England, as well as between England and the USA. In each case the term oscillation presupposes that the textual elements referred to can be separated out into contrasting poles, differences which can be represented through the analogy of oscillation as opposites or contrasts.

All the concepts in theoretical arguments have their basis in the use of analogy, which is a means of abstracting typical trends, patterns and processes in concepts that can be regarded as general. By the same account, Critical Theory develops often by pointing out the sometimes inappropriate uses of analogical concepts and by developing new ones more appropriate to the situation under study. That is to say that we cannot use any concept in contemporary theory uncritically. We must be aware of the history of its development as a concept, of the specific uses to which it has been put, of the ways in which it has become currency in theoretical discourse. Many thinkers will take great pains to define terms precisely as their argument develops, and this is very important as it helps readers get a firm sense of what is being argued. However, given what I have said about the relation between theoretical discourse and everyday discourse, we should be aware that no precise definition will be able to neutralize or pacify the clamour of historical, cultural and everyday discourses that necessarily inhabit and infect the theoretical term that is fundamentally parasitic upon them. Thus, there is no real alternative to the consistently self-critical or self-reflexive use of theoretical terminology that characterizes the work of so many of the most influential thinkers. You will doubtless find that much theoretical writing today fails to consider this important point and this results in apparently jargon-laden texts which reflect the fashion of the moment for certain concepts that have achieved academic currency (and which often filter into use in the popular media).

Economy Notice my own use of analogy here, the analogy of 'currency', likening the use of current coinage in a relatively closed economy to the use of language in relatively closed institutional contexts. The concept of economy is, as we shall see, very important and has wide-ranging uses in contemporary theory. What it disallows in theoretical language is the use of any term that can stand alone, outside or beyond the system that gives it currency. In other words, all concepts have an integral relation not simply to others in a relatively closed system, but to all other concepts in a language, as well as to a range of sometimes quite difficult choices with regard to translation. The concept of oscillation, for instance, might indicate frequency or periodicity, concepts associated with regularity and recurrence; but it also might, rather differently, indicate change-ability, under which term it shares similarities with fitfulness, transience and agitation. Oscillation is also understood in relation to concepts regarded as opposite to it, such as disorder and discontinuity (if oscillation is thought of as periodization), or stability, permanence and fixture (if it is considered as 'chopping and changing'). All this reveals is that the single concept 'oscillation' is capable, depending on context, of meanings that are potentially opposite to each other and therefore mutually exclusive. In principle this capability is a feature of all language.

When the need to translate a concept arises, quite precise attention to the context is necessary, as well as a knowledge of current uses in the language it is being translated into. Oscillate in the German might be *oszillieren* or *schwingen* if the context is physical; or it could be *schwanken* for the lie detector as well as for a great many of the analogical meanings that we have used where *oszillieren* would sound odd in the German. The concept of 'translation' too works to an extent in analogy with the concept of 'currency', as coinage can be translated ('changed') by virtue of a 'rate of exchange' into any other currency. The same is true, of course, for any word, although precise translations are impossible because we cannot at the same time translate the whole system to which the one word belongs. Such a system is by no means fixed and unchangeable but undergoes a continuous process of transformation. As I will show throughout this book, theory must operate very much on the boundaries of fixity and change in critical thought, and is consistently concerned with the family of concepts concerning translation, analogy and exchange.

Objects   Having complicated the notion of 'concept,' I shall now discuss the ways in which the concepts of Critical Theory relate to their special objects. First, what is the object or what are the objects of theory? Before we can answer that question we must ask, what is an object? As with all important concepts used in theory, it is necessary to explore the constructions, histories and conventional uses of the concept 'object', in order to tease out the deeper implications of its use.

In the physical world, it would seem, there is no difficulty in establishing what objects are. An object is simply a thing presented or capable of being presented to the senses. What this means is that an object is something that can be observed. If we begin with the least problematical examples we can easily see what is involved. The most basic kind of object that can be observed is a material thing, something in the world like a rock, a tree, a dog or cat, a man, a woman, a child. Leaving aside for the moment (although we will come back to this directly) the fact that rocks and people are conventionally considered to be objects with very different qualities, their shared status as objects in the most basic sense remains the same. That is, each thing can be regarded as existing outside and as being independent of the mind observing it. This indicates already that the concept 'object' has its most basic sense in relation to a correlative concept, that of the 'subject' who does the observing, who is in possession of 'a mind' and is thus capable of understanding the concepts (like rock, tree, dog, cat, man, woman, child) which stand over against the objects in the world (the things to which those concepts are said to refer). Now, because the concept of 'subject' is supposed to refer to the very being that does the observing, it is not surprising that it is one of the most difficult concepts in the history of theory. The subject is the one who sees and who sets things into view. Once we have said this, of course, we see an inherent difficulty. If the concept of 'subject' is already part of a way of setting things into view (the objective way), how can the subject itself be the one who does the setting?

Anyway, an object is, therefore, not simply some discrete thing standing passively around in the world but something in the world that has been set into view in some more or less specific way by the subject who observes it, or at least by subjects who habitually observe things in specific ways. In other words, rocks, trees and people share the same status as objects but are viewed in very different ways by different people, i.e. as having different qualities. An object is something upon which attention, interest or some emotion is fixed. A botanist will see an oak tree in a very different light, will 'set it into view' in a different way, to the way a painter or a person walking in the country or a lumberjack or timber-merchant would. It is possible to say that each of these different people has a different interest in the tree, and thus see it as a different object when his or her respective attention is fixed upon it. In the case of people, things become very complex. A child might be the object of a parent's love or irritation, siblings may be the objects of each other's envy; a stranger may be the object of someone's secret desire. In principle the situation remains when, rather than an individual, a whole group is taken as an object. An identification of 'racial type' or a gender is a way of objectifying a group, possibly as being 'other' or 'different'. These concepts can then be (and often are) applied to individuals in a way which also reflects the attitudes of the subjects who have set their objects into view in this way. There are also concepts, such as virtue and crime, that seem not to refer to any object that is in any basic sense 'in-the-world'. This reveals all the more that concepts denote objects in an active, productive way, creating their objects rather than simply reflecting or representing them.

People collectively are actually the objects of disciplines such as anthropology, sociology and psychology, in which case concepts like 'behaviour', 'group dynamics', 'personality' or 'attitude' govern the ways in which people are set into view. And because those disciplines aim for scientific status, they must find legitimate criteria for objectivity, to help reduce the tendency for subjective interests to inform observation. So means are found for making generalizations. People can then be understood objectively thanks to empirical methods like the statistical analysis of measurable segments of society. But the scientific viewpoint is itself a 'point of view' or, more specifically, a particular way of setting objects into view. And the 'subject' of a scientific viewpoint is no less subjective for being scientific. This is not to suggest that contemporary theory should abandon science, but rather it is to suggest that the scientific viewpoint is, in contemporary theory, made more self-critical in its awareness of the styles by which different disciplines (both theoretical and practical) set their objects into view. There is no pure objectivity. Traditionally, objectivity would be a condition under which objects could be described and/or acted upon that was not coloured by sensations or emotions. In a more significant formulation it would also be a condition under which objects could be described and/or acted upon uncoloured by any way or style of setting things into view at all. But there is no way of setting things in view that is not coloured by a way or style of doing so. There can be no pure objectivity because the attitude of the subject always intrudes and intervenes in an active way. Take the example of science. We have become so used to adopting a technological way of speaking in the modern world, especially where academic disciplines are concerned, that we often fail to see that technological ways of speaking themselves constitute a positive style. In other words, while such ways of speaking attain to a condition of transparent description and, ultimately, to objective truth, they are in fact part of a system, a set of tendencies, habits of thought and conventional laws of operation.

So the concepts that are developed in contemporary theory are designed to allow us access to elusive objects. But these 'objects' are very often the creation of the system that gives their concepts currency. And their use often implies a breakdown in any hard and fast distinction between subjects and objects. The concept for this chapter is 'theory' itself, and I have demonstrated the way in which a theoretical point of view can proceed by questioning the very grounds of the theoretical point of view itself, which is simply one specific way of setting objects into view. We can use the analogy of framing and say that theory frames its objects in specific ways. You can take this to mean both in the way pictures are framed to provide tidy boundaries around what they depict, and in the way a person charged with a criminal offence might complain that s/he 'was framed' or 'set up', meaning that s/he didn't do it. The first sense indicates the way objects must be defined, conceptualized, bounded and brought into view in a particular light. The second sense indicates the intrusive, active way in which concepts 'produce' meanings, add meanings on to an object (an object does not necessarily mean anything independently of the concepts attributed to it) or even produce their object (an object may not exist independently of its concept, as is the case with *Hamlet* or the unicorn). There is no alternative to the potentially criminal production of meanings, the risks we must take of 'mis-representing' our objects; all theoretical work insists that concepts are created and used, and such use is always an addition and an intrusion. So contemporary practices generally accept a responsibility not only for making their own backgrounds and presuppositions clear but also for questioning them, as I am doing in this chapter. This questioning is not negative and destructive, as some people think, but is productive. It improvises concepts, in a way, for theories that are intended to account for the very specific situations that require questioning in the first place, situations that are cultural and historical and thus always in a process of change as they fall inevitably into their unknown but often surprising future.

Contemporary theory does not simply rely on past theoretical systems, developed say in philosophy, social theory, anthropology, linguistics and textual criticism. These must be used, certainly, because we have no already developed system of concepts that could possibly account for the situations that call for understanding and interpreting. But theory too must be questioned and read in a carefully critical way, so we can use it to arrive at new conceptions, while as far as possible avoiding the deep-seated prejudices that underlie all of our thinking (just by using available concepts we are making implicit judgements). Thus, theory operates on two levels. On the level of objectivity, now understood as being impossible in any pure sense, we need to identify the situation that we are both conceptualizing and intervening in. On the level of conceptualization itself, we must self-critically develop our concepts and arguments through careful readings of existing theory, locating contradictions and problems, and developing each time a workable framework for the specific engagement that we wish to make.

Contemporary theory cannot be thought of as belonging to any specific discipline. Theory informs many disciplines, especially in moments of crisis and self-questioning, but it occurs generally as a process that is not reducible to any discipline (certainly not 'its own', which would be a contradiction). Theory puts the notion of a discipline under constant interrogation – not so that traditions can be undermined in any naively subversive sense (although much contemporary theory is subversive) – but so that traditions can be opened up to the possibility of their changing in productive ways, both in terms of their concepts and in terms of their activities, in short, their politics. But while theory has its own mode of proceeding and must be regarded as operating outside the strict boundaries of existing disciplines, it cannot be thought of as existing simply independently of any discipline. Theory is what happens when the grounds or the boundaries of disciplines are questioned and altered, certainly, but nothing like that could happen unless theoretical terms and concepts already existed. And only traditional and everyday discourses have them. If contemporary theory became an independent and autonomous discipline with its own philosophy and conceptual framework, it would no longer be theory but yet another discipline in the arts or social sciences, itself vulnerable to theoretical critique and resistant to anything perceived as 'not belonging' within it. In this respect it is instructive that the most influential authors, texts and arguments in contemporary theory consistently resist easy disciplinary categories. A critical approach can work productively and often subversively within, as well as between, disciplines and traditions.

Summary   As I have shown, the problems that tax traditional theories in academic disciplines are general. The difficulty of arriving at stable concepts that can accurately stand against often enigmatic objects troubles all participation in everyday talk, as well as the discourses of the mass media and all practices that characterize a given culture. And, just as the traditional sciences must ignore these difficulties in order to proceed, so too must the participants in everyday discourses ignore their own problematic grounds in order to get on with their lives. What I am calling contemporary theory aims to expose those problematic grounds. So concepts used in everyday discourses may be regarded as constructions, meanings that have been imposed on objects and which thus to an extent create those objects. Everyday concepts, no less than those of a science, are specific ways of setting things in view and framing them. For participants in those discourses, however, these concepts will often appear natural or transparent. In other words, only their objects will appear and they will appear is if independent of the system of concepts that has played such an important role in constructing the way that they appear.

One final observation now needs to be made. Despite the need in academic disciplines for consensus, that is, a set of shared assumptions and definitions upon which practical and objective work may proceed, a brief history of any period in a discipline's development will invariably reveal dispute and criticism at the deepest level. If this is the case in science and philosophy, it is even more so in everyday discourse where meanings are by no means shared. Meanings can be regarded as sites of struggle, which implies that a culture tends to be made up of individuals who are related only tentatively by shared values and norms, and those relations are often better characterized by mutual antagonism, incompatible interests and struggles of power. A concept in everyday discourse gets its 'naturalized' sense only at the cost of other contradictory senses that would reveal a determination from many sometimes contending positions.

2 Philosophical Impossibilities

If we can look back over more than two millennia of philosophical thought to witness a project whose main aims are impossible, that doesn't mean we need to reject the whole tradition. Rejection of past thought is actually one of the impossibilities of philosophy, so we know we cannot. It is possible, rather, to affirm the impossible in philosophy, as a good thing, as if impossibility was in these instances a positive attribute, a kind of power. The ancient Greeks used the word *aporia* to describe any problem or question that turned out to be insoluble. An *aporia* brings any discussion or argument to an impasse in such a way that the structure of the argument shakes, including its presuppositions and predicates (first principles), and needs to be reconstructed on the basis of what proves to be impossible. So *aporia* is similar to crisis, and is thus intrinsic to the processes of Critical Theory. The following sections chart some of the arguments in the tradition that most powerfully bring philosophy to its own *aporias* or impossibilities in such a way that, independently of historical context, the arguments and their failures become resources for current thought.

I The Ancients

We must let our destination be decided by the winds of the discussion. (Plato, *Republic* 394d)

Philosophy What, then, determines the problems that relate to critical study? As we have seen, the main problem is one of constructing an adequate theoretical frame. In this chapter I will use 'Philosophy' as a generic term for describing the way attempts are made to outline the conditions for constructing such a frame. The magisterial history of academic and intellectual thought always reveals an at least implicit but often explicit philosophical basis for theory, in whatever discipline.

Philosophy is not just a generic term. It is the history of philosophy as a discipline that provides our means of analysing the problems that arise for anyone attempting to clear such a ground. And history reveals the contradictions and paradoxes that emerge in those attempts. We will also find that there are forces that help to form thought that are inextricable from those that help to form history. So this is not a history of ideas. A theoretical treatment of ideas and history must look for ways of assessing what makes these ideas and this history possible in the first place.

The history of philosophy is not one of steady progress from humble beginnings through the gradual accumulation of knowledge to a position of greater understanding. Certainly, profound advances and giant leaps have since the earliest times contributed to fields of technics like medical knowledge and mass communications. But rapid developments, especially during the modern period, have been matched by the consistent failure to develop anything like a total knowledge, or even any sense of certainty in knowledge. Furthermore, in fields such as politics, morality, legislation and aesthetic judgement, there remain so much controversy and disagreement that we could hardly justify the belief that, while there have been undeniable developments in science and in technics, this is also true in the more general fields concerned with notions like humanity. In fact, the most successful forms of advanced knowledge have such a technical feel that it is sometimes feared that advanced technics will overtake the destiny of humankind and the whole of nature to the impoverishment of both. Undoubtedly, though, simultaneous technical achievement and moral frustration in history are inextricably linked.

The history of philosophy reveals a number of often audacious and singular attempts to clear the ground for adequate knowledge about goodness, truth, legislation and science. The classical philosopher wanted a single and permanent principle that would account for all the different, changeable things that occurred in the finite world. But in so far as the philosophers we examine operate in terms, systems and styles that are their own, they do so only with reference to their heritage, i.e. with what is already possible in the realm of thought. So we can see already that a problem is likely to emerge regarding the tension between all the different things that have already been thought and the kind of singular truth that we want to arrive at. In order to arrive at knowledge we must first have a way of assessing previous knowledge. But the only available resource is previous knowledge. How can we use previous knowledge for constructing a theory that goes beyond previous knowledge?

In fact, for many philosophers all previous knowledge is nothing more than an encumbrance to thought, a deceptive time-waster and a lure that entraps the mind. For others it is a passageway through history that must be worked through and then sublimated or transcended in the thought that evolves beyond it. For still others it is a resource for learning how to think, how to be critical and how to construct theories, but never a means to knowledge itself. We will see that the problem of deciphering the role and meaning of this previous knowledge is a key to philosophy as such.

Deception   The problems that have faced philosophers since the earliest records of western thought (at least) give us the best clue to understanding what philosophy is trying to do. Nearly all influential early philosophers agree at least that people are chronically vulnerable to deception. They are deceived by myths and stories, believing them to be true, even if they were intended as allegories. They are deceived by the authority of powerful men and men of repute (and repute itself) into believing that their authority has rock-solid foundations, even if the authorities themselves declare a suspicion of authority. They deceive themselves into thinking that their own beliefs and thoughts are representations of the world as it really is. They are deceived by signs of things and fall into the error of believing that the signs *are* the things themselves. Signs have a peculiar ability to efface themselves as signs. And so a basic problem of philosophy concerns the difference between illusion and reality.

Our thoughts and beliefs about the world as it appears to us, however natural they make it seem, constitute a subtle and complex deception, woven together from stories and desires, passions and beliefs that take effect from the earliest experiences of childhood. Thus, according to this philosophical argument, it takes extraordinary discipline and a rigorous application of the rational faculties of thought to break through the deceptive web and grasp the way things are in reality. The ancient Greek thinkers named this discipline philosophy (*philo*, love or friendship, and *sophia*, wisdom), the desire for wisdom. So philosophy, at first sight, seems to be the aim of being able to distinguish between reality and illusion.

Socratic Dialogue   The problems are easier to grasp than the solutions. Which is to say, it is easy to show how the most committed convictions and beliefs on the weightiest as well as the most trivial matters are inconsistent, incoherent or just plain false. It seems far less easy to communicate the truth about those matters, even when the teacher apparently knows it.

The method that characterizes the arguments of Socrates, the philosopher whose thought is often regarded as the cornerstone of western philosophy, involves the disturbing process of unsettling cherished convictions and exposing false reasoning and failures of logic in others. The aim is always to arrive at an objective knowledge, free from opinion, deception and complacency, to help others break free of their own deceptions. The process, called dialectic (*enchelos*), is consistently negative, and it involves a form of refutation that makes use of the interlocutor's own definitions to refute the premises on which they are based. Socratic philosophy could not be done without the presence of an interlocutor, whose false convictions and honestly but mistakenly held beliefs are the means by which the light of reason emerges against its dark negative in deceived thinking. What we need to hold on to here is that the so-called light of reason seems not to shine independently of the confused thoughts that tend to obscure it. It is only by stripping away those confused thoughts that reason makes itself known. If there were no confused thoughts there would be no reason. To follow the logic of the analogy of light, we might be tempted to think that the veil of falsity hides truth. But it would be closer to Socratic thinking to imagine truth as a light, which comes on through active questioning.

That is why Socrates never wrote anything down. The only access we have to Socrates is via the more influential intermediary, his student Plato, whose philosophy emerges as a series of dramatizations. Plato's dialogues feature Socrates in a range of adversarial debates and discussions with fictional characters (often, though, like Socrates, based on actual people) whose beliefs and convictions are systematically shaken by irony, rational argument and ultimately undone when their attempts at definition and clarification collapse in contradiction. So although in the early dialogues Socrates never presents a theory of reason, let alone an attempt to define it once and for all, the nature and circumstances of the debates, i.e. the arena or theatre of his philosophy, give us a clue to his notion of reason. It is essentially a living activity of argument that involves the necessary participation of an interlocutor in face-to-face debate. It is clearly not something that could simply be defined and dogmatically presented to a passive reader who would then absorb it as the truth. That very passivity is one main route to error. Two and a half millennia later we may allow ourselves the suspicion that this refusal to write and this unquestioned assumption of the rational virtue of the face-to-face debate might itself harbour a deception and an unthinking prejudice. If that is the case it is one that lies at the very basis of western knowledge.

Plato's Theatre How do we know what Socrates really said as he roved the markets and parks of Athens, unsettling everybody's most cherished convictions? (In questioning conventional attitudes he posed a threat to the authority of the law itself and was executed in the end for insurgent activities, forced to drink a flask of poison hemlock.) Plato forms something of a bridge between Socratic philosophy, which is essentially oral and aporetic (designed to expose puzzles), and the written documents that characterize philosophical works afterwards, which are more likely to be demonstrations and logical arguments presenting, defending or attacking some thesis. But Plato does not say anything directly. The entirety of his corpus is constituted by fictional debates. It is not possible to say with certainty what Plato's conclusions were or even if he had any. And although his dialogues might seem to pose the same kinds of problem as a literary drama, where we must be careful not to confuse the statements of a character with the beliefs of the author, we must be very cautious about reading them as if they were simply literature (Plato is often confusingly compared to Shakespeare).

On one hand, the fictions are clearly designed to guide a reader to a philosophical conception of the truth about things. Although Socrates did not write, his teaching informs Plato's representation of it. Plato writes where Socrates did not but he writes the words of Socrates. Socrates speaks through Plato's writing. Nevertheless, it is Plato who puts words into Socrates' mouth. Most commentators believe that the earlier dialogues represent a more accurate (true to life) Socrates than the later ones, where (it is assumed) Plato's own maturing philosophical vision increasingly informs his text. This seems fine except that it would be structurally impossible to show, even in the very earliest dialogues, where Socrates ends and Plato begins. This is a genuine *aporia* in which it is structurally impossible for us (or anyone) to say for certain what either Socrates or Plato actually (really) believed. But that is no real problem. So long as that is recognized as being the case, then Socrates' basic premise is maintained. Everybody is vulnerable to deception and the only foil against it is a singular and active quest for the truth about things through rational argument. What matters, in other words, is what and how *you* think, and by extension here, how you read.

On the other hand, to regard Plato's philosophy as simply literature would be to hold to a vast unquestioned assumption about what literature is. And in a sense derived from Plato, which will gather urgency as the centuries roll forward, that is another problem that lies at the heart of philosophy. I began by saying that one key to the problem of philosophy was the question about interpreting the role of previous knowledge; and I said that another basic problem of philosophy is the distinction between illusion and reality. Now I am saying that it is also the question about what literature is. The question is more urgent when we ask, what, precisely, *is* the difference between Plato's dramatizations and literature? What is the difference between philosophy and literature? Who decides? We now need to explore the ways in which the problem of previous knowledge, the distinction between illusion and reality and the question of literature are decisively entangled at the very heart of the philosophical project.

Nous (Mind) The first problem that philosophy teaches us, then, is this: we are all in the dark. No matter who you are or where you are, you are badly in need of some good clear thinking to free you from your illusions and deceptions. Otherwise you just let others do your thinking for you. From the very beginning the answer to the problem is always singular. There is only one truth yet many ways of error. Before there was philosophy it appears that people had to rely on myth to augment their understanding of their world and reflect on their place within it. In a later chapter I will explore the role and concept of myth in some detail. The Greek cosmology of symbolic gods – including the figures of Zeus, Ares, Aphrodite and Athena (chaos or Deus, war, love and wisdom) – and the endless cycle of stories involving the gods with man comprised a complex series of allegories, which helped to give meaning to the Greek experience. Each god is symbolic for some force (love or war for instance) and the narratives show how these forces are related in the whole (the cosmology), which thus constitutes a massive allegorical narrative that reflects human experience. In other words, myth provides an explanation. But this is not the sort of explanation that philosophy aims to provide. The philosopher in ancient times emerges as a figure whose aim is to free people's thoughts from mythology. Myth doesn't work. People end up believing in the figures as if they were real (they believe in real gods). They miss out on an understanding of the single truth.

In 500 BC, while the ancients were still developing the field of thought later to be called philosophy (long before Socrates), someone called Anaxagoras arrived in Athens and said some things that seemed to capture everyone's imagination. He said:

> Together were all things, infinite in quantity and smallness. Mind [*nous*] is something infinite and self-controlling, and it has been mixed with no thing but is alone itself by itself. And mind arranged everything – what was to be and what was and what now is and what will be – and also this revolution in which revolve the stars and the sun and the moon and the air and the ether which are separating off. (Barnes 1987: 228)

Let's not try to understand all this too quickly. It was written a very long time ago and this is a transcription of the original, of which only a fragment remains. It is the first recorded occurrence of the use of the Greek word *nous* in the philosophical sense that it later gained. *Nous* means 'mind'. In parts of England you will hear people use the Greek word in a colloquial sense; e.g.

'anyone with any nous ... ', meaning anyone who knows or who has understanding or uses their head, any reasonable person. Here it denotes the controlling power of the very universe itself. In a universe that is, according to the convention of the time, ruled (albeit in a rather capricious way) by gods, this statement rather stands out. First, mind is a faculty of the human soul (in Greek the *psyche*). And this gives to the human agent a power that mythology hardly allows. Secondly, *nous* is described as 'something infinite and self-controlling'. This means that it is never used up, it is eternal, and that it is not contingent on anything else.

This is very important. In the finite world of experience absolutely everything is affected by other things. Everything is an effect of some cause. In the modern world the light in my study at night is caused by a number of things: my hand on the switch, the live electrical energy lying latent in the wiring, experiments by nineteenth-century chemists, the generator, the millions of tons of burning coal, the archaic forest that is turned into coal deep underground, this terrible desire for light. No one has ever seen the first cause,

---

Allegory

The most basic meaning of the word 'allegory' is when we say something but mean something other than what is said. It comes from the Greek *allo* meaning other and *goreo*, which was the platform on which political orators and rhetoricians stood while speaking. So allegory is literally speaking otherwise. It emerges as a form of political rhetoric describing the way politicians would weave stories into their speeches that would act as coded commentaries on political situations. In modern times it is more or less exclusively used to describe certain kinds of literary writing. The epic tradition (which goes back to Greek Homeric poetry) is constituted by long stories that are supposed to stand for some extra-literary message, to which the reader is led by the narrative. So, for instance, Spenser's *The Faerie Queene* can be understood as being at once a long epic poem and a set of allegorical commentaries on religion, ethics and politics (including a clear allegorical allusion to the court of Elizabeth I, retaining the political sense that the term seems to have had since ancient times). For Spenser it also acted as a disguise for his political views, which were always in danger of courting the queen's displeasure.

In the context of Hebraic and Christian religions, allegory is a use

however, so that is God or the big bang or whatever, something supposed to be out there beyond experience. To call it mind seems pretty daring. Thirdly, it is 'alone itself by itself'. There is a beautiful purity in the thought. Mind is not compromised by its relations or attachments to any other thing. It moves by itself, it is independent, autonomous and, according to Anaxagoras, it is the only thing in the universe that is.

Philosophers through the ages have celebrated this concept of mind, even though most of them express some disappointment that Anaxagoras chose not to explore the nature of human mind a bit more. Plato, about a hundred and thirty years later, was disappointed that 'the man didn't use his mind at all – he didn't ascribe to it any explanations for the arranging of things'. Plato would have preferred to see a development of the ways in which the human mind arranges human experience. For him the examination of the human mind should arrive at the truth of experience. But that is Plato's project. Plato's *Republic* is a book about how a perfect community might be set up on the sole principle of reason. This singular controlling power, if

of language that has become necessary since the loss to Man of the perfect language of God, thought to be capable of both creating and naming that which is created, a loss referred to by the allegory of the Tower of Babel. It is thought that Man's abstract referential language can at best only approximate God's concrete, immediate language so Man can communicate God's truth only through allegory. Thus allegory stands in for a truth that can otherwise not be spoken. The religious interpretation of the world as a shadowy reflection of God's divine world has been threatened increasingly throughout the more secular modern period. Although allegory has played a less central role, it is still evident as a literary technique as in political fables such as George Orwell's *Animal Farm*, in which a plot involving animals taking over the farmyard has an allegorical reference to the Bolshevik revolution.

Some types of contemporary criticism, which would seem to deny the possibility of any perfect original language, employ a kind of allegorical reading. Allegory is the only possibility in language because all language demands decoding. As a key, however, allegory is fundamentally unreliable. It is argued that language contains no guarantees as to any final singular meanings that we might wish to arrive at.

properly applied, would ensure smooth functioning in whatever changing and otherwise unpredictable circumstances. Plato, notoriously, disqualifies poets, dramatists and artists from his Republic on the basis of the tendency for people to be deceived by the representations of imaginative writing and art, including, of course, mythology. We must come back to this point later.

Plato's famous student Aristotle (whose influence on later philosophy is hardly calculable) has this to say in *Metaphysics* about Anaxagoras: 'Someone [Anaxagoras] said that just as in animals so in nature mind is present and is responsible for the world and its whole ordering: he appeared as a sober man compared to his predecessors who spoke at random.'

G. W. F. Hegel, the nineteenth-century German philosopher, translates Aristotle as saying that Anaxagoras stood out as a sober man in the company

---

Contingency

In Greek philosophy (and ever after) it is conventional to divide what can be known into two categories. Things are either *necessary* or they are *contingent*. A necessary law (like the laws that govern the movements of the planets) will always apply in any situation and at any time. A contingent event is something that can happen but might not (meeting an old friend in a crowded city). Contingency plans (putting money away for a rainy day, taking out insurance) are made *in case* something unpredictable occurs. Necessary laws govern the universe. Contingent events are unpredictable, ruled by chance, and are determined randomly. The philosophical system since the Greeks makes necessary laws primary and contingencies secondary. Relating the two in this way, however, leads to some interesting paradoxes. Necessity must be the case. Contingency might be the case. Now, for the philosopher, everything must have aspects that are both necessary and contingent. Take a human being. What is necessary about being human and what isn't? Are there necessary laws governing human understanding and behaviour? Do they govern the ability to use language? Is the question reducible (as Plato thought) to rationality? What then is contingent? Colouring, relationships, gender? Some people would say that these are necessary aspects of individuals. Others would say they were contingencies. Contingency also implies dependence while necessity implies autonomy. Philosophy very often insists on this distinction but it is possible to ask, what if contingency was itself necessary?

of drunkards. The suggestion is quite powerful. A party of drunks with their random and nonsensical theories, bitter arguments and disconnected ideas is put to shame by the sober thought of this early philosopher whose concept of mind grounds all philosophy on a principle that will bear on the beginning of science. Does Anaxagoras sound sober to you?

Plato's Cave   Perhaps rather disconcertingly, one of Plato's most affecting and influential arguments is an allegory. In *The Republic* he describes a long cavernous cell, which he also calls a 'prison house', deep underground. There are people who have been down there since early childhood. Their legs and necks are tied so that they are forced to face the back wall of their cave with firelight flickering behind them. Between their backs and the fire is a wall, about the height of a conjurer's table, behind which are people carrying little model artefacts, statuettes and toy animals which stick up out from the wall like puppets. The puppet masters talk to each other all this while. So what the tied-up people passively experience as their complete reality are the echoes of the sounds of talking and the shadows of the puppets flickering in the firelight. (Incidentally, 20,000-year-old cave drawings of hunters and hunted animals are suspected of inducing a kind of ecstasy in the cave dwellers as the figures flickered in the firelight at night.) The elements that compose their only reality are the echoes of sound and passing shadows of puppets. Plato says that we are all like that. He then asks us to imagine what it would be like for one of these people to turn and loosen their bonds, to face the firelight and the truth about their existence. How much harder would it be for someone then to proceed beyond the fire and out ultimately into the light of day, to gaze at the sun, which for Plato stands for the light of reason itself? A difficult process, certainly, but Plato also points out that anyone who had been outside would be reluctant to return to their former unenlightened circumstances. If they did, then which of the cave dwellers would believe or understand what he had to say? And here, in a nutshell, is the task and the desire of the philosopher. The modern version of Plato's cave would comprise the globally networked mass media, the uncountable layers of consumption and reception of information beyond which we may hardly dare to aspire in a search for Platonic truth. We must come back to the question of the media in a later chapter. In a milieu where forces over which we have little control mediate just about all our knowledge for us, Plato's problem clearly still stands.

What is the relationship between Plato's use of allegory, on the one hand, and the myths, the dramas of the Greek theatre, and the great epics of Homer, on the other? In other words, what is the difference between philosophical allegory and literature? Plato's answer is that the poetic form (like a picture) presents a whole and complete image. The gods are there in their richness, fleshed out with character and narrative density. The drama presents a complete action, a ready-made to be consumed by its audience. An epic brings its characters to life in their actions. Mythology gives you the gods themselves. Plato's allegories, on the contrary, leave out the very thing they are designed to instruct us about, the process of thinking itself, the truth as such. They show us the truth only in negative. They tell us that what we think of as the truth is not the truth at all. But they do not ultimately give us the truth, for that, Plato insists, is transcendent and cannot be pictured in the finite world. So any picture or description of the ideal truth, the truth of mind, is necessarily false for Plato. The allegories of philosophy must refrain, therefore, from attempting to represent it *as* something. Plato can show us the cave but he will not tell us what we will find once we have emerged from it.

If we recall that Anaxagoras described the mind as infinite we can quickly get a sense of why it is not strictly representable. The cave, in Plato's description, can represent our experience of the finite world. Being finite is, of course, one of the most frustrating aspects of existence. Everything is limited. We will never have enough time to know everything there is to know. (One common experience of anyone embarking on serious study, e.g. in higher education, is that the more you find out the more ignorant you feel. Knowledge seems to tower above in greater and greater magnitude the closer you move towards it. It is like walking towards a mountain where, at first, gentle hills make the ascent comfortable, yet the further you go the steeper is the climb and the more immense appear those increasingly distant peaks.) But even if it were possible, say with the help of some as yet barely imaginable computer, to document all knowledge (the Internet and CD-ROM only prove the point), knowledge seems not to be containable, it is not strictly a matter of quantity. There are infinite relationships between all the parts of knowledge. As will often be the case, the example of language can help us to understand why. If you documented all the meaningful sounds and marks in all known languages you would have a huge volume of dictionaries. You could even imagine someone very clever who could learn a large percentage of these marks (call them words for the sake of argument). Then if you added everything that has been written to this already quite large library you would have a huge database. There are, however, two things missing. If you tried to add all the possible marks or sounds, not so far as we know meaningful (yet) in any language, your library would already be tending towards infinity. If you then attempted to add all the books, articles, fragments, whatever, that might be written (but haven't been yet), your library would indeed be infinite. And it would probably take you several lifetimes of browsing to find even one coherent phrase.

Searching among the chaos of infinity for ordered systems is like searching for life in the immensity of the universe. There is hardly any. But that is what being finite means; our very real restrictions at least let us communicate with each other across time and space, in a necessarily limited way. The other thing is the future. The modern period has given us probabilities but never guarantees. And the various means of forecasting the future – e.g. dream analysis, astrology, divining of various kinds, fortune-telling – are notoriously unreliable. We know that misfortune, bad weather and ultimately death will come for us but we don't know when. The future is missing in our universe and we, even now, can only vaguely guess at it. One thing we can be quite sure of is that it is very dangerous. Infinity, beyond space and time, into the future, that is what lies outside finite experience, and that is the domain that philosophy, from its earliest days, has failed to make its own.

Ideal Objects   Plato does appear to believe that a scientific (properly philosophical) approach is possible. The philosophical concept called *eidos* or 'idea' by Plato is the universal type of all its imperfect copies in the finite world, in the same way that the abstract existence of a geometrical form like a triangle is the universal type of all such triangles (drawn or modelled) in the finite world. But while Plato certainly assumes that the ideal shape of a triangle has always existed, there are some ideas that appear in history. What do the following have in common: a wedding; a production of Shakespeare's *King Lear*; the 1995 Penguin edition of Jane Austen's *Pride and Prejudice*; a copy of the Magna Carta; a totem pole; a print of John Constable's *The Hay-Wain*; a photograph; a washing machine; a motorcar; Bow Street Magistrates' Court; Pythagoras' theorem; a table? One obvious answer is that they each represent something that originated in culture and is historical. But less obviously perhaps we can also say that they each embody one of various kinds of *ideal object* like the right-angle triangle. Each stands as a particular example or representation of a general type. An ideal object ought to be able to exist independently of its embodiments. Once the principles of the electric washing machine exists any number of actual machines can be made. In the same way, each time a particular type of wedding ceremony is performed we can say that an ideal ceremony is embodied in the actual event. No two ceremonies will be exactly the same the vicar may stumble over the words during one, the bride or groom may cry or giggle or faint, it may take place in a church, a register office, even on a ship and so on – but essentially the same ceremony is performed. Where, then, does this ideal ceremony exist, to be repeated in slightly different ways but many times (potentially infinitely)? Plato suggests that there is an ideal realm of forms or types, which exist outside time and space but which are embodied by their examples in the empirical world (the world as we experience it). We get the word 'idea' from the Greek word that Plato used for these forms or types, *eidos*. According to this theory it doesn't matter how many times you draw a right-angle triangle, or make one out of wood or some other material, the ideal form of the triangle itself remains absent for the senses because all the triangles we see are simply copies of that

---

Technology

From the Greek *techne*, skill or craft, and *logos*, scientific or rational discourse, we get *technologia*, meaning systematic treatment. Technology has since the Greeks been contrasted to nature (in the Greek *physis*) and indissolubly linked to human beings and their activities. The mythical story of Prometheus is supposed to represent the arrival of technology in the world of humans. Against Zeus' wishes Prometheus, who sympathizes with the humans' abject and slavish, miserable state, gives them the gift of fire (for which he is rewarded with eternal and vile punishments). Along with fire the humans acquire the following attributes: language, writing, money, mathematics. That is, technology. Beyond myth, all we can say about these things is that they have always been with us. There is no document, for instance, that does not record the existence (obviously!) of writing and that includes those enigmatic 20,000-year-old cave inscriptions. In that sense the human just is the technological. Modern technology, however, does have a historical character and a social and cultural development that is specific to the West. To distinguish this development from the more general sense of technology we use the term 'technics'.

1. The Greek and Roman civilizations developed advanced technics of war, government and civil sanitation, among other things.
2. Technological development in the West lay low in the so-called dark ages (the medieval period) which was characterized by feudal systems of social organization and the development of powerful Christian authorities.
3. From the end of the seventeenth century technology is linked to both theoretical and applied science in very complex ways. As the values of rationality and freedom of individuals fight free of the yoke of religious authority, advancing scientific knowledge bears tremendous technological benefits in medicine, cosmology and

abstract original. Each of the historical and cultural examples I have listed can be understood in the same way.

The idea of this 'other realm' outside space and time defies both experience and common sense, but there have been remarkably few convincing alternative explanations for the existence everywhere of what we are calling ideal objects. What does Plato mean when he says that these ideas (like the

other branches of knowledge. Print as a medium for written works (generically literature) gives us the first instance of a mechanical reproduction that will come to dominate the modern period. Economic developments involving free trade and global exploration signal the power of capital and the pursuit of the production of profit for its own sake.

4. With industrialization taking off in the nineteenth century and the free pursuit of undreamed-of wealth spreading into the farthest reaches of the globe, the West enters the machine age. Technics seems inextricably shackled to the interests of capital and the increasing wealth of the wealthy but at the same time promises undreamed-of comfort, entertainment and health, if not for everyone then at least for those who can afford it. The promise lies in the ideals of democracy.

5. Against this promise dissenting voices speak out against advancing technics. Mary Shelley's *Frankenstein: Or the Modern Prometheus* can be read as an allegory warning against attempts to reproduce life technologically without nature or the female. But the Hammer Films versions of the *Frankenstein* story can show us the extent to which the widespread dissemination of the Frankenstein motif of technology-gone-out-of-control is itself a function of the reproductive technics of cinema.

6. Technology becomes global and is no longer controlled unqualifiedly by western political and economic interests. The cybernetic character of late twentieth-century technics – the possibility of self-ordering or the automaton – begins to neutralize the distinction between automatic machines and living things. The Internet offers the promise of a life in cyberspace where everything becomes a neutral function in the continuous processing of information. The question of technics is more than ever a central problem for critical theory.

idea as such) are universal? If something has the quality of being universal then it is available everywhere and at all times. This is the case for right-angle triangles of course, but it is true also for ideas of every kind. Remember that an idea is only ever represented; it can never be made present in itself. If an idea is universal then it can be made present only in the form of an example or a representation of it, a particular wedding, for instance, or at least an account of a possible one, even a fictional one, or a drawing of a right-angle triangle. As with all the most important philosophical concepts, the concept of universality is linked inextricably with another concept, sometimes re-garded as its opposite, the concept of particularity. An example of a particular triangle is this one here: ▼. Now while it should be easy to see that the universal idea of the triangle can be made present only in its particular worldly forms, it should also be easy enough to see that without its abstract universal form no particular version could appear at all. The same law seems to apply for cultural and historical objects as well. If the wedding ceremony did not have its universally knowable and repeatable abstract existence, a wedding would be only a one-off, something two people and their guests did once, never to be repeated (which paradoxically is often the way people think about their particular weddings, but a wedding is only unique for the ones who participate in it). In principle the template of the service can be repeated perhaps infinitely, performed as many times as there are people to do it, legally or illegally. In practice of course cultural objects do change with the times, though sentimental people can always revive old-fashioned forms. The point is that there is something that allows the infinite repetition of a singular form in different particular embodiments. These embodiments will never be exactly the same.

The concept of universality also carries the sense of availability. No one is in principle barred access to a universal idea. Any two people may get married. The marriage ceremony itself is universally available and takes on whatever significance is appropriate in the context, even if this is outside legal bounds – as with the marriage of two gay men in the United Kingdom or of two people one of whom is already married – and even if it is staged, as in Shakespeare's *A Midsummer Night's Dream* or in children's play. Anyone can make a washing machine or a combustion engine, given that they take the time to learn how and can afford the materials, but not everyone is *allowed* to make an Ariston or a Ford. Ariston and Ford are names given to ideal objects like domestic machines and motor vehicles so that only the authorized manufacturers can legally copy those particular types. One can see, then, that the laws of copyright and patent respond to the complex relationship between universal ideas and particular (historical, cultural, legal, economic and political) processes. Repeatability of ideas makes things possible. But it also makes problems when we consider the law. Or, rather, isn't it this that makes laws necessary?

Plato was so taken with the mathematical abstractions that inform his theory of types, or ideas, that he filled his academy (one of the first and most influential strictly philosophical institutions) with mathematicians. Here several threads are found together that emerge centuries later as the complex of relations between philosophy, science and technology. Literature and art will have been firmly relegated to a less powerful office.

The Visible and the Invisible We began with three problems to which philosophy in its early days seems to have been responding. First, the problem of previous knowledge, in whatever form, constitutes the only knowledge available. All that we can think is made possible by what has already been thought. This is often contradictory and rarely reliable and certainly offers no guarantees for knowledge about the present or future. Second, the problem of the difference between illusion and reality emphasizes the fact that we might always be deceived, taken in, by the things we regard as knowledge. What we think is reality might always be just an illusion. Third, once we have established a way of distinguishing between illusion (deceptive knowledge) and reality (true knowledge), how do we maintain that distinction? Plato considered poetic and artistic works to be the most dangerous forms of previous knowledge. Poetry was for him a kind of mythology, meaning fictional stories that people none the less believe to be true. In other words, unguarded dissemination of mythical stories might deceive people into believing what is false.

Socrates and Plato, developing a precedent set in earlier Greek philosophy, establish some powerful and influential answers to these problems. First, the application of persistent questioning will help individuals free their minds from their unfounded beliefs. This involves pushing notions, opinions and beliefs through to their logical conclusions until some *aporia* (some insoluble puzzle) has been reached. Second, the persistent valorization of what is abstract, what is theoretical in the strictest sense, will enable the philosopher to attain independence from the grip of worldly illusions. Third, this valorization of abstraction can be disseminated, communicated, even taught, by the use of a kind of allegory that works in a different way to mythical allegory. Plato's allegories are pictures, tales, representations of the powers of abstraction. The model of mathematical and geometrical abstractions can be used as a basis for theories of just about anything. Look again at how this works. A right-angle triangle, in whatever shape or size or colour, whether drawn in the sand or carved out of stone, always and everywhere has the same abstract geometrical properties. Therefore all right-angle triangles are just versions of a more original abstract right-angle triangle that has no existence in the finite world, except in its embodiments, which are its imperfect copies. It is thus possible to say that this triangle has an abstract, theoretical reality that is prior to and independent of worldly existence. The abstract one is necessary. The embodiments of it are contingent. Furthermore, everything else in the world can be said to operate on the same principles. Given the multitude of tables of all shapes and sizes, we can say that there exists beyond this world the abstract, theoretical idea of a table. These rickety wooden ones and this sloping stone one are pleasant enough but they are just imperfect copies of the single abstract ideal. In which case this whole finite world is just an imperfect copy, partial and fragmentary, of the perfect world of perfect abstract forms to which only the human mind has access, through its theorizing abstractions.

Now it's not difficult to see that this supersensible world of Platonic ideas,

---

Example

I'm still in awe of my old German washing machine, which after many years of violent moves, inhospitable kitchens and the accumulated encrustment of dust and mould, still performs its cycle with impeccable efficiency, a worthy embodiment of the ideal form. The only time it stopped working I received a lesson in the demise of Platonism among service technicians. The machine has long since lost its logo (the emblem that names it) and I do not know the make. This flummoxed the service technician who came round to fix it. If it had been an Ariston and was failing to pump water the answer would have been a specific part number. But this unknown machine that was failing to pump water had no correlative in the manual. The technician, who understood only the particularities of brand name, left me to puzzle it out for myself. This was not difficult in fact as all machines have water flowing in and water flowing out (whatever name they have). An abstract picture in my mind of how the various parts of a washing machine need to be ordered helped me orient myself among the myriad circuits and pipes that emerged chaotically from its innards. So I was quickly able to locate the blockage in the outflow pipe that stopped the pump from working. I think my reading of Plato helped me at the time but it might have just been common sense.

if we take it literally, is going to have the same effect on us that Plato feared from myth. Clearly, all concepts, ideas, types, are infinitely repeatable. That cannot be doubted unless you want to deny the infinite – which is always possible. Nor can it be explained just through empirical observation (the answer *must* be supersensible). Careful geometrical and mathematical manipulation can indeed produce inventive technological marvels.

The theoretical response, however, which is the one I am promoting here, must ask the question about the emergence and force of the idea that underlies all this, that is, the idea of 'mind' itself. I'm fine about the repeatability of forms; everything that can be understood must be repeatable in some form. But what is this infinite and independent mind, disembodied, disinterested and disengaged like most of the gods? It should not have escaped our notice that a very specific kind of myth about human reason is emerging in place of the more ancient Greek mythologies. That emergence seems to go hand in hand with the development of what already feels like a modern science. Plato seems to be promoting a type of allegory that does not complete the picture, on the one hand; but he gives us allegories that do seem to give a complete picture, on the other. It is a complete picture of a world in which something essential is missing.

One further complication lies in the fact that Socrates introduces the allegory of the cave in Plato's *Republic* to illustrate not the truth as such but an analogy that he has just given. We know already that Plato's picture of the

---

Analogy

An analogy is a comparison between things that are different but have some similarities. It is often used to explain an unfamiliar or difficult phenomenon by a familiar one or one that is more readily understood. Aristotle provides the basic logical form of analogy and writes it in this way: A is to B as C is to D. I might embody the abstract form of analogy by making the following observation: the Colt 45 is to the western as the ray gun is to the science fiction film. Or you could describe the workings of the human heart with reference to a simple pump. Thomas Aquinas observed that, as there was no literal way of speaking about God in Man's fallible language, analogy was the way to do it. In this sense analogy can provide an explanation of something that cannot be known (or doesn't exist) through something that can (or does).

world is divided into two dimensions. It is this theoretical, or hypothetical, distinction that the analogy of the visible and the invisible presents, so called because one side of the division represents the visible world and the other represents the intelligible (which is not visible). The visible dimension describes everything that we perceive of the world through the senses. This is also, therefore, called the sensible or the palpable and it composes the basic experience of what we call the empirical.

The intelligible dimension, on the other hand, describes ideas and thoughts that are independent of empirical experience. For this reason it is closely related to what is called the 'ideal' and, by further extension, the 'transcendental'. The empirical dimension is grounded in the world as we experience it, apparently through our senses. It is composed of perceptions, memories, images and expressions of all kinds. The intelligible dimension gives us that part of the world that has meaning, relationships, thoughts, concepts and ideas. Plato divides each side into two again in order to construct an analogy that can give us an idea of what the pure abstract world of ideas is like. The analogy is often called the *divided line*.

The Divided Line

/ - - A - - / - - - - - B - - - - - / - - - - C - - - - / - - - - - - -D - - - - /

reflections   things   hypotheses   truth

visible   intelligible

On the left-hand side the visible is divided into two. The extreme left is supposed to represent images of the next bit. So on the left you find shadows and reflections, while in the next section you find actual animals and trees and things that we perceive directly. The left-hand portion of the right-hand side represents all the geometrical and mathematical abstractions and hypotheses that serve as shadows or reflections of the ideal forms. So the fully ideal and intelligible realm is just unattainable. But we know of it in the same way that reflections or images presuppose the things that they are images or reflections of. So A is to B as C is to D. Or reflections and shadows are to empirical objects as hypotheses and geometrical figures are to ideal objects. The final dimension of the analogy is as follows: A is to B as AB is to CD. In other words the relationship between images and objects is the same as the relationship between the empirical dimension and the ideal one. The world we see, hear, touch, taste and smell is just a shadow of the ideal world of abstract forms. The real complication here is that the hypothesis itself is this analogy, the analogical or hypothetical form. We never get beyond it. We understand the reflections (look at something in a mirror). We understand the actual things (look from the mirror image to the thing). We understand geometrical shapes and analogies (which belong in the intelligible dimension). But we never go further than that into the final section of Plato's line, as he freely admits. We always get to a kind of last stop before the real last stop, as if your train to King's Cross had stopped at Finsbury Park but as you waited for it to continue the journey you saw that that's where the tracks ended with buffers and nothing beyond them; you have reached the end of the line before the end of the line. King's Cross is where we are going but we cannot get there. Unkind critics might suggest that Plato assumes he is at King's Cross even though he never got as far and Platonic philosophy remains stranded at Finsbury Park. But don't be taken in by the levity of my analogy. If this failure to arrive at the final destination is a serious problem for philosophy it is a major resource for Critical Theory. This is an *aporia* because while we are forced to admit that the empirical world alone cannot account for all human experience, it is nevertheless difficult to fill in what is missing without creating mysteries, myths and stories. The analogy is one of the finest manifestations of this *aporia*: something visible is used to describe something invisible. Plato's answer to this problem takes the form of a *closure* because it closes off the empirical world and asserts that the abstract truth about it cannot be accessed.

Plato's use of the cave allegory is thus a further remove from what we are already removed from. Speaking of the relationship between the allegory of the cave and the analogy of the visible and the invisible, Socrates says: 'This entire allegory you may append to the previous argument; the prison house is the world of sight, the light of the fire is the sun, and you will not mis-apprehend me if you interpret the journey upwards to be the ascent of the soul into the intellectual world' 517c (Plato 1961: 749).

The cave, or 'prison house' is our whole universe. The relation between the sun and what we see is analogous to the relationship between truth and what we can know. It illuminates and allows us to see more clearly. Look at the presentation of Plato's argument. There are at least three layers of rhetorical device. First there is the fictional dramatization of a dialogue between Socrates and others. Second, the argument is presented in the form of an analogy (the divided line). Third, the analogy is illustrated with an allegory (the cave or prison house). At each stage the notion of truth, the final destination, is presented as unattainable, hence the need for allegory. His chain of dramatical–analogical–allegorical arguments is itself beautifully clear but none of the arguments ever takes us to the truth itself.

The Empirical and the Transcendental This final *aporia* resides in the nature of allegory itself. The possibility of allegory (saying something but meaning something other than what is said) is so basic to experience that it is very difficult to examine objectively. Can you think of an allegory for the possibility of allegories? What about Plato's allegory of the cave? Allegories, Plato says, can lead to illusions. That is the truth. But the truth can be presented only in allegories, which are potentially deceptive. The possibility of the truth thus lies in the possibility of allegory. It is therefore possible to argue that the reality of human existence is something like allegory, in so far as we are always gesturing otherwise in the things we think and say. In that case the truth would not be simply elsewhere in the sense that if we worked hard enough we would arrive at it. Rather the truth would be the impossibility of arriving at the truth. To say this would be to say that the only true account of human existence is one that avoids arriving at the abstract truth. Critical Theory today is one way of engaging seriously with this possibility.

II Greek/Jew: Closure and Opening

Greek Many people have observed that western thought throughout its formative stages is dominated by two towering traditions. The first is the Greek or Hellenic tradition established by philosophers such as Socrates, Plato and Aristotle. As we have seen, this tradition is characterized by the institution of a great hierarchy where ideas, rationality and mind have privilege over material things, sensible experience and the bodily passions. The hierarchy takes a fairly systematic form once the categories have been sorted out. We can easily list them, as Aristotle does in *The Metaphysics*, so that each category falls on either side of a definitive boundary:

Material	Ideal
Empirical	Transcendental
Body	Mind
Matter	Form
Passion	Action
Sensible	Intelligible
Perceptions	Concepts
Visible	Invisible

This is all fairly abstract, of course. Well, so it should be. It is, after all, a theory. We will later see how other categories, more culturally determined ones, get added to the list. But you should be able to see also that it is a theory about the place of theory. It is a hypothesis, an abstract figure pointing us towards the ideal truth about things. And it puts that ideal truth on one side of the boundary. The boundary itself is supposed to represent the difference between the transcendental (ideas, concepts, thoughts) and the empirical (stuff we see, hear, taste, touch and smell). Now, throughout philosophy there are endless variations, hypotheses, arguments, debates and discussions about what constitutes the difference between these two dimensions. Some people have even tried to argue that there is only one or the other side of it. A 'materialist' might try to argue that there is only matter and that the independent mind is just a myth. So what is the stuff of myth? An idealist or an 'immaterialist' like George Berkeley, the eighteenth-century British philosopher, would on the other hand argue that there is only the ideal dimension. The world we perceive is not material but made up of ideas sent by God. In each case the argument doesn't abolish the other side. Rather it attempts to explain it and in theory nothing changes. But generally there is hardly any question about the existence of the difference itself. It is in fact very difficult to think without taking for granted, taking as unquestionably given, that there are both sensible and intelligible dimensions to experience and that they are different. The difference is what leads the philosophical tradition to see the two sides as being categorically opposed. In theoretical terms they are *binary oppositions*.

Take the experience of consciousness. The moments pass without my being quite able to pin a moment down, to arrest the sweep of time. But the space around me seems fairly stable and while I blink nothing much changes, even though I am very much aware that the space I can see is only a tiny fraction of what there is. You know that there is more to all this than meets the eye. Our senses let the world around us in for the duration but we also have thoughts about it, which we bring to it, add to what we see, even though the thoughts may be dreamlike, half-formed, learned from others, hypothesized. Thoughts may also be brought to bear on the empirical world so that these trees, this road, those buildings, these people can be ordered into categories, understood in certain ways, set into view in a particular way. As we have seen, that is the basic activity of theory. It is a gift from the Greeks who set into view that way of setting things into view.

So it's not enough simply to say that there are things out there and lots of different ways of setting those things into view. To say that is to subscribe to the philosophical notion of *Weltanschauungen* or world-pictures, which suggests that there are lots of different conceptions of the world depending on the historical period and cultural placement of the viewers. Any notion of cultural difference based upon the idea that my experience is determined by the dominant perspective of the culture I belong to, and that different cultures set the world into view in different ways, must also take into consideration the fact that that is itself a particular way of setting the world into view. The notion of a world-view is possible only if we maintain the classical western distinction between the transcendental and empirical dimensions themselves. The empirical is a concept that makes it possible to posit a straightforward world of objects; and the transcendental is a concept that allows for different subjective perspectives. The subject–object distinction is, however, a conception itself and as such belongs on the 'transcendental' side of things, leaving open a massive question about what an empirical world indeed *is*.

Binary Oppositions

Certain pairs of words can conventionally be contrasted in a number of ways. The strongest of these are *antonyms*, which are words opposite in meaning such as 'good' and 'bad', 'light' and 'dark'. Sometimes this tendency becomes quite systematic and what appear to be merely linguistic oppositions are revealed to be value-laden systems of categorization. Such systems are especially powerful in myth. They are based on analogies that have disguised their analogical nature. Take the example of the antonyms 'male' and 'female'. Each of the two terms has a number of synonymous associations. *Synonyms* are words that denote the same thing but with varying emphases and often different connotations. For instance some synonyms of 'female' are woman, lady, dame, bitch, cow, courtesan. 'Male' also has the corresponding synonyms man, lord, master, dog, bull, courtier. Once we line them up as binary oppositions we can get a sense of the often unnoticed connotations that are attached to particular concepts. By extension a whole structure of thought is revealed once we look at mythological systems, where synonyms are often only hinted at, or made to seem natural and obvious. The male–female one is very common. It is not difficult, in fact, to align this mythical difference with the philosophical one. Notice they each have their own symbols as well:

FEMALE	MALE
Dark	Light
Passion	Action
Moon	Sun
Body	Mind
Nature	Culture

In the East these oppositions are presented under the terms *yin* (female) and *yang* (male). Such systems provide a kind of shorthand, a shared language and a system of associations that allow people to understand and discuss their experiences and their environment. We cannot do without that side of things. The downside is that we tend to forget that our version of our environment, our shared experience, is just that: a version. Things as they appear to us are mistaken for things as they must always appear to anyone at any time at all, so long as they use their senses (or their intelligence). We forget that our version of the world is a system or that our world, in fact, is a system. Looking at the widespread existence of these systematic ways of associating concepts through binary opposition, it is possible to see how the philosophical oppositions, the difference between transcendental and empirical dimensions, fits snugly into the great mythology of man and woman (or conversely perhaps the great mythology of man and woman fits snugly into the philosophical system). This has not, of course, gone unnoticed by contemporary historians of theory. This way of establishing systems of binary opposition is a popular method of cultural analysis today. Now it is possible to show that the difference between transcendental and empirical dimensions of experience can lead to specific types of mythology. The question remains, however, doesn't the difference between the transcendental and the empirical also constitute a transcendental determination in theory?

Empirical–Transcendental Difference

If there isn't an empirical world then the transcendental cannot be transcendental at all because it has nothing to transcend, which means it must itself be empirical. That is, there are ideas *only* in experience and the actual real world is not attainable by conscious perception. That means that the empirical itself transcends the (empirical) transcendental. And so on. Questions about the very conditions for thinking anything at all, instead of arriving at answers, reveal at the basis of thought only paradox and *aporia*. But these can be productively mobilized.

Jew The other major western tradition is, as I have already suggested, the towering and contradictory edifice sometimes called Judaeo-Christian thought. Western thought is not, therefore, a twin edifice exactly, but a triumvirate, at the very least. If Christianity is to be thought of as an extension to and an attempt at closure of its Judaic past, as history suggests it must be, then whatever we say about Christianity is going to be qualified by its relationship to Jewish thought. The question about how Christian thought (and institutions) and Greek philosophical principles come to be so eloquently combined (by the scholastic philosopher-monks of the middle ages) concerns the basic conditions in the western world for the history and experience of what people today call *modernity*. The great 'civilizing' missionaries from crusaders of the thirteenth century to the nineteenth-century parson in the heart of the colonized world always held the metaphorical combination of the Bible (Old and New Testaments) in one hand and Plato and/or Aristotle in the other. Writers from William Shakespeare in England to Johann Wolfgang von Goethe in Germany (to name only two of the most widely respected), whether consciously or not, assumed the Judaeo-Christian-Greek system in all its glorious complexity and specificity for their own extraordinary expressions. Philosophers throughout western history have taken as their basic problems those that emerge from this triumvirate. For these reasons contemporary thinking often returns to those basic questions as they emerge in the form of modernity, as we know it. We can see already why the role of Judaism should be a point of real concern.

Recent work in Critical Theory has drawn increasingly on influences informed by the Judaic tradition itself, so this is a good point at which to introduce some of the terms of what turns out to be a very interesting tension. The best way of thinking about it may be through the problem of interpretation. After all, interpretation is what we're talking about and doing throughout this book. It's important to take as little for granted here as you possibly can. Interpretation traditionally implies some kind of *Hermeneutics* (a science of interpretation and explanation) and therefore, like everything else, a theory. Hermeneutics (from *Hermes* the Greek messenger) developed systematically as a branch of theology setting out laws according to which the meaning of the Scriptures should be determined. Whenever you have laws you can be certain of two things. First, a situation has demanded, called for or encouraged some kind of legislation. And second, a situation (not necessarily the same one) has granted some authority the force of legislation.

The link between interpretation and legislation will become much clearer when we deal with the problem of politics but for now it is enough to note that if legislation has been called for there might be an unexpected or unexamined reason behind it. This is an important clue. Why do you need laws for interpreting the meaning of the Bible? Why is the meaning of the Bible not self-evident in what is written there? Well, if the Bible is not *just* the tip of a vast iceberg – and its status in the history of interpretation means that we have to take it rather seriously – it *is* something *like* the tip of an iceberg because it is only a conspicuous example of the evident inability of any existing or possible text to guarantee a definitive single interpretation. In order

How to Lay Down the Law

It obviously wouldn't do you any good just laying down laws unless you could decisively enforce them. In modern democratic cities you sometimes come across people standing on soap-boxes on crowded pavements laying down laws for passers-by: 'You must do this, you must do that,' they yell, usually referring to some fundamentalist religious or political doctrine. They are usually ignored as harmless cranks until the police arrive to move them on or take them away. In other situations people (like university lecturers) have institutionally validated authority to lay down laws within certain limits defined by their qualifications and fields of expertise. However, their authority is such that, with the right tone of voice and just the right sense of vatic sententiousness, even their most arbitrary and unsound pronounce-ments can have the air of authoritative truth. Beware! Journalists, theatre critics, literary critics, book reviewers and fashion designers all play roles in laying down laws and each has more or less authority depending on the situation. In all cases the institution of authority for laying down laws is extremely complex. People often react antagon-istically to and rebel against what they believe are unjustifiable laws. If enough force is behind it, however, authority needs no further justification. Aristotle, in his *Ethics*, points out that a legislator is better off laying down laws that people are already prepared to obey because they already simply believe that they are right. An incompetent tyrant will have to work hard to protect himself from rebellious forces. A good legislator, on the other hand, can remain in power by adopting laws that have already been internalized by his subjects as something like good common sense. What we call good common sense may well be as powerfully legislated over as the most tightly governed republic. My reference to the authority of Aristotle should not, of course, be taken to mean that he is necessarily correct.

to say of the Bible, 'It means this and only this', you absolutely *need* to lay down laws because it can be interpreted in God knows how many different ways. But it is the necessary absence of the single (monotheistic) God that is behind all this, as we shall see.

One of the important assumptions shared by Judaism, Christianity and Greek philosophy (though *not* Greek theology) is the need to affirm a dimension of irreducible and eternal singularity: one truth (for the Greeks); one God (for the Judaeo-Christians). And for both, this essentially singular truth is (devastatingly) absent. Even though you can neither see it nor in any way prove its existence as such, you still feel that you must insist on it, believe in it, maintain irresistible faith. And so the Christian hermeneutic tradition concerns itself with commentaries and exegeses on passages of the Old and New Testaments of the Bible, insisting that a single spiritual truth is each time enfolded within.

There is, however, an alternative tradition of biblical exegesis, called Midrash, which denotes various rabbinical investigations of Old Testament writings and includes many self-consciously conflicting interpretations. The commentaries of the ancient *Midrashim* emerge from the Jewish oral tradition and appear in writing between the second and eleventh centuries. Midrash

---

Dogmatism and Criticism

When a teacher lays down the law his or her teaching can be regarded as being *dogmatic*. When a teacher poses problems for you to solve, his teaching may be regarded as being *critical*. Most teaching falls between these two poles. A dogma is something held as an established opinion, a definite authoritative tenet, or a code of such tenets. By the same token, a dogma can be regarded as a point of view or tenet put forth as authoritative but lacking adequate grounds. By extension the word dogma is used to define the doctrine or body of doctrines concerning faith or morals formally stated and authoritatively proclaimed by a church. The Latin *dogma* translates the Greek *dokein*, which means 'to seem' or 'to seem correct or decent', and it still has that sense for us. A dogma, whether right or wrong, is just what *seems* right and proper and is maintained by the proper authorities. The critical approach, of course, is the topic of my text but it would be *nothing* without the tension it represents with regard to instituted dogma, which we can never entirely leave behind, even if we really want to.

itself is divided into the Halachah, which deals with the legal sections of the Bible (the ones that record the laying down of laws), and the Haggadah, which includes the varied history of interpretations as well as commentaries on civil customs and doctrines. A crucial difference between Midrash and the Christian tradition lies in the text itself. Where the Christian Bible is based on a relatively unambiguous Greek text, the Midrash is concerned with the Hebrew Bible (the Old Testament), which is much less stable as a text and has many alterations, emendations and alternatives, with obscurities that demand scholarly interpretation in nearly every verse. So while the Hebrew text might be difficult it nevertheless has the virtue of being richly readable, whereas the Christian text lends itself more to dogmatic and unreflectively singular readings. The differences that result between Jewish and Christian exegetes and preachers point to a fundamental difference in the interpretation of religion itself. The Jewish tradition concerns the potential plurality of interpretations, which can be considered neither true nor false, for nothing in the Hebrew Bible can be regarded as a definitive singular statement. Yet the Christian tradition is based on a dogmatic notion of singular fundamental truth, which must be defended against the permanent danger of falsification by fallible interpreters. It is this that calls for legislation.

Singularity and Plurality The point here is to show that the difference between the Jewish and the Greek traditions involves something like the difference between a law that governs diverse and plural interpretations, which never get back to a singular truth, and a law that governs singular interpretations, which always gesture towards a singular truth that itself stays none the less out of reach. It is the difference between the plural and the singular.

It is important to understand that deciding on one or the other of these alternatives cannot solve the question of interpretation. Rather, the difference and the productive tension between the singular and the plural may bring to light a situation that allows us to rethink the basis of interpretation itself. The formulations of the tradition can be a great help in this. The tension between the singular and the plural is everywhere. Thomas Aquinas, the great Church father who perhaps did the most to sew together the Greek and Christian teachings, gives a clear exposition of the problem. He tells us that because humans lack a perfect language we cannot speak unmediatedly of a single God. If we could the result would be what he calls a *univocal* utterance. That is an utterance that means only what it means, means it once only, and cannot be used to mean anything else at all, ever. Catholics know the problem. All kinds of people speak of God, including pagans, but they do not speak of the same God (the same idea of God) – and only the Catholic *really* knows what the word God means. In other words, 'God' is an *equivocal* word in so far as it means lots of different things in different contexts. Because we have no access to univocal language, Aquinas tells us, we must make a compromise. So we use *analogy*, which he says lies somewhere between equivocality and univocity. As we have seen, analogy, and its whole family of rhetorical devices like *metaphor* and *allegory*, do an excellent job of standing in for concepts or things or even whole dimensions (i.e. the transcendental) that are radically, drastically and chronically absent from the finite world of everyday empirical experience. And, as we have seen, *analogy* is the concept *par excellence* of concept construction. Is there anything else? It looks as if Christian dogma is reduced to laying down the law but only by analogy, for there are no grounds available for lasting authority on these things. Enter the need for faith.

So far I have been focusing the discussion on trends and tensions to be discovered in the writings of the Greek, Judaic and Christian traditions but it is important to see that the problems uncovered here can be used as veritable resources by any Critical Theory and it is precisely these problems that persist in the later stages of what we are calling modernity. They are decisively historical yet we might resist reducing them too hastily (in a dogmatically historicist gesture) to localized historical periods if we want to see the relevance of history for our own critical condition. Hermeneutics develops as a form of religious interpretation but Aquinas's problems (and his solutions) are maintained throughout all secular realms of interpretation and they crop up again and again during the modern period, in surprising contexts; for instance, wherever the problem of the difference between the singular and the plural is posed. It is the problem of language that mediates the questions of truth (for the Greek) and of God (for the Christian). In the modern period it is language and the question of meaning that brings the grounds of the whole puzzle to light.

Opening and Closure   These are deceptively ordinary concepts. They are apparent opposites. To close something (a box, a road, a factory, a shop) is to act on and thus to change its condition of being open. To open something, on the other hand, either reverses its former condition of being closed (in the case of a box or a shop) or institutes a condition that is new (in the case of a road or a factory). I am not being unduly simplistic (simplicity is what we crave here, so go with me on this) when I say that these two opposing concepts are fundamental and deserve clarification. In the world of the Hebrew exegete there is a fundamental openness of interpretation (no 'single right way' closes down the possibility of alternative readings). In the case of the Christian preacher, however, reading imposes a form of closure. Closure prevents newness and is always reactive – you don't begin something by closing it. You can, however, bring closure to an end and that (oddly enough) brings about a new condition. Opening Pandora's box (in the Greek myth) brings sin into the world. Opening a new Ford factory brings employment to Dagenham. The great closure of western theology and metaphysics attempts to promote everything that is missing or said to be missing from the finite world to a fabulous beyond in which all things infinite, eternal, perfect and true reside. The opening is a straightforward consequence of the metaphysical and theological failure to maintain that desired closure.

III Modernity

What do people mean by the modern period? A number of significant events that occurred in the first half of the seventeenth century allow people to date the emergence of a distinctly modern period from then. But there are those who would put the birth of the modern even earlier, using the term 'early modern' to describe the rapidly changing and turbulent times once referred to as the Renaissance. To date the modern period from the first half of the seventeenth century is to locate the emergence of some leading though often contradictory assumptions, which are supposed to form the basic attitudes of modernity. But we need to make one more qualification before proceeding. In the form of a question (like so much Critical Theory), is the concept of *period* adequate to account for what we mean when we talk about the experience of modernity? The answer, strictly speaking, will be 'no', but we will give reasons for this later on. In the meantime, the following concepts and trends will help us to excavate the site of what we call modernity.

Empiricism Empiricism usually denotes a specific way of thinking about knowledge, about where it comes from, what knowledge is, and how much or how little can actually be known. So while you might read about empirical philosophers such as John Locke, David Hume or John Stuart Mill (all British, notably), you will also come across references to the 'empirical sciences', which dominate until well into the twentieth century. But apart from explicitly and avowedly empiricist trends we find that empiricism dominates even those who oppose it. Empiricism teaches that all knowledge is derived from experience and must be tested only with reference to palpable evidence. That is, at its extreme, everything we know concerns what we can actually see, hear, taste, touch or smell. The world is just as it appears to us through the senses and can be understood only through painstaking empirical analysis. Empirical thinkers, then, dispute any knowledge said to be derived from supernatural, transcendental, mysterious origins and direct our attention to things, facts, matters that can be understood as having real existence. This way of thinking, as you can guess, leads to what we now know as 'good common sense'. As we have seen, even those who oppose empirical thought as such would be unlikely to deny the existence in some form of things that are apparently real, but they would deny the lofty status that the empiricists ascribe to them. What is important here is that empiricism simultaneously draws limits to what can be known – knowledge is restricted to the empirical sphere – yet it opens knowledge up to the promise of completion. Ultimately it denies any such sphere as the ethical or any metaphysical foundation that lies beyond finite empirical experience; but in so doing, it provides a basis for the development of something like a total science. The assumption is that the more we can understand about the universe on scientific grounds then the more control we should be able to exercise over it. It is difficult within the terms of modernity to deny the extraordinary advances that have been made in the development of scientific thinking and in technological progress, much of which must be at least connected with modern empiricist trends. But some of the most effective and radical developments in critical and cultural theory have been made against empiricist assumptions, often apparently against good common sense. That no doubt leaves theory open to ridicule from certain points of view, which we will have to examine quite carefully. However, the logical conclusion to be drawn from empiricist thought would suggest that we ought to be able to do without theory altogether. And that already rules out any notion like empiricist *thought*.

Rationality   The very fact that empiricism has another side ought to be enough to draw it into question. But rationality, its alter ego, is generally constructed as being its opposite. Throughout the eighteenth century a philosophical battle raged between empiricists on the one hand and rationalists on the other (with a decisive victory for the empiricists towards the end of the eighteenth century until the ground-breaking critical philosophy of Immanuel Kant entirely shifted the terms of the debate). So where the empiricist claims that knowledge is available through the senses alone, the rationalist asserts that there is a transcendent source of knowledge in the human mind (Anaxagoras's *nous*, of course) and this is needed to organize and understand the world of empirical experience. The privileged example for rationalists (following Plato) is the realm of mathematical and geometrical proofs which demonstrate a kind of universal truth beyond deceptive and capricious empirical finitude. It is striking, in this respect, that both Gallileo and Descartes can be found independently asserting the possibility of a mathematical understanding of the universe and its contents. The assumption of a rationalist is that the universe is itself rational. Only much later, in the twentieth century, do scientists and mathematicians start asking awkward questions about phenomena such as cloud formations and coastlines, which do not seem to conform to traditional mathematical principles. These questions lead, via what will be called 'Chaos Theory', to an entirely new and very interesting mathematics.

Freedom   It is not by chance that a certain concept of freedom comes to be valorized and affirmed at the same time as the tension between empiricism and rationalism becomes more tightly defined. As the clarion call of Enlightenment during the eighteenth century, the concept of freedom signals both an empirical problem and a rational principle. Jean-Jacques Rousseau begins his famous and influential *The Social Contract* (1762) with the observation, 'Man is born free, and everywhere he is in chains' (Rousseau 1997: 41). And towards the end of the eighteenth century the critical philosopher Immanuel Kant describes Enlightenment as 'Freedom from Man's self-incurred tutelage' (in 'What is Enlightenment?'). Notice the assumptions that inform both these statements. First the concept of freedom used here suggests something like an original state, which has been lost. (The echo of Rousseau in Joy Adamson's story about her life with lions in Africa, *Born Free*, and the sentimental song that goes with the film version of it are simplistic reminders of this Enlightenment notion of freedom.) Freedom, according to these conceptions, is a natural and original state that has been lost to Man but might somehow be regained in the process of his emancipation. In that case modern civilization must be regarded as being in some sense a form of enslavement, enchainment or like a prison. The analogy with Plato's cave, then, is not so far behind these conceptions, for it is Man's essential freedom of *thought* that is supposed to mark him out from machines and the brutes. The fact that this notion of freedom emerged while the slave trade was at its height, and while the notorious middle passage between Africa and America was at its busiest, is a telling indication of the contradictory historical processes at work in modernity. The other important assumption in both Rousseau's and Kant's formulations involves the concept Man. To the greatest extent, it seems, Man ought now to be able to take centre-stage in the unfolding of his world. Not only do his scientific (both empiricist and rationalist) projects allow a hitherto undreamed-of understanding of the objective universe, but his freedom allows him to intervene instrumentally in the process of his own history. So, on the one hand, freedom and science march forward together; but, on the other, they are fundamentally opposed because where science is concerned with uncovering unchanging necessary truths, freedom concerns Man's intervention in a world considered in terms of its absolutely unpredictable contingency. What is more, Man's thought doesn't seem to be constrained or determined in the same way as his body is governed by, say, the laws of gravity. There are no established principles that can be used to predict the actions of Man. Man is free to make a science of his universe but he cannot make a science of his freedom. One of the urgent tasks of much eighteenth- and nineteenth-century philosophy thus becomes one of reconciling the claims of scientific necessity and moral freedom.

Man   Who, then, is this 'Man'? Now *that* is a question. Some would argue that for eighteenth-century thinkers Man is not, as was overtly affirmed, just anybody, but covertly Man turns out to be based on the image of a specifically modern rational western white bourgeois educated male. This would thus exclude madmen, women, lower classes, children and members of other races and men from other (selected) historical eras as well as machines and brutes. But despite the now obvious sexism and racism that hindsight allows us to pinpoint with easy clarity, the notion 'Man' is a bit more enigmatic than that and deserves further elaboration. Man is not, in itself, a new concept. Nor is freedom. Aristotle, in *The Politics*, qualifies his statement that '*Anthropos* is a political animal' by saying that this is a being that is capable of both the best and the worst of actions – hence the need for a politics. And in the late middle ages controversies about 'grace' concerned precisely the level to which Man could be held responsible for his own actions. But in each case Man (or *Anthropos*) is characterized in terms of a teleology that is beyond him. A teleology is a long-term system or plan that gives a final purpose to the things that fall under it. So the human race, in the late middle ages, could be characterized in terms of what lay beyond the finite existence of its individuals – some kind of after-life – all part of God's great plan. But mythical notions of destiny and fate, far from falling out of use altogether, become covertly disseminated within the new scientific vocabulary that begins to take over from religious cosmologies in providing representations of the world as such. So where the ancient conceptions of the universe rested on the consolation of richly detailed mythologies and theologies, the new scientifically oriented conceptions place the emphasis firmly upon the shoulders of Man himself, who thus becomes a new mythology rigged out with a rationality supposedly equal to the new calculability of the universe in its entirety. So if God was *strictu sensu* unknowable, Man, who takes over the transcendental role, tends to become his own blind spot in an otherwise increasingly transparent frame of vision. In other words, the enigma behind the question 'Who is Man?'

turns out to be just that – enigmatic in a necessary way. The answer would spoil everything.

Progress Progress is a name for one of the ways in which mythological fate, or Man's destiny, becomes disseminated within the new vocabulary of modernity. We have already learnt that empiricism has limited the field of knowledge to the finitude of empirical experience. The effect of this is to transform that finitude (which has since Plato and throughout Christianity been nothing more than an impoverished and imperfect temporary condition) into the rich and fecund totality of existence itself (if it wasn't for some pesky reservations that we must come back to shortly). It's not that finitude is any less impoverished just at the moment (as it were). Rather, the new conception involves the belief that this finitude can be transformed by the scientific and moral manipulations of rational Man himself until it becomes that perfect world which everyone hitherto had assumed was in some fabulous beyond. Modernity thus involves a spectacular shift in the experience of time itself.

Arguably, contemporary Critical Theory evolves as a set of responses to certain crises or problems with the general condition of what is often referred to as modernity. This can be considered in terms of philosophical, aesthetic, historical, economic and technological developments that have occurred in the modern period, beginning in the sixteenth century. However, modernity does not become visible as such without certain important trends within it, which reflect back often very critically upon it. These self-critical trends are often seen most clearly in the various forms of aesthetic production known as artistic or literary modernism. What is striking about these modes of self-reflexive critique are, indeed, the aesthetic strategies. Modernism is both a reaction to and a constituent part of modernity that involves a set of engagements utilizing a variety of aesthetic, political and ideological strategies. The modernist avant-garde, especially, attempts to shake up consciousness of the present and to rethink relations to the past and to the future. The problems of modernity become clearer in the kinds of conspicuous engagements that are made in the name of modernism and these engagements thus constitute a vital source for critical theory.

Centrism Modernity becomes visible only when the conditions that modern subjects take for granted emerge as problems. These taken-for-granted conditions, then, turn out to be the consequence of an evolution of ideas, a historical development, which imperceptibly governs the thoughts and experiences of modern subjects. Modernity thus names the constructed field of historical ideas and attitudes that underlie the experience of being modern. A constituent part of that experience, however, is its naturalization. That is, the modern subject implicitly assumes that his or her experience and view of ordinary things like the self, the world and other people is the normal or natural view to take. Scientific rationality (a uniquely modern perspective) is equated with a certain 'common sense', which only primitives and the insane or stupid would refuse. Other perspectives tend to be relegated to the past (primitive cultures) or to the margins (third world cultures, women, lower classes and so on). This experience thus involves certain forms of *centrism*.

ETHNOCENTRISM   Ethnocentrism involves implicit or explicit privileging of one ethnic region over all others (which are thus placed on or outside the margins). As the political, technological, aesthetic and philosophical achievements of the West develop, a parallel set of assumptions about the primitive and regressive nature of other parts of the world are developed too. Whenever problems have greeted the progress of the western cultures, on the other hand, a corresponding hyperbolic praise of exotic 'others' around the globe has often accompanied the response. The result of ethnocentrism is usually a forgetting of the specific ethnicity of the centralized ethos (western culture). Instead, that is either regarded as the *universal* against which everything else should be measured. Or else it is regarded as not quite finished, needing only this or that imagined quality to complete it.

ANDROCENTRISM   This formulation comes from the word 'androgynous', meaning hermaphrodite, from Greek *androgynos*. Being androgynous could mean either having the characteristics or nature of both male and female, or being neither specifically feminine nor masculine. Or it can mean having traditional male and female roles obscured or reversed, as in an androgynous marriage. Whatever, the meaning implies a neutralizing of the differences between the sexes. Androcentrism, on the contrary, implies a normalization of one sex (in western culture, men) to the exclusion of the other. So sexual difference, it is assumed, does not matter in the basic definition of what it is to be human. This assumption, together with the highly stratified accounts of the actual differences between men and women, comprise one of the central contradictions of modernity. The implicit assumption is that there is only one sex and that sex is male as opposed to female. If we tried to live according to this contradiction the feminine could only cause trouble, which, of course, it does, to the impoverishment of actual women's experience as they are forced to live inside this kind of representation.

PHONOCENTRISM   This is a slightly surprising one, but since the work of the French philosopher Jacques Derrida began to appear in the early 1960s we are getting used to the fact that this version of centrism is crucial. Phonocentrism implies the standardization of the phonetic unit as the key component of language. What this means is that the spoken word tends to be privileged over the written one. Somehow speaking, which seems very close to breathing, comes to be correlated with meaning. The living truth of what I say begins its journey of compromise and corruption only when it is written down. Hence the phonic unit ('*a*') is privileged over the written unit ('*a*'). As you can see there's no real difference, is there? However, what I say and what is written down bear no relation to each other whatsoever, except via the conventions by which we unconsciously associate the one (*a*) with the other (*a*). As we go on we shall see that this type of connection (i.e. absolutely no relation) comes to trouble and determine all attempts to identify and assert any unit of language whatsoever. Research has revealed that this prejudice against the graphic mark is based on a desire to maintain belief in something that cannot be presented to experience but must none the less be affirmed, that is, the notion of transcendental truth.

LOGOCENTRISM   Logocentrism involves the belief in the existence and identity of meaning beyond and outside the various modes of representation, such as language and other sign systems. Sign systems include aesthetic genres as well as ideas, encompassing both epistemological ideas such as *understanding* and *reason* as well as moral ones such as *virtue* and *crime*. In many cases philosophers have had to conclude that even the basic elements of experience, like perception, memory, imagination and surprise, are formed of systems of representation, and that the world we experience is at best the consequence of human modes of framing it. The logocentric belief accepts the vulnerability of representation but asserts an independent truth, or a realm of meanings that we get access to only through the most painstaking philosophical and/or scientific labour. Generally, then, logocentrism involves the stubborn rejection of the inescapable power of rhetoric to make or break the world. A committed Critical Theory is obliged to respect this attempt, as it reveals, on the one hand, the inescapable power of rhetoric and, on the other, possibilities towards an outside or beyond that would allow for any development or change from oppressive forces. Such an escape is not likely to be possible but that needn't mean we have to rest within oppressive systems and institutions of meaning, as we shall discover.

Descartes' Judgement   The philosophy of René Descartes represents, along with a number of other developments, a peculiarly modern way of thinking, one that reaches into all domains of thought and action. What distinguishes Descartes from earlier forms of philosophy is the way in which he establishes the relation between thought and the world of objects. As with Plato, the hierarchy remains. Ideas inform our knowledge of the world around us. Ideas are not sensible (reducible to the senses). They are intelligible and belong to a dimension of thought that operates independently of the empirical dimension. Descartes' project, as he presents it, is to establish a method for arriving at precise judgements about the world. He therefore begins with the need to form clear and distinct ideas as a basis on which to build a more complex but no less precise epistemological edifice. The interest that Descartes provides for a developing Critical Theory lies in the succinct elegance of his arguments. Descartes contributes lasting treatments to (at least) three philosophical concepts. First, the *subject* of philosophy, which stands over against the world of objects, has never before been given so much attention. But the activity of the theorizing, objectivizing subject is for us another embodiment of philosophy's great *aporia*, the difference between the empirical and transcendental dimensions. The Cartesian subject is in principle entirely disembodied and free and is therefore entirely transcendent. The empirical world lies at his disposal. Once the right method is learned, Descartes argues, the subject can advance his knowledge unhindered. Second, the precision of the *judgement* by which clear and distinct ideas are applied to the world of objects allows a knowledge of the universe and everything within it that had hitherto been impossible. It is on this basis that we also witness the rapid growth of modern scientific thinking. Third, the idea of *infinity* as a clear and distinct idea replaces embodied notions of the Christian God. Descartes argues that one of the most basic ideas we have is of God. But once we read the texts carefully, we see that this God is essentially unknowable except as the idea of infinity. Now, in this section I am going to explain how the privileged role of the subject, the refinement of the judgement, and the idea of infinity combine to give us a picture of the activity of theory. Before looking at the philosophy of Descartes in more detail, let's have a look at the problems that it must respond to.

Otherness, Infinity and Difference   Philosophy has always been concerned with relations to what for want of a better term we may call 'the other'. Philosophy's 'other' is anything that cannot be conceptualized, that lies beyond the representations of the mind. Many would argue that the feminine is one such other, philosophy being resolutely masculine (I wouldn't argue that unreservedly but there is plenty of evidence to show that the philosophical norm is often simply masculine). Many would say that western notions of otherness concern other cultures, peoples who do not fit the western philosophical interpretation of humanity, which contrasts humans with animals and machines. There are problems with these notions of otherness, not least because, strictly speaking, the other is unpresentable. Otherness in general constitutes a philosophical problem in so far as it has no concept – it has no repeatable ideal form – so there is often a tendency for people to slot some empirical object in its place (it is possible to show that the woman and the African, for instance, are both 'others' for certain powerful nineteenth-century westerners for whom the white male constituted the norm). The problem is thus the relation between thought and its outside, and the identity of the thinker. If you don't have a concept of the other (as black and/or female, for instance) then it is as difficult to come up with a definitive concept of the self.

So the problem of otherness had its correlative in seventeenth-century philosophy as the problem of maintaining a single unified subject who could remain objective in a world of plurality, difference and change. If thought belongs to a mind (as Anaxagoras described it) that is both infinite and independent, then what is the relation between this naked singularity and the many objects that surround it? What is the relationship between the one and the many? You can always bring strange objects into your domain by attempting to categorize them under concepts. But will there ever be an end to it? Will there ever come a time when all the possible objects of knowledge have been categorized and stored up in ordered hierarchies?

The short answer to that is 'no'. For a start, 'the many' certainly looks like being infinitely many. But also, and more importantly, this infinity is not simply the number of particular others that would need to be taken into account by a total knowledge. Rather, this infinity is what remains absent in the finite world (including unheard-of arrivals and events that might occur in the future). All this points to the existence in the finite world of something that at all times resists knowledge: otherness. What this means is that otherness has something important to do with the infinite and, crucially here, something to do with the possibility of knowledge, which seems to come into being as a need in the face of otherness. It is, paradoxically, a part of knowledge that lies outside knowledge, infinitely. It is what is always missing from knowledge.

When I *know* a table I frame the object with my concepts of table (its status as furniture, its relation to chairs and to other tables, other types of table, the materials to which the concept of table gives shape and purpose, the wood, the glass, the metal), I add a whole network of ideas, beliefs and relations to what I see on the surface. My knowledge looked at in that way is a set of restrictions that enables me to understand my world. I share this knowledge with many others. They include designers, manufacturers and retailers of tables, who know what they are to be used for and must thus follow the very conventions that also activate my knowledge of what to do with them, though many fashionable designers would stretch the conventions to their limits. They also include my friends, relations and acquaintances, who often gather together around tables for eating, drinking, talking and related social rituals. When westerners visit the East for the first time they may become 'confused about certain things. What are those low ornate boards around which silk cushions are arranged? The presence of containers on these boards signals that they serve in the same way as tables do in the West. But how do you sit? On your knees or squatting or with legs crossed? Cultural difference often reveals knowledge to be limited, conventional and, of course, cultural. But it is important to see that 'otherness' is not 'other cultures'. Otherness is what makes other cultures (including yours) possible and it is the strangeness that intervenes between cultures (making both yours and mine strange).

Science fiction writers and film producers (maybe even set designers) have to consider unknowns beyond their cultural background. What would a table in the twenty-third century be like? The future is unknowable but it can be represented. Isn't that a terrible paradox? How can you represent something that has never been present? How can you represent the future? The answer is through fiction – this is not a twenty-third century table; it is just a fiction. Furthermore, the fiction is unlikely to depart very far from the conventions of a particular cultural background – you've got to think of your audience, after all. But the paradox is not limited to science fiction. Otherness is not just the future. The unknown surrounds us like a night fog. When something emerges from it or when we enter into it with the torches of our knowledge flaring we can understand it (whatever it is) only by the light of the concepts we already know, which we then apply until 'the other' is no longer other. Indeed, the effects of otherness may change our knowledge, but never by giving us otherness itself. Otherness (like the future, infinity, aliens and so on) remains always and by definition beyond the frame of our conscious gaze. If there is something we cannot know we can still represent it through the possibility of *inventing* it. This possibility seems to infect the possibility of all our knowledge.

The example of something as humble as a table is complicated enough but what then do I mean when I say I know a person? How much more complex it all is when compared to the conditions for knowing a table. What does it mean when I say that you are 'not acting yourself' or 'that's not like you'? It's all very complex. The sentence has both a literal meaning and a more involved *implied* meaning. Literally, the sentence says, 'the way you are acting does not conform to the way you are'. There is a discrepancy between what you are and the way you are acting. The more involved implied meaning suggests that the way you are acting does not conform to the norms that my concepts of you provide. Less analytically, if you like, the way you are acting does not conform to what I think of as 'you'. What that actually means depends upon context. Perhaps you have fallen out of love with me and show less interest in me than you used to do. Perhaps you are drunk and I want to censure you. Perhaps you are being rude to someone and I want to caution you. On the other hand, perhaps you have fallen in love with me and have given me a present. Perhaps for the first time in months you are not drunk but articulate and sober, like Anaxagoras. On another tack altogether, perhaps some devilish professor has created an android that looks just like you but hasn't quite got the fine-tuning sorted out. Or maybe your twin has turned up out of the blue as in some banal soap opera plot.

Where then does my concept 'like you' come from? When I meet someone for the first time I have to rely on some very flimsy presuppositions in order to form a preliminary knowledge. Appearances help; dress, gender, age are all things that can help me form a preliminary category or concept because there are conventions in all societies that through habits of practice and representation (television, film, advertising, magazines) allow us to make quick assumptions. Anyway, I have nearly always already formed quite involved concepts on those issues. Previous knowledge can help; what I know by what other people say or by repute may give me some idea of what to expect. But of course appearances can also hinder – they are deceptive – and reporting by others, as we know, can be extremely unreliable. In any case I cannot avoid prejudice – now hold on, *I'm* not prejudiced – but yes you are; knowledge depends on prejudice, making judgements about an object before impartial judgements can be made. To an extent all these prejudices (at least in terms of the basic judgements, if what I see is, say, a twenty-eight-year-old woman wearing jeans and a T-shirt or a forty-year-old man in an expensive suit and tie) can be tested when measured against repeated behaviour and things said and done. My concept of you will be gradually 'enriched' as time goes by just through your repeating certain anticipated ways of behaving. (Depending on my psychological state I may well be capable of completely missing 'uncharacteristic' ways of behaving if the 'characteristic' ones are repeated regularly enough, which simply means that I see what I want to see.) Only when you act 'out of character' (out of concept) does the concept need modifying. In a world where the likelihood is high that even one's closest friends and relations might suddenly and unannounced act out of character or do something different, it is no surprise that so much is invested in making things 'the same'. Difference is disturbing. It is as if getting to know someone is a form of domesticating his or her difference. But at the same time we desire difference, as if mechanical repetition was somehow unreal. As if a relationship would get dull or stale unless it was with someone for whom your concept was never complete. Things will be all right as long as there is always the risk that after, say, twenty years of being together one of an apparently happy couple might suddenly leave the other. If that did happen, of course, it would reveal an aspect that was never evident, acknowledged only in retrospect while the bereaved lover's concept of the beloved undergoes its inevitable crisis. What has happened? The lover's other, the otherness of the beloved, has outstripped the will-to-knowledge of love.

The problem of course is not just restricted to our dealings with other people. As the philosophers never tire of explaining, knowledge, whether passed on by others or gained through painstaking observation, is intrinsically capable of deception. This is why scientific knowledge demands so much rigor and painstaking empirical research. Knowledge can take you in. You might always have been wrong. On the one hand this is clearly a bad thing for the philosopher who wants to know things with certainty. But on the other hand, with the concept of 'otherness' (which, remember, is not a concept at all), it is possible to begin to see this 'bad thing' as being also something that makes things possible. What would you have without the other? Everything would be reduced to your own thoughts, cut off from the world of legislations, negotiations and love. Take it a step further: without the possibility of such associations would you even have your own thoughts? Don't your concepts already come out of some other domain in order to be applied to the domain of the other? Otherness: without it knowledge would be nothing. Otherness is the possibility of knowledge.

How to Not Define the Other   The point to be clear upon is this. *The other* is not a concept, not a name for some thing or someone. It doesn't name an object. It is used to gesture towards that which is noticeable only ever by its absence. How then is it possible to know it? It isn't. Knowledge of the other is precisely impossible. But it is possible to present accounts that demonstrate that this impossibility is absolutely necessary. Remember that Plato uses analogy to gesture towards a truth that cannot be represented. (The truth is this: the truth is impossible to represent. Here is a good single-sentence précis of Plato: 'it is impossible to represent the truth and that's the truth.')

It is also possible to communicate by analogy the importance of not defining the other. Psychology tells us that there are cases of people whose nervous disorders cause them to see *nothing* as a terrifying and persecuting presence, a 'no-thing'. Beginning with the absence of, say, the mother's breast, they develop a pathological fear of absences, spaces, gaps, that each time represents the monstrous no-thing, which seems to reflect back upon them the sense of their being nothing. In place of nothing a terrifying monstrous presence is hallucinated. What these cases illustrate is that in order to cope with existence we all must learn to cope with the vivid and threatening experience of the no-thing. The very transition from infantile dependence to independent adulthood seems to be about learning to cope with absences, lacks and unconsummated desires. But we often do this by replacing the nothing with a something that supports the sense of self that I believe completes me, fills in the gap that is *my own otherness*.

Philosophy too sometimes seems not to be able to cope with the absences that foil aspirations to total, universal knowledge, the absences that make philosophy for ever incomplete, fundamentally open (that's what calls for the closure). So even things that cannot be named get named anyway and in the place of the absent other some innocent third party fills the role.

SUMMARY   Here are the problems.

1.   *The other* has no concept. But there is always a trace of the other. Knowledge, which operates through its concepts, must therefore engage with something that resists it.

2.   Finitude is the condition of the knowing subject. Quite simply we are limited as to the space and the time we have for developing knowledge, let alone anything else. You know that corny old phrase 'so much to do, so little time'? Well, that is the big philosophical problem. It seems that we humans are incapable of passing our knowledge around with any efficiency. To be sure, we can now gather vast stocks of information but that is demonstrably not the same as knowledge. Once a wise person dies the sum total of their wisdom dies with them. All that remains is what they have been able to pass on through teaching and writing. Then it becomes yet more of that 'previous knowledge' contradicting the working remains of all the other scholars. Anyway, what did anyone's 'sum total of wisdom' ever amount to? Certainly not enough for anything like a total knowledge. We think Einstein knew a lot. Compared to others, that is surely true. But even that much is put to shame by what he didn't know. Anyway, finitude is not just a limitation on time. Time itself is a limitation – remember all those notes you took for classes three years ago? How much of that knowledge do you actually remember? As we learn new things we forget old ones. When you think about it the whole idea of a total knowledge begins to look absurd.

3.   Language is the only means of communicating knowledge. Yet as

nearly every philosopher will say, language is a big problem. A proposition can so easily be misunderstood, quoted out of context, repeated by people who only *think* they understand it. When you try to put your knowledge into words, it doesn't matter how clearly you express it, you cannot guarantee that your reader will understand what you say in the way you meant. We will look at this problem in more detail later.

Cogito Ergo Sum   It is convenient to use Descartes as a reference point because so much of what is distinctively modern is found with him. His statement *cogito ergo sum* ('I am thinking therefore I am') was from early in his writings an example of one of the few most basic, 'clear and distinct', ideas a philosopher could have. The statement asserts the certainty of my existence as a consequence of the mere fact that I am thinking. So long as I can be sure that I am thinking I am sure that I exist. A lot hangs, then, on this 'I am thinking'. Descartes' most sustained and widely read demonstration of this is to be found in the first two of his *Meditations*, which can be recommended in their entirety. What comes to be known (admittedly rather absurdly) as *The Cogito* (the 'I am thinking') concerns the faculty of human judgement. What he is concerned to do in *The Meditations* is to prove that judgement in his sense is free of deception. If he succeeds, of course, then there's a nice ground for human knowledge indeed. Clearly, he is attempting a fresh reading of the already traditional search for a ground for truth. It is this sense of 'fresh reading' that is crucial here. The problems of philosophy, charted in the preceding sections, are only clouded further by slavish adherence to traditional authorities like Plato and especially Aristotle. The point of judgement ought to be free from all forms of deception, like stories and myths, certainly, but all old previous thinking, the whole cultural heritage, including the hazardous wastes of rhetoric. Furthermore, human imagination and, worst of all, the fallible evidence of the senses each in their own way serves to compromise the clarity and distinctness of proper thinking. Thus a mixture of geometry and philosophy produces what we now know as Cartesian method. Cartesian *doubt* is one way of characterizing this and, to be fair, Descartes certainly encourages such labels because his most influential book, *The Meditations*, is built upon a cunning narrative; he calls it 'a fable of the mind' in which the philosopher takes his addressees through several stages of doubting. It is advisable not to play down the literary aspects of his writing, for this will lead the casual reader into the error of taking his *demonstrations*, which are almost explicitly theatrical acts, as a kind of authoritative knowledge. For instance, when he complains of the multiplicity of philosophical authorities, none of which provides a convincing account of the grounds and first principles of knowledge, we may be forgiven for assuming that Descartes is announcing a historically based crisis, the breaking down of epistemological foundations. He would thus represent, as has been argued, a shift from medieval thought to a peculiarly modern one. However, this would fail to do justice to the argument as we find it. Descartes' point is not much altered from Plato's. The thinker must each time start from scratch in order to be sure of his or her knowledge. The real question is to what extent is this escape from the multiplicity of sensuous distractions ever possible? The demonstrations are, at the very least, suggestive of the necessity for the kind of theatrical cunning that Descartes himself employs to get his 'Archimedian point' across.

Having first of all doubted the words of the authorities (which is always easy to do – why should we believe Aristotle or Plato when even they often contradict each other?), he moves on to the evidence of his senses. Why should I believe that what I experience – what I see, hear, touch, feel or taste – is real, or even a true representation of the object world to which I get this sensuous access? The question is, now, can I successfully doubt that my experience is real? Descartes uses a number of examples. Sometimes my dreams seem to be as real as when I am awake. I cannot, therefore, be certain that I am not dreaming. There are some madmen who think they are made of glass or that they are kings when they are really just poor beggars. Controversially, Descartes says, 'but these people are mad and it would be extravagant if I followed their example'. Instead, he follows a different kind of extravagance. If I hypothesize a demon, who systematically tricks me into

---

Frontiers

The problem raised by frontiers (both as distinguishing marks and as loci of passage) is that they reveal the multiplicity of ways in which persons and communities interact with those from whom they are or wish to be distinguished. This multiplicity is often regarded as a *bad infinite* because not only does it describe the multiple conditions of similarity and difference that define association per se, but these frontiers can be marked only with reference to the particularities of a given and specific community. The bad infinite is thus finitude itself, history and historical specificity, and as such it subjects us to all the distressing vagaries of contingency and chance. In this respect the Cartesian judgement remains tied to the metaphysical tradition in which it emerged first of all as a concept.

believing that all my experience is real when in fact it bears no relation to actuality, how can I be sure of anything at all? Added together, the doubting and the hypothesizing prove one thing for certain (while all else remains in doubt), that is, that I am doubting and that I am hypothesizing. The invention of the evil demon may of course be an invention of the evil demon too, but the fact that I can doubt even this cannot be doubted. Therefore my capacity to throw all aspects of my experience into doubt, except that fact of doubting itself, ought to be able to serve as a ground for certain knowledge. It is called *cogito*, 'I am thinking'. Notice that when *I* adopt Descartes' *I*, I do not say, for instance, 'Descartes thinks therefore he is'. That would simply not work. It works only for what he calls 'this "I"'. The *I* is a philosophical subject that remains constant in the statement, whoever occupies that place. So the auto-biographical aspects of Descartes' *Meditations* are purely fictional in so far as any *I* ought to be able to occupy that slot in the demonstration. Descartes calls his method *analytic* as opposed to *synthetic*. Traditionally the *synthetic* method would set out a theorem and follow it with a series of proofs. What Descartes is interested in here is putting the addressee into the position of the philosopher going through his hypotheses and doubts.

Along the way, Descartes gives a couple of crucial demonstrations of what this 'thinking', the Cartesian *judgement*, involves. At a certain point in the demonstration Descartes says, 'when I look out of the window I say that I see men passing by'. He then points out that this is an error caused by habitual ways of speaking. These passers-by might be automata clothed in robes with hats and masks (more Cartesian extravagance). Rather, says Descartes, 'I judge what I see to be men'. Hence the faculty of judgement gives sense to what is visible and, once again, a version of the difference between the transcendental (judgement) and the empirical (the visible) comes to organize the argument. And, once again, the rhetorical field is the frontier between the two.

The Cartesian Subject is Not a Subject   As we have seen, Descartes' texts reveal a desire for reasonably certain grounds among irreducible cultural and philosophical difference. Furthermore, Descartes' subject, now canonically referred to as the *Cogito*, is often today described as being in crisis.

This identity is often equated with the social identity of the modern subject – an identity before anything else who is capable of making free and rational decisions. For this reason Descartes is a good place to go in order to discover the conditions out of which such an identity so powerfully emerges. What we learn is surprising, because if we consider the sense of 'social or cultural identity', we find that the so-called Cartesian subject is actually not really a subject at all.

In 'Rule Twelve' of the *Regulae ad Directionem Ingenii* (*c*.1628), Descartes describes how knowledge of the outside world passes through five relatively discrete operations or events of perception, culminating in the reasonable judgements and understanding proper to the operation of 'native intelligence' or 'mind'. I want to make special reference to Descartes' qualification here, which is typical, that he 'lacks the space to include all the points which have to be set out before the truth about these matters can be made clear to everyone' (Descartes 1985: I, 40). It would be a mistake to regard this as a passing comment, contingent on the purpose of the work in hand. Descartes' method is predicated on the desire for a certainty that is always 'embarrassed' by the so called 'bad' infinite: lack of time and space, prematurity of reason, infinite regression in solving complex propositions, infinite computation with respect to probabilities and so on. Indeed, in *The Meditations* the same problem emerges as reason for not assenting to the standard interpretation of Man as 'rational animal.' He writes 'from one single question, we would fall un-wittingly into an infinite number of others, more difficult and awkward than the first, and I would not want to waste the little time and leisure remaining to me by using it to unravel subtleties of this kind' (Descartes 1992: 75). As a consistent response to this problem, Descartes' method, learned not only from geometry but from the allegorical arts as well, involves setting out 'as briefly as possible [...] the most useful way of conceiving everything within us which contributes to our knowledge of things' (Descartes 1985: I, 40). The method of explanation, which as such implicates judgement with the ability suc-cessfully to communicate the judgement itself, allows the reader to follow a chain of 'suppositions' that otherwise 'detract not a jot from the truth of

---

The Subject in Crisis

This is probably most marked in work following Julia Kristeva and Jacques Lacan who both demonstrate a tendency to see Sigmund Freud and psychoanalysis as having decentred a subject commonly described as 'Cartesian'. In Jacques Lacan's *Ecrits* we read: 'the forma-tion of the I as we experience it in psychoanalysis [...] leads us to oppose any philosophy directly issuing from the *Cogito*' (Lacan 1997b: 1). And in *Four Fundamental Concepts of Psychoanalysis*, Lacan uses Des-cartes to assert that while the subject of psychoanalysis is of Cartesian origin, it emerges only in the wake of the signifier (Lacan 1986: 47). We will go on to explore these positions in a later section.

things', a chain exorbitant to the truth that none the less makes 'everything much clearer' (I, 40). This kind of abstraction, based in part on the abstractions of algebraic geometry, subordinates logic to figuration.

In demonstrating the first phase he asks us to conceive the process of passive corporeal sense perception as one in which senses are 'impressed' by data, 'in the same way in which wax takes on an impression from a seal' (Descartes 1985: I, 40). In this way Descartes can generalize all sense perception under the term shape ('nothing is more readily perceivable by the senses'), including colour, which is his example here. He writes: 'we simply make an abstraction, setting aside every feature of colour apart from its possessing the character of shape, and conceive of the difference between white, blue, and red, etc. as being like the difference between the following figures or similar ones' (I, 41). His diagrams show three figures as follows: one is constructed of five equidistant lines of equal length drawn vertically; the second is a square divided into sixteen; the third is a larger version of that square but with diagonal lines bisecting each of the sixteen internal squares. The given figures are entirely arbitrary, so colour is to be understood through the abstract principle of differentiation per se. The generalization is therefore regarded as being sufficient owing to the special quality this time of a *good* infinite. He writes: 'The same can be said about everything perceivable by the senses, since it is certain that the infinite multiplicity of figures is sufficient for the expression of all the differences in perceptible things' (I, 41). And, because infinity can be grasped neither by the senses nor by the imagination, we know that the intellect will never run out of means (figures) for representing its objects in abstraction. Again, in *The Meditations*, Descartes asks rhetorically:

> Is it not that I imagine that this wax, being round, is capable of becoming square, and of passing from a square to a triangular figure? No indeed, it is not that, for I conceive of it as capable of undergoing an infinity of similar changes, and as I could not embrace this infinity by my imagination, consequently this conception I have of the wax is not the product of the faculty of imagination. (Descartes 1992: 85)

So the frontier between the object world and the transcendental judgement actually constitutes the meeting point of two types of infinity. The first is the multiplicity of worldly forms and the second is the ability of human judgement to find potentially infinite substitutions for representing them. Descartes' philosopher is thus the master of a universe of signs, which each time need the perpetually creative activity of interpreting judgement.

The mind is thus simply the name for an exorbitance, the excess that infinity suggests, which lies between the subject and the outside world. The difference between good and bad infinity thus characterizes the frontier itself as an absolutely necessary condition of representation and, as we would see if we took a sufficiently complex range of the colour spectrum and represented each difference with a graphic mark, writing. This just *is* the *Cogito*. Writing in this sense in fact defines Descartes' universe not only as semiotic but also as constituted essentially by a relation to 'the other' as potentially infinite and randomly determined addressee.

Authority and Enlightenment   It is interesting in this respect that Descartes' writing abounds with masks, guises, performances and representations of all kinds, all acting as mediation for the otherwise absent light of reason itself. More than a hint is given here as to Descartes' participation as a social subject. 'Actors', he writes in his very early *Praeambula* (*c*.1619), 'taught not to let any embarrassment show on their faces, put on a mask. I will do the same. So far, I have been a spectator in this theatre which is the world, but now I am about to mount the stage, and I come forward masked' (Descartes 1985: I, 2). There is no proper scholarly context for this passage although it does bear traces of the Renaissance and baroque traditions that surface from time to time in Descartes' texts. But this 'I' we will gradually come to think of as the *Cogito* itself, as 'this "I"' in *The Meditations* (II, 17); and *Discourse on Method*, Descartes' 'autobiography', is in fact a biography or as he calls it 'a fable' of reason (I, 112), in which reason adopts the role of the good citizen, pretends to accept the most conservative, normative and dominant of historically and nationally established principles for a 'provisional moral code' in order to demolish them and rebuild them on firmer grounds (I, 122–31). On this note what will come to be known as the call of Enlightenment is sounded.

The status of the *Discourse* itself is important. On the one hand it demonstrates the way that a single philosopher arrives at a level of certainty from which to proceed in developing a well-founded knowledge. The demonstration is, as Descartes is at pains to point out, at best a history but perhaps better understood as a fable, like the pictorial representations of Renaissance art:

> I shall be glad to reveal in this discourse what paths I have followed, and to represent my life in it as if it were a picture [...] but I am presenting this work only as a history or, if you like, a fable in which, among certain examples worthy of imitation, you will perhaps also find many others that it would not be right to follow. (Descartes 1985: I, 112)

So the *Discourse* may offer examples for imitation, but imitation should be understood here in a specific way. What the *Discourse* reveals in this passage is that the very grounds for the certainty of any given singular understanding can be represented only in the ungrounded rhetoric of fable or resemblance, the 'being-like' of allegorical representation. Descartes' rationalist legacy emphasizes rather too easily the role of mathematics in an epistemology understood in terms of exactitude conditioned by order and measure. The rationalist aspects of Descartes' legacy was developed *par excellence* by Leibniz, who substituted the logical structure of judgement for Descartes' suspension of assent. But we are able to read in the writing of this early modern philosopher that resemblance and exactitude are neither coincidental nor opposite (which we know is true of all relations of difference and identity). Rather, both are grounded in the infinite frontier itself, which is *difference*, understood by us as the *Cogito* – 'I am thinking' – my existence as representability. Thus the notion of imitation that Descartes employs is quite subtle and must be understood as a term in the series of models, masks, fables and representations of all kinds that characterize his work, the importance always of choosing one's authorities, or models, with prudence. Thus what is to be imitated might perhaps best be thought in terms of imitation itself: 'Fables make us imagine many events as possible when they are not. And even the most accurate histories, while not altering or exaggerating the importance of matters to make them more worthy of being read always omit the baser and less notable events; as a result, the other events appear in a false light' (Descartes 1985: I, 114).

So the *Discourse* combines fable (which conventionally offers an allegorical version of proliferating images, doublings and subtle illusions) with the necessary idealizing finitude of a history, with its lacunae and arbitrary overemphasis on selected aspects of an otherwise chaotic constellation of events and relations (the bad infinite). This very important qualification, which again points to Descartes' consistent philosophical practice, must be taken into consideration when reading the fable/history of the *Discourse* itself, which records a vast pretence.

Architectural Metaphors   The nature of the pretence should be regarded as a kind of 'temporary accommodation', in line with the architectural metaphors he uses. For instance, he says: 'before starting to rebuild your house, it is not enough simply to pull it down [...] you must also provide yourself with some other place where you can live comfortably while building is in progress' (Descartes 1985: I, 122). This metaphor is of course constructed upon the subtle foundations of a whole allegorical system of architectural metaphors, which develop as a response to the familiar problems.

With regard to philosophy (as we have already observed), not one of its problems is not subject to disagreement (Descartes 1985: I, 115). And this situation is repeated in the empirical world where Descartes, while mixing with people of different humours, ranks and races, discovers 'almost as much diversity as I had done earlier among philosophers' (I, 115). So the problem of diversity is answered through the concept of singularity, and the architectural metaphor goes to work:

> Buildings undertaken and completed by a single architect are usually more attractive and better planned than those which several have tried to patch up by adapting old walls built for different purposes. Again, ancient cities which have gradually grown from mere village into large towns are usually ill-proportioned, compared with those orderly towns which planners lay out as they fancy on level ground. Looking at the buildings of the former individually, you will often find as much art in them, if not more, than in those of the latter; but in view of their arrangement – a tall one here, a small one there – and the way they make the streets crooked and irregular, you would say it is chance, rather than the will of men using reason, that placed them so. (Descartes 1985: I, 116)

Paradoxically, Descartes' aesthetic would favour new cities like Singapore or Milton Keynes over London, Venice or Dublin, while enjoying the particular buildings, squares or even neighbourhoods of the latter over the former. But no single architect could compose a well-ordered whole out of eccentric individual visions. Again, for Descartes, the randomness that seems to have determined the way cities have grown is representative of the way individuals, who are sometimes capable of reasoned judgements, find that they are mere parts in an irreducible and chaotic diversity when faced with each other. This passage by Descartes is echoed by the twentieth-century Austrian philosopher Ludwig Wittgenstein in a famous passage from the *Philosophical Investigations* where he compares language to an ancient city: 'Our language can be seen as an ancient city; a maze of little streets and squares, of old and new houses, and of houses with additions from various periods; and this surrounded by a multitude of new boroughs with straight regular streets and uniform houses' (Wittgenstein 1958: 8).

In Wittgenstein's description the 'new boroughs' seem to conform to Descartes' ideal of 'orderly' planning, overlaid, as Rationalism itself is supposed to have been, on ancient foundations, chaotic yet brilliant with baroque beauty. But both descriptions (one just after the beginning of modernity, the other just before the end) are linked by a single thread by which the bad infinite becomes good in analogy. Citizens are already subjects who must speak in the peculiar metrics, write in the labyrinthine marks associated with the places where they live.

In the work of the Swiss linguist Ferdinand de Saussure (see Chapter 4, 'Structuralism') we read about the myths of language-change. In Part Three of *The Course in General Linguistics* he notes that, in the view of the early linguists, 'anything which departed from an established order was an irregularity, a violation of an ideal form. Their illusion, very characteristic of the period, was that the original state of the language represented something superior, a state of perfection. They did not even inquire whether that earlier state had not been preceded by a still earlier one' (Saussure 1978: 162). Saussure then proceeds to demonstrate that 'the main factor in the evolution of languages, and the process by which they pass from one state of organisation to another, is analogy' (162). And it is precisely analogy that serves to 'counterbalance the diversifying effect of sound change' (160). Analogy turns chaos into regularity. It coverts a bad finite into infinite possibility for change. It demonstrates yet another way in which reason is necessarily linked to the exorbitance of rhetorical processes. And it reveals a notion of chance that is consonant with necessity. Language, if only in this sense, belongs to the generalization that reveals a massive tendency to inertia in community: the more participants there are who may influence change, the less chance there is for fundamental change to occur. F. de Saussure again observes that:

> Legal procedures, religious rites, ship's flags, etc. are systems used only by a certain number of individuals acting together and for a limited time. A Language on the contrary, is something in which everyone participates all the time, and that is why it is constantly open to the influence of all. This key fact is by itself sufficient to explain why a linguistic revolution is impossible. (Saussure 1978: 74)

This is more or less what Descartes is saying with the architectural metaphor:

> We never see people pulling down all the houses of a city for the sole purpose of rebuilding them in a different style to make the streets more attractive; but we do see many individuals having their houses pulled down in order to rebuild them, some even being forced to do so when the houses are in danger of falling down and their foundations are insecure. This example convinced me that it would be unreasonable for an individual to reform a state by changing it from the foundations up and overturning it in order to set it up again; or again for him to plan to reform the body of sciences or the established order of teaching them in the schools. (Descartes 1985: I, 117)

Here, Descartes' pretence to conservatism with regard to issues of education and state reform is in fact a radicalism regarding the desire to construct the grounds for individual critical distance from existing social standards and norms. Citizenship is the mask of a subjectivity that ensures social existence but that is open to a radical exorbitance – the exorbitance of the *Cogito*, or writing, or analogy – which all name the possibility of a substitution that cannot be named in fact.

So the architectural metaphors are not merely metaphors. They do the very work that the metaphors describe: they offer the exorbitant ground of a surrogate vocabulary without which 'rebuilding' would remain one of the transient dreams of imagination; analogy offers the possibility of an exterior locus to the temporary accommodation of historical conditions. More crucially, analogy does the work of architecture itself. As G. W. F. Hegel writes in his *Introductory Lectures on Aesthetics*, the task of architecture

> lies in so manipulating external organic nature that it becomes cognate to the mind, as an artistic outer world [...] It raises an enclosure round the assembly of those gathered together, as a defence against the threatening of the storm, against rain, the hurricane, and wild beasts, and reveals the will to assemble, although externally, yet in conformity with principles of art. (Hegel 1994: 91)

Architecture thus resembles the ways in which communities guard themselves against the chaos that is their outside, it 'resembles' them and offers a kind of communal identity in style and structure. Martin Heidegger in the twentieth century also writes on the purpose of a Greek temple:

> It is the templework that fits together and at the same time gathers around itself the unity of those paths and relations in which birth and death, disaster and blessing, victory and disgrace, endurance and decline acquire the shape of destiny for human beings. The all-governing expanse of this open relational context is the world of this historical people. (Heidegger 1971: 42)

Here the specific nature of the architecture stands not only as the symbolic representation of a historically grounded people, but it also determines the essential experience of their world in its entirety.

It is a possibility, however, that architecture always exceeds its limits and sculpture, 'for the limit of architecture [...] is that it retains the spiritual as an inward existence over against the external forms of the art' (Hegel 1994: 91). The 'spirit' of a community is never 'contained' as an inward form; it is rather already the sculptured exterior of architecture itself, because architecture inspires its material and forms 'as the determinant content on behalf of which it sets to work' (91). In other words spirit builds its dwelling place around itself against a hostile outside, but that dwelling always bears the inventive trace of spirit itself, thus externalised in the becoming-sculpture of architecture, the dwelling itself. Spirit just is the sculpture of its external form. What all this says, very briefly, is that the essence of humanity is what it builds itself, whether out of the ruins of inherited legacies or bravely, independently, against the storm. This hint of heroism is never far from the modernist version of things. If the analogy between architecture and language is taken seriously, then the suggestion is that the human is no more or less than the milieu of the historical, cultural edifice, in language or in buildings, where the human must dwell, for this dwelling just is the human. If so, then we dwell in a radically unfinished project.

Responsibility The modern subject, then, may seem something like an infant, shrouded in a terrifying authority which it needs in order to define itself; or it is something like Descartes' *I* masquerading in the guise of the good citizen in order to be the true philosopher, enclosed by the architecture of geographical and historical forms but opening those forms up at their limits to an exorbitance that is spirit, or reason, nothing but this exorbitance.

Descartes solves the problem of cultural difference with reference to the infinity of figures available for representation. But the masquerade of subjectivity can be overcome only through the recognition of selfhood *as* masquerade, i.e. by reason. Reason, however, as otherness itself, can only ever be manifest in the extravagant forms, the fables and fictions of the philosophical *oeuvre*, the extravagant fashions and necessary chances that help construct the bizarre cities of modernity and postmodernity. Only an engagement with the exorbitance of the frontier itself will help account for the conditions and responsibilities of the modern (and the postmodern) self. We should just add that any attempt to understand cultural frontiers within an already established framework (the finitude of a conceptual system) would discover that the frontier is not reducible to the available concepts. And because these limits to political thought are points of potential transformation, potential for change is thus conditioned by this infinite frontier.

3 The Political

I Being

Rhetoric There is a connection between the various domains of knowledge that reveals a common basis in rhetoric. This rhetorical bridge proves to be decisive and wide-ranging, linking anthropology, psychology, politics and aesthetics, as well as the variety of natural and social sciences. Notice that in the distinction between the types of science a rhetorical and, even from a scientific point of view, entirely unsatisfactory boundary has already been drawn between the natural and the human. It is as if the two realms are utterly different, and require different types of logical procedure; two incommensurable types of logic (with no logical connection between the two). Aristotle divided knowledge into its natural and political dimensions, so that in his texts we read about the universe, about physical and biological nature, on the one hand, and aesthetics, politics and ethics, on the other. There is even a text in Aristotle's work that sets out a philosophical ground more fundamental than this distinction. This text came to be known as *The Metaphysics* (meaning 'after', 'on' or 'about' the physics) and it deals with the most general questions of philosophy, notably 'thought' and 'being'. However, a number of Aristotle's works deal with what we would now recognize as the field of *discourse*. The extant remains of his *Poetics* (most of which has never been recovered) deals with the nature and function of tragedy in art and manifests an extremely sophisticated aesthetics. His *Rhetoric* charts the ways in which discourse functions to persuade and construct arguments. His *Interpretation* examines the relation of thought to language. His *Logic* begins what was to unfold over centuries as a systematic exploration of the processes of human reasoning. A careful reading of Aristotle would reveal that the *rhetorical* investigations (interpretation, rhetoric, aesthetics and logic) could be reduced neither to nature nor to politics (in Aristotle *phusis* and *politeia*). But rather, the works on knowledge itself, including the *Metaphysics*, show that a rhetorical dimension affects and compromises each attempt on Aristotle's part to arrive at a clear and unchanging ground for understanding in *any* of the

95

relatively distinct areas. The explicit or at least implicit assumption of any metaphysics (which can take numerous diverse forms) is that something, some logic, some order, whether hidden or essentially discoverable, determines things and thus can itself become the object of knowledge. An inescapable meta-knowledge is thus implied, a knowledge on or about or after knowledge. Aristotle was not the first to attempt to chart knowledge, systematically bending knowledge back on to knowledge itself (asking, what can we know about the process and the ground of knowing?) but his metaphysics is among the most influential and systematic. At its heart are the problems of rhetoric.

The Being of Things   What is implied at the very basis of metaphysical questioning is the question of Being. Here things get broken down into empirical and transcendental dimensions. In natural knowledge the empirical is made up of what appears to us: e.g. rocks, trees, skyscrapers, sun, moon and stars. The empirical thus reaches out to the infinite heavens beyond which we may only imagine. The empirical is the dimension of beings, that is, things that are (as in the phrase 'there is a moon'). The question of being thus concerns the dimension of the phrase 'there is'. What is involved in asserting 'there is' (there is a moon, there are stars)? We seem to assert of particular beings an essence or some kind of essential predicate, that is, their being. In traditional western thought, which is a sophisticated grafting of diverse theological and philosophical traditions, *being* as an essential predicate takes the form of a transcendental determination, a determination from beyond and outside empirical experience. 'The eternal', 'the infinite', 'the being whose existence is essence', 'God', 'the order of things', each of these phrases indicates some sense of how the transcendental realm is systematically opposed to the empirical. The eternal can be assumed to exist only outside and beyond mutable worldly existence. Plants, animals and people die, as do suns and planets eventually. The infinite as such is outside experience, though the mathematical versions of it are suggestive and can inspire startling intuitions of infinity, as can certain kinds of poetry. 'God' or, in one Catholic version, 'the being whose existence is essence' is just everywhere, wherever there is existence God is its essence. According to this account, if something exists the source of its existence is God. Everything else is a creature whose existence is owed to something not itself. 'The order of things' may refer us to the obscure but perhaps real system of ordering of the universe and all the things in it. Discoveries in cosmology always strongly hinted at an order to the universe even though there are innumerable chaotic counter-examples. The development of modern empirical science always hinted strongly that there was an order that eventually scientists would discover, in the meantime adding up all the accumulated facts until a total picture emerged. This supplemental faith links science to the great world religions in its own way. Sadly for many scientists this kind of faith is no longer possible. The point, finally, is this. The transcendental indicates a kind of ordering or structuring of the empirical, an ordering that cannot be discovered or embedded within our experience. We assume, without witnessing, the existence of some universal or grand principle of ordering, which in its absence needs to be intuited or hypothesized on the basis of what we do have. We have access only to our traditions, histories and customs, the appearance of things in the world, our mode of reasoning and the events and actions in which we participate. In the absence of that universal principle of ordering we do have a range of rhetorical strategies for producing critical yet faulty versions of 'the universal' that may stand in, as it were, temporarily.

Being and Beings One of the most important, yet controversial, philosophers of the twentieth century, Martin Heidegger, concentrates his attention on the relation between finite beings and their Being by focusing on the phenomenon of finitude itself. Thus predicates like time, anxiety, guilt and death, come to organize his earliest writings (specifically 1927's *Being and Time*). *Dasein* ('being here') is the name he gives to that being for which Being is first of all a question (i.e. philosophers like you and me) and an issue. Very briefly put, we can say that Being (in the English translations with a capital B) stands for the modes of interpretation that constitute what traditionally would have been the transcendental determination of empirical experience. The separation of the transcendental from the empirical is seriously compromised by Heidegger, increasingly so after his major work (*Being and Time*) ground to a halt uncompleted. (It was published anyway after pressure from his university authorities; nothing changes in this sense, I am thinking, as I type this section at a rate of knots you wouldn't believe.) The importance of Heidegger's work is reflected in terms of its influence on our reading of the tradition. His understanding of western modernity is based upon a series of quite extraordinary readings of traditional philosophical and poetic texts, from the pre-Socratics to his own contemporaries. It seems odd to think that a deep understanding of the ancients should provide him with prophetic insights into the most modern trends of modernity, specifically the direction of technology and the uprooting of cultures that many have observed is the key to postmodernism. But this would follow as a matter of course if his most consistently stated thesis turned out to be the case. That is, that *Dasein* is grounded in its historicity – humanity is a historical being – and in the modern era this has been forgotten as technics takes over and dominates every other mode of being. Technics, in this sense, is not just technology and machines; it is, rather, a specifically technological interpretation of the world. The greatest danger, thought Heidegger, was that the alarming successes of technology, which reaches deep into the earth and stores up its energy as standing reserve, would enslave and ultimately destroy humanity on the basis of a promise to cure the inevitable condition of finitude (*Dasein*'s temporal and finite condition). Being is in fact essentially ungrounded but watched over by poets, artists and philosophers, who remember the modes of interpretation by which experience is produced. The key distinction is between the *ontological* (Being) and the *ontic* (beings). The former is the dimension of ungrounded historical being. But no access can be achieved to the realm of Being without passing first through the dimension of the ontic, which we know through our particular modes of being (e.g. Caucasian professor of literature in a South-East Asian university). The difference between the two (my particularity experienced empirically and my Being, barely glimpsed) becomes known as the *ontic–ontological difference*. However, it is a little difficult to think about what is meant by this difference unless we recall our previous discussions of the alterity of the other. Heidegger, it seems, is determined to think Being through as a kind of presence or event towards which only the greatest effort is required. But, as I am suggesting, our only real access to the universal ground of our existence and responsibility appears to be radically absent, so I suspect that we will never arrive at Being – that radically there is *no* Being.

II The Political

Aristotle's famous phrase, '*Anthropos* is a political animal', was intended to resonate beyond what is often regarded as the political field today. But he did intend a clear distinction, in so far as there are other beings that are not in his sense political. It is his version of what marks out the human from all other things, and what makes the human special. What is the definition of human? Aristotle would say, 'the political'. Just as there have been numerous diverse attempts to discover the underlying order of beings in nature (*phusis*) there have been numerous diverse attempts to discover the hidden order of the political. In the wider sense the political concerns the organization of social relations. In a more focused and personal sense it implies the problem of ethical action. So the distinction between the empirical and the trans-cendental is operative here too, in almost the same way as with the order of things. The empirical stands for actions and passions of people in their historical, geographical specificity. It implies relations of economics and force. The transcendental thus implies a realm where these relations are determined.

Aristotle's *Politics* charts the different modes of government that are possible and explores the conditions upon which one might arrive at the best form of government.

What lies at the heart of the problem of government is the evident fact that people are different and they have different interests. Some desire more freedom, others wish for greater wealth. Some require better transport or healthcare. Some require more security, more policing. Others require less. There are some interests that often go unnoticed or that represent the needs of those with little influence or power (the homeless and hungry). Yet in some cases a minority may have influence over decisions that affect everybody, thus

---

Best, Most and Generally

In order to arrive at a general sense of any being, Aristotle's analysis sets out to find a model for the best example of the thing under analysis. The function of the thing is first established. What is an eye for? It is to see. What is the best kind of eye? It is an eye that sees well. What is a government for? It is to govern with an eye for everyone's interest. What is the best kind of government? It is the government that most approximates the ideal of government where all interests are taken into consideration in matters of legislation. The circularity of the argument is a genuine problem. But implied is a strong teleological factor. To ask about the final purpose of something, is to ask what is its *telos*? When Aristotle asks the question of man (what is the function of *anthropos*?) his answer is a little obscure. The function of *anthropos* is *praxis* or ethical action. But *praxis* has no example that can be generalized (like the seeing of the eye). A brave action may not be brave if I just copy someone's bravery in a different context. *Praxis* demands the simultaneous skills that make up deciding and acting in the midst of unpredictable contingencies. Thus, according to an inescapable logic, humanity is perpetually indefinable. The essence of the political is in perpetual retreat. It is as if the *telos* of humanity, its final purpose, is somehow just itself, which means that individuals must write their own *telos*, their own final purpose. What is the function of man? The function of man can be discovered with reference to the best of men. Who is the best of men? That is the kind of question that will cause fights. Again, the circularity of the argument is likely only to get us in to trouble philosophically.

putting them in a position of privilege (Members of Parliament with business interests). Furthermore, it is impossible to predict in advance what particular antagonisms might arise. We never go for long without reading about some dispute between neighbours. Someone has loud music playing. Someone else grows his or her trees too high. Neighbours have been known to fight, often with fatal consequences. The courts are flooded with such disputes. Analogous situations occur on every level and, in severe cases (though never rare), neighbours wage war. Therefore any conception of justice, on whatever level, must include laws according to which one can act but with enough leeway to account for situations that cannot be predicted according to those laws. The keeper of these laws must also be their interpreter in such cases that arise. The judge is also always an arbitrator – a perpetual third party who must decide according to principles divorced from the immediate empirical interests of the two parties. Even when one of the parties is right that right does not belong to his selfish interest but to the law as neutral arbitrator. In this way it is possible to promise (if not to deliver) a universal or 'human' right.

The transcendental thus stands for all those modes of theory that attempt to approximate the obscure order of things that would solve the ills of social relations (whether within a state or internationally). And, in a more focused way, it stands for the hidden imperative of a moral law that seems always to be off the edge of experience. In so far as laws are unavoidable they are based upon some existing rationale. That rationale, in its rhetorical dimension, will always have been a gesture towards a transcendental determination.

The argument for sovereignty might run as follows: why must I give my money to the king? It is the king's law. Where does the king get the right to make such a law? As the king it is his divine right. Against this type of argument it would always be possible to oppose a kind of empiricism. According to the above logic, people would owe fealty to a ruler only in a social environment where belief in the divine was dominant. Once that is shaken then the divinity argument is going to look a little fragile. But it takes seismic cultural shifts of immense historical structures to shake such arguments. And the appeal to the bluntly empirical must itself assume the rhetorical power that makes such ungrounded belief possible in the first place. So the empirical cannot simply be opposed to the transcendental. But rather, empiricist rhetoric can be opposed to transcendental arguments. Rhetoric would then be in the service not of right or truth but of an alternative power base. Once again it is the absence of a universal principle that comes to organize the political, for a universal principle seems always to be what is desired. We are stuck with a subtle play of often-antagonistic forces each gesturing outside to some unimaginable exterior that would ground them all.

III False Consciousness

In the modern period the subtle yet powerful forms of fealty, which I have just simplified with my example of the king's divinity, come to be known as types of *false consciousness*. False consciousness is a notion that allows the philosopher or critic to assert and demonstrate that our most deeply held beliefs about ourselves and others, about right and wrong, about the universe in general, are based upon assumptions about these things that are complacently accepted and culturally produced. Our culture is made up of stories or narratives that support a dominant version of things that is generally accepted as true. The stories are not simply false, of course, but rather they are related to the true situation by distorting it, disguising it, distracting from it and lulling its subjects into the false way of thinking. Analysis of false consciousness tends to aim for a kind of enlightenment that provides an understanding of (1) how the false situation came about and (2) what the true one is. The problem for contemporary Critical Theory is that the narratives of false consciousness are in no clearly discernible or final way less fragile

---

Figurative Language

Figurative language is the language of tropes. A trope is a form of substitution whereby a metaphor, simile, allegory or even parable stands in for another way of speaking. The ideal form of discourse is often regarded as the literal. However, the phrase 'literal language' is an oxymoron. An oxymoron (itself a kind of trope) puts two contradictory words together and is often used in poetry. William Wordsworth's description of his experience of a trickling mountain stream as 'peopled solitude' is a good example. The notion of literal language is a *logocentric* dream because language, just in terms of what it is at the most basic level, already stands in for something other than what it is (for what we assume it means). So by the same account the phrase 'figurative language' is a tautology. A tautology (which is also a kind of trope) is a phrase which more or less says the same thing twice (e.g. an 'evil devil'). A literal use of language takes advantage of the essential ability of language to stand-in-for things other than itself. Thus, literal language is just a particular form of language generally. The condition of being always somewhat literal and somewhat figurative (somewhere between contradiction and tautology) marks language.

than the narratives they would expose. The narrative of false consciousness opposes a rhetorical procedure against another rhetorical procedure.

There is a story by Jorge Luis Borges called 'The Circular Ruins' in which a wizard goes to the jungle and arrives at the ruined temple of Fire. There he dreams a man into being with the help of the god of Fire. This man believes he is real and is terrified by fire, but the wizard knows that he is not real and thus also knows that fire cannot harm him. The story can be understood as a fictional commentary on narratives of false consciousness. In the western tradition Plato's allegory of the cave is the best-documented reference point. The cave itself represents the finite world of our experience, the empirical, which, Plato assures us, is a deception. However, in order to move beyond the deception Plato's only resources are the very means of representation that are also the sources of our deception: allegory, analogy and metaphor. These sources together add up to the field of discourse that we call in general figurative.

In order to step outside the cave – to see it, as it were, from outside experience, that is, from a transcendental viewpoint – the cave has to be constructed and represented. In other words we are still inside the cave but now looking at a representation of it in order to imagine what it might be like to get outside if only it were possible. Imagine that you enter the town hall and find yourself looking down at a model of the town with the town hall in beautiful scaled-down reproduction. You are stuck in there, says Plato, and you cannot get out, except by means of representational models like these. This is the basic pattern of the false-consciousness narrative. It involves a kind of rhetoric that builds a representation of the world as somehow being contained within a larger one, which we can imagine only by virtue of the representational model. Of course you can leave the town hall but can you ever get beyond your own experience? What is important to understand about this is that, without getting us to an outside, the rhetorical dimension is still able to take us beyond experience. The beyond is not necessarily what we'd happily call *real* (remember fire in the story of Borges's dreamed man), as Plato demanded. But if representations like the cave and the miniature town hall could not have been made, then what kind of experience would ours be? Doubtless it would be entirely different. Experience would not be what it is without the possibility of these representations. Thus something of the empirical does always seem to involve a passage through what we are for the moment calling the transcendental. This is the dimension that traditionally is called *theory*.

Graven Images   The narratives of false consciousness move through several variants throughout western history and each deserves careful analysis. Here I can provide only a few directions and pointers. I have already introduced the medieval Dominican scholar Thomas Aquinas, whose writing is among the most majestic and impressive. He managed systematically to integrate Christian teaching and Greek philosophy, through a series of close commentaries on Aristotle's texts that run parallel with readings of the Christian pedagogy. For our purposes we should focus on two related issues. The first is iconic representation and the second is language more generally. Iconic representation occurs when a figure or an image of some kind stands in as a sign for something, often an elusive entity like a god. Every culture, it seems, has some image of their god, representing the object of their belief. Pictures of saints, the Christian cross, carved Buddhas and the ancient Greek statues of Zeus are all totemic images or icons. In the strict sense an icon is symbolic or representative of something. Christians worship in front of an image of Christ on the cross as a symbol of Christ himself and his suffering sacrifice. Thus, the word 'icon' comes to mean any kind of symbolic image, including the icons on your computer screen, which are images of pathways into some densely written store of digital information. This icon stands for 'My Computer' on the Microsoft desktop:

Nowadays you can replace the stock icons by downloading uncountable alternatives, from characters from *Star Wars* to animated figures of all kinds, which will give you a personalized shortcut to wherever you tend to go in the digital universe. What makes this possible is no different from the conditions that make all substitutions of tropes possible, the tautology 'figurative language'. So an icon might look like the thing it symbolizes (a tiny computer screen for my computer) or it might not (a *Star Wars* Gungan can be used instead). In the case of religious icons we are dealing with representations that are often images of something no one has ever seen. They are sensuous personifications of abstract or otherwise impossible concepts. Notice in that last sentence that the difference between the empirical (sensuous, visible) and the transcendental (spiritual, invisible) is strongly implicated. Aquinas, working with a Christian theological philosophy that owes as much to Greek as to Hebraic influences, can make use of a pattern of thinking, a teaching in fact, that is common to both. This has to do with the supposed tendency of fallible and mortal creatures (men and women) to fall into the worship of false images. A representation of the spiritual realm can become *fetishized* and be taken for the thing itself.

In the case of both Hebrew law and Platonic philosophy, icons too easily become objects of devotion themselves, no longer simply symbols but actual manifestations of the divine. So in Yahweh's commandments from Exodus we read the following:

> Thou shalt have no other gods before me. Thou shalt not make unto thee any graven image, or any likeness of any thing that is in heaven above, or that is in the earth beneath, or that is in the water that is under the earth. (Exodus 20: 3–4)

Fetish

The word 'fetish' is very interesting here. Its etymology, from the Latin *facticius* meaning factitious, via the French and Portuguese, *fétiche* and *feitiço*, associates the word with senses of artificial or false. It comes first of all to describe an object (perhaps a small stone or wood carving of an animal) that is believed to have magical power which can protect or aid its owner. A lucky rabbit's foot or other mascots are often brought to competitive sports or exams. The use of the term fetish implies the recognition that these are objects of occult superstition. So, more broadly, fetish comes to describe a material object regarded with superstitious or extravagant trust or reverence. People also come to *fetishize* ordinary belongings or things, which become objects of irrational reverence or obsessive devotion. In the domain of sexuality, of course, a fetish is an object (for instance, a whip, leather gloves, suspenders, or stilettos) or a bodily part (for instance, breasts, feet, fingers or toes) whose real or fantasized presence is psychologically necessary for sexual gratification. The fetishized object thus stands in for the supposed real one. It is an object of fixation to the extent that it may interfere with complete sexual expression; a fetish sometimes becomes a barrier to the thing itself. In each of the above examples, the fetish has come to stand in for the supposed real object of devotion or trust. When Karl Marx coined the phrase 'commodity fetishism' what he had in mind was the fetishizing of things in terms of their commodity value, divorced from their actual use value. The trouble with using the notion of fetish is that it too easily refers us to some as yet unanalysed 'real', some thing-in-itself beyond the circulation of substitutions. In other words, the word 'fetish' is itself a fetish, implying an extravagant trust in the real on behalf of its user.

The commandment is decisive. There is only one God. And nothing in experience, nothing in the universe, can represent it. Hebrew monotheism and Hellenic philosophy thus have in common this insistence on a single spirit, a single truth, a single good, that nevertheless cannot be represented or embedded in the world, which is otherwise full of shadows and graven sensuous images. Aquinas explains the situation in terms of language and, specifically, analogy.

We have observed that he insists on only one God and that everybody worships the same one. Even pagans worship the same single God, though

---

Logocentrism

According to the dream of the univocal word, or the logocentric dream, a word should always have the same meaning. Because the dream cannot possibly be fulfilled, words have to be held in check by strategies of containment, hierarchies and oppositions, which authorize and, strictly speaking, institute meanings. In other words, the dream (or naive assumption) is maintained by an attempt to relate marks to each other in a more (rather than less) fixed way. Actually, though, the dream is rather more involved and has its source in higher and brighter concerns, i.e. truth and God. It has always been known that words fail in their assumed task (to represent meanings univocally). The knowledge is the source of a metaphysical hatred of writing, the language form which best exemplifies the failure of the univocal word in so far as written expressions most clearly exemplify a tendency of addressees to *mis-understand*. The dream and its failure support each other in so far as the unchanging identity of that which is more or less well represented by the word (or concept), the transcendental truth or God, must remain untouched by the miserable failure of human language, especially in its most alienated form – writing. In other words, the finite and fallible languages of man have always been a handy demonstration (through negation) of the perfection of the truth that they can in no way approximate. So logocentrism involves the belief that meanings are anchored by a principle of identity of meaning. The logocentric assumption accepts, even affirms, that languages are shifting and con-text bound while meanings are invariant (i.e. what I mean is what I mean but what I say may not convey it well and may certainly be misunderstood).

they may have many gods, with many different names and diverse icons to represent them all. They just do not realize it. The Christian, on the other hand, *knows* what God is so when he worships he worships the true God. Why, then, does Aquinas think that heathens fall into error? He suggests that the error is connected with a failure of language. He shares with his tradition an assumption about language that holds until well into the twentieth century. That is, in an ideal situation, words should be used *univocally*, they should have a single meaning in whatever the context of use. But they don't. Words are *equivocal* in so far as they tend to mean different things in different contexts. Now the assumption, which we can recall here as *logocentrism*, isn't about the words themselves but their meanings.

Nomos

Nomos is the Greek word for law. Significantly, Aristotle introduces his notion of analogical predication during the central discussion of the *Nicomachean Ethics*, where he discusses the nature of the social bond, that is, the essence of *the political* itself. The usual distinctions are made, as follows: humans obey a law (*nomos*) that is not a law by nature (*phusis*). It is a law by convention and is designed to bond people in a community. The law works through analogy, which can be seen in the example of economic exchange. Tailors and bakers need to exchange their goods but a robe is worth a good deal more than a loaf of bread so a single measure must be assumed that would square the baker's labour with the tailor's. So the labour is broken up into units of exchange, according to which its price can be calculated. Because needs and quantities are always changing, the 'single measure' that would determine the relative prices of everything in the market place cannot be fixed. However, the *idea* of the single measure remains in place as the principle of analogical predication by which tailors and bakers are put into relations of economic justice. A is the Baker and B is his labour (bread). C is the tailor and D is his work (clothes). A is to C as B is to D according to price (which determines how many loaves are equal to a robe). This example is supposed by Aristotle to account for the totality of social relations. What is important is that this single measure (analogically it is the same as Plato's transcendental truth and Aquinas's God) cannot actually be fixed and embedded in the world. It is a principle only. But it seems that we cannot as political animals do without it, ever.

So Aquinas can assert the unchanging necessity of the single and absent God with reference to the shifting languages of fallible man. He says that only divine language can be univocal and thus there are many names for God because human language is equivocal. It is Aristotle's notion of *analogy* that serves to square things in this instance. Analogy lies somewhere between equivocality (difference) and univocity (identity) in so far as it gestures towards the same yet it involves finding a relation between differences, squared only in the relation. When pagans worship their multifarious gods and goddesses they all in fact worship the single Catholic God *by analogy*.

Some of the terms we have explored in this section can briefly be repeated here because a relatively consistent pattern is emerging. Analogy lies somewhere between *univocity* and *equivocality*. The naive and simplistic univocal dream, that a word always means just what it means, is often mistaken for what we can nearly always recognize as a *literal* use of language. So equivocality might be mistaken for *figurative* uses of language. However, all language is figurative to the extent that substitution is always implied. The key terms upon which these oppositions rest are, in fact, *identity* and *difference*. In the logocentric dream it is assumed that identity-of-meaning (what a word refers to) is represented by something different (language generally or a figure, i.e. metaphor, metonymy, simile, analogy). But it is figurative language that grounds all discourse and all expression. By no coincidence we also find that in the earliest accounts, from the ancient Greeks onwards, some pattern which is precisely equivalent to figurative language accounts for the political bond that holds people together in social relations (association). Social relations, too, are grounded in the difference between *identity* and *difference*. For this reason these terms will come to play an increasingly greater role in working through the problems of the political.

Ideology   The best-known versions of the false-consciousness argument are contained in various versions of the term 'ideology'. The joint influence of Karl Marx and Friedrich Engels cannot be disputed. For many years the political was simply equated with Marxist or, more broadly, left-wing political positions. The Enlightenment notion of 'emancipation' is important here, but what we have with Marx and Engels is a specific mode of critical engagement with the intent to foster revolutionary change. The most famous quotation from Marx is the ninth of his 'Theses on Feuerbach', which reads: 'The philosophers have only interpreted the world, in various ways; the point is to change it.' A careful review of the first two theses would reveal in what ways that change is expected to come about. Marx writes:

The chief defect of all hitherto existing materialism (that of Feuerbach included) is that the thing, reality, sensuousness, is conceived only in the form of the object or of contemplation, but not as sensuous human activity, practice, not subjectively. Hence, in contradistinction to materialism, the active side was developed abstractly by idealism – which, of course, does not know real, sensuous activity as such. Feuerbach wants sensuous objects, really distinct from the thought objects, but he does not conceive human activity itself as objective activity. (Marx and Engels 1969: 15)

The point he is making here constitutes a dialectic between what traditionally is conceived as the empirical (real) and transcendental (ideal) realms. The contradiction is found where the object is regarded as sensuous thing and the subject is regarded as abstract thinker, with no actual relation between them but the object's passivity in the gaze of the subject's understanding. Marx, on the contrary, considers the *subjective* realm of ideas to be worthy in itself of objective understanding. Ideas are concrete images, constituent components in the world of actions. So understanding must turn back critically upon its own ideas, systematically (dialectically) locating them within the historical process. In other words, the very notions of philosophical subject and passive object are also objects, ideal objects (subject/objects), susceptible to dialectical upheaval. For Marx the consequence was a contradiction not only in philosophy, but also a corresponding one in the world of social relations, most famously, in class contradiction.

The materialist doctrine concerning the changing of circumstances and upbringing forgets that circumstances are changed by men and that it is essential to educate the educator himself. This doctrine must, therefore, divide society into two parts, one of which is superior to society. The coincidence of the changing of circumstances and of human activity or self-changing can be conceived and rationally understood only as revolutionary practice. (Marx and Engels 1969: 13)

Revolutionary practice would thus involve a position that goes beyond the ideology that disguises, or distorts, the economic reality of social relations. It would involve manipulation of changing circumstances in terms of the contradictions that underlie ordinary experience. So the proletariat (the labouring classes) who are supposed to be alienated from their economic interests by an ideology that distracts them from the facts of their exploitation, should be enlightened and then emancipated through the revolutionary activity of intellectuals. Marx's version of false consciousness does not, unlike many of the others, gesture to some actually existing truth, but to a reality of struggle and contradiction that is discovered only in the contingency of social relations.

An understanding of ideology is thus a means of engaging socially within the intellectual sphere. This has not prevented certain dogmatic assertions from arising in the name of Marxism, of course, and a continual critical vigilance appears always to be necessary.

The study of ideology, begun in the eighteenth century, sets out to understand the effects of ideas on consciousness and raises the question of what an idea, as a historical and thus concrete entity, actually is. You remember that, for Plato, an idea is only ever represented by its repeatable and imperfect real forms (e.g. writing). Plato's philosophy also serves as a prototype of theories of ideology in so far as his analogy of the cave provides an image that describes the world of our experience as fundamentally false and posits a real truth somewhere outside the cave in a wonderful yonder that we unfortunately cannot experience.

Marx and Engels are responsible for the (often contradictory) statements that form the basis of contemporary notions of ideology. The following quotations, from *The German Ideology*, will give an idea of the various things ideology can mean: 'The ideas of the ruling class are in every epoch the ruling ideas [...] The class that has the means of material production at its disposal, has control at the same time over the means of mental production' (Marx 1970: 47).

In the era of bourgeois capitalism the ruling class is the class which controls the means of material production – factory owners and industrial investors for the most part. Thus the quotation might suggest that the ruling classes have their specific ideology, in that the class of industrial investors and factory owners imposes a set of beliefs, values and ideas upon the whole of society. Beyond the era of bourgeois capitalism, the notion of the dominant or ruling class can be generalized beyond the class arguments of Marx and we see similar approaches in studies of ethnicity and sexuality, in which various racist, homophobic and misogynistic ideologies can be seen to be at work in cultural texts. There are more complex variations, however, as a second quotation illustrates: 'If in all ideology men and their circumstances appear upside down as in a *camera obscura*, this phenomenon arises just as much from their historical life-process as the inversion of objects on the retina does from their physical life-process' (Marx 1970: 25).

This notion (another philosophical analogy) suggests that ideology is a false consciousness that alienates subjects from political and economic reality (and their own interests), both veiling the reality of social relations and naturalizing the alienated condition. Marxist criticism (and Marx too in places) can thus be criticized for having a spurious claim to the *actual truth* (not dissimilar from Plato's sense of truth). In his own critique of Feuerbach, which we examined above, he finds an unanalysed aspect of material ideology in Feuerbach's text (the ideal). However, Marx himself retains an unanalysed element in his own discussions. That truth, in classical Marxist terms, is the *political economy*, which lies outside and beyond the rhetoric of substitutable (thus supposedly false) tropes. A yet more sophisticated version is suggested by the following quotation:

> We do not set out from what men say, imagine, conceive, nor from men as narrated, thought of, imagined, conceived, in order to arrive at men in the flesh. We set out from real active men, and on the basis of their real life-process we demonstrate the development of the ideological reflexes and echoes of this life-process. (Marx 1970: 25)

This last statement gives rise to a dialectical consideration of the *mediation* between what Marx and Engels call 'real life-process' and 'ideology'. The dialectic mediates 'real life-processes' and types of discourse, 'what men say', the words, images and ideas of (actual) men, the discursive habits of human subjects as well as images and ideas *about* men, the mythical human subject as dreamed up in discourse. Underlying these types of discourse – what men

---

Fake Snuff

A number of recent Hollywood blockbusters, including *8mm* and *The Matrix* appear to be peddling false-consciousness narratives. *The Matrix* is basically Plato's cave without the sun. The premise is as follows: late in the twentieth century humanity has destroyed the clear sky leaving only a bustling civilization and a ruined world complete with scorched earth. The machines, dominated by intelligent computer technology take over. Mankind is now bred in captivity and used for body energy, stored in little cave-like structures embedded in huge cavernous walls. There the little humans spend their lives plugged into what is called the Matrix, a computer-simulated version, complete with taste, sound, colour, light and feelings, of late twentieth-century civilization. Things have been like this for some time. A few are able to resist the Matrix and live as outlaws eating tasteless food and entering into the Matrix only sporadically. These last are Hollywood's latest incarnation of Plato's enlightened philosopher. Clearly the Matrix stands for the fake transcendental while the empirical is the dull outside. In *8mm* Nicholas Cage plays a detective hired to discover whether the apparently real on-film killing of a young teenager was actually real or faked, thus

say and the men that are 'spoken' – is a kind of substratum, a 'reality' of actions and passions manifested by economic relations. The ideological forms might include all media (books, newspapers, journals, broadcasting, cinema, advertising), all manifestations of distinction and class, traditions, artistic movements and tendencies, while the mediation between these and 'real life-processes' can be considered in terms of the role of institutions: i.e. church, family, school, university, media organizations. The mediation involves the participation and the lived experience of subjects who thus have some agency in opposing and contesting ideologies. In cultural and Critical Theory, reading protocols become one of the main focuses of attention.

The implicit argument of the canon of false consciousness is not only that you are deceived, but that you are the deception itself, a doubt in the face of which even Descartes' subject might tremble. What the canon sometimes tries to say in its subtlest moments is that the narrative of the origin of narrative is another narrative of origin; consciousness of false consciousness is more false consciousness; the account of the origin of myth is just a myth of the origin of myth (and so on).

For these writers the empirical (and objective world) always has to be fitted

---

tapping into the mythology of the snuff movie. The film thematizes the real through a number of carefully constructed oppositions, centrally contrasting the uniqueness of the single copy snuff film (on 8mm) to the repeatability of the pornographic video. The fake snuffs, oddly, are made in the Philippines. The only way he can recognize that they are fake is because in two of the films the same woman dies. The emphasis seems to be on the repetition of pornographic (fake) death and it affirms, by its negation, an off-screen reality that not even *8mm*, with its armoury of gothic devices (heavy rain, wetness everywhere, huge gothic arches, graveyards and dark contrasts) can attain. The rhetoric of the film, as with *The Matrix*, is designed to illustrate, describe or evoke an actual reality beyond rhetoric, which it cannot do. In this case the pornographic is the denigrated paradigm for a fake reality nevertheless too close for comfort to a dull and horrific real that only love (well, this is Hollywood) can redeem. Many other contemporary films could be considered in this light. There seems to be an obsession on the part of the mass media with their ability to produce fake realities and their corresponding inability to produce reality as such (given that cinema promises precisely this).

in to the 'matrix' of principles, axioms, rules, laws, cultural representations, patterns of memory, before the subject has access to it. But that too is a construction based upon the opposition between the empirical (object) and the transcendental (subject), and fails to account for the iterability that remains its principle.

As for false consciousness: on one level an argument would presuppose the possibility, existence (or something) of a true or correct consciousness (e.g. authentic as opposed to illusory being). This kind of argument can take all kinds of different forms. On the one hand, the empirical world is a false representation of a true one, either (A) to which we cannot get access, or (B) to which we can get access only in certain ways. Or, on the other hand, the empirical world just is the real one and all assertions of a transcendental reality or truth are themselves false pictures of the world. In each case the opposition of truth and falsity is based upon the opposition between the transcendental and the empirical. On another level (that of appearance, perhaps) an argument about false consciousness might refuse to accept the opposition true/false and reinscribe falsity as the condition per se, i.e. deception with no reference to the truth. At this stage the dialectic is radically incomplete, the telos is absent and particularity is given free rein in every direction to satisfy its needs, accidental caprices and subjective desires. So it destroys itself.

Even the enigmatic twentieth-century philosopher Ludwig Wittgenstein should be included in the growing canon of false-consciousness arguments. He talks of the metaphor of waking from the dream (as so often, echoing Kant), but also of being 'held captive' or being 'taken in' by pictures, propositions, similes and repetitions. He says that 'Philosophy goes to work when language goes on holiday.' For him it is to the peculiar ability of language to create false pictures of the world that the philosopher must attend: 'What we do is bring words back from their metaphysical to their every-day use.' He

---

Iterability

Iterability contains the two senses of repetition and difference, or same and alteration. It is the name that Jacques Derrida gives to the law of repetition: what repeats must be the same but can never be identical. We explore this law in detail in Chapter 5, 'Derrida and Deconstruction'. It is out of repetition that all identities emerge. Yet in the repetition identity is always corroded by its difference.

claims that this is necessary because language, like pictures, can produce false appearances. His sentences are 'correctives' to be transcended, 'Then you'll see the world aright.' The following argument is typical:

A simile that has been absorbed into the forms of our language produces a false appearance, and this disquiets us [...] if only I could fix my gaze absolutely sharply on this fact, get it in focus, I must grasp the essence of the matter [...] One thinks that one is tracing the outline of the thing's nature over and over again, and one is merely tracing round the frame through which one looks at it. (Wittgenstein 1958: 47–8)

The metaphorics of light and dark shade Wittgenstein's pictures. In the introduction to *Philosophical Investigations*, he says: 'It is not impossible that it should fall to the lot of this work, in its poverty and the darkness of this time, to bring light into one brain or another' (Wittgenstein 1958: viii) (that is the – 'unlikely' – power to *stimulate* thinking). And, pointing out what is wrong with this picture, he manages to dissolve one false-consciousness myth by opposing another false-consciousness argument to it:

The evolution of the higher animals and man, and the awakening of consciousness at a particular level. The picture is something like this: Though the ether is filled with vibrations the world is dark. But one day man opens his seeing eye, and there is light. What this language primarily describes is a picture. What is to be done with the picture, how is it to be used, is still obscure. Quite clearly, however, it must be explored if we want to understand the sense of what we are saying. But the picture seems to spare us this work: it already points to a particular use. This is how it takes us in. (Wittgenstein 1958: 184)

Access to the Transcendental

Dialectic first of all is the Platonic way; interlocutors are brought to the way of truth via the permanently negating activities of Socratic dialogue. *Analysis* would be the Cartesian way of presenting a demonstration through the phenomenology of the 'I.' *Aporia* would be the way of the sophist, revealing your assertions and beliefs to be based upon contradictions you cannot go beyond. *Empirical research* would describe the recourse of the Enlightenment scientist, convinced that the truth lies in the direction of simple provable facts with the power of safe prediction. The modern logician might rest on the repeatable and immutable consequence of *mathematics*. But the list is endless.

The quotation finds Wittgenstein exploring the so-called picture theory of meaning. The result of this was the famous statement, 'Whereof one cannot speak, thereof one must remain silent' (Wittgenstein 1961: 74). I would argue that where Wittgenstein leaves off, Critical Theory begins. The ethical and political obligation of contemporary critical thought is to affirm what cannot be spoken of, not as a reality or a ground upon which we must some day hope to land, but as the impossible space that makes politics and the social relation possible. There is no universal ground. Instead we affirm its singular absence.

4 Structuralism and Semiotics

I Saussure

What is Structuralism?   Structuralism is the name given to a wide range of discourses that study underlying structures of signification. Signification occurs wherever there is a meaningful event or in the practice of some meaningful action. Hence the phrase 'practices of signification' or, more often, 'signifying practices'. A meaningful event might include any of following: writing or reading a text; getting married; having a discussion over a cup of coffee; a battle. Most (if not all) meaningful events involve either a document or an exchange that can be documented. This would be called a 'text'. Texts might include any of the following: a news broadcast; an advertisement; an edition of Shakespeare's *King Lear*; the manual for my new washing machine; the wedding vows; a feature film. From the point of view of structuralism all texts, all meaningful events and all signifying practices can be analysed for their underlying structures. Such an analysis would reveal the specific system that makes such texts and practices possible. We cannot see a structure or a system per se. In fact it would be very awkward for us if we were aware at all times of the structures that make our signifying practices possible. Rather they remain unconscious but necessary aspects of our whole way of being who and what we are. It is easy to see, then, that structuralism ought to be able to offer insights into what makes us the way we are.

Structuralism first comes to prominence as a specific discourse with the work of a Swiss linguist, Ferdinand de Saussure, who developed a branch of linguistics called 'Structural Linguistics'. Saussure died before he was able to publish his material but we have the meticulously recorded notes of several of his students made during the courses between 1906 and 1911. The theory was still at a developmental stage then, and has remained in a developmental stage ever since. There is nothing authoritative about Saussure's theory and even now it is open to debate and controversy. Yet there has been an extraordinarily diverse and fecund range of work, including a number of schools of thought in Eastern Europe, the United States and, particularly, in Japan,

115

based upon readings of his initial insights as documented by his students. The reconstruction of his lecture courses can be found in *The Course in General Linguistics*. This is essential reading for anyone who seriously wants to understand the basis of structuralism and semiotics. For those who don't have the time, a summary of basic points follows. Bear in mind that I am reading with hindsight and have probably added some insights that belong to critical readings of Saussure.

The Course in General Linguistics   Saussure's demand for a *general* linguistics is what leads to his most startling insights. Previously there had been many explanations of language but there had always been something missing and, thus, the absence of a ground to explain all of language. An empiricist like John Locke, for instance, explained language by claiming that words were used to refer to things. All the discrete objects in the world (trees, dogs, cats and men and women) each had a word in the vocabulary that pertained to them. Some words are general (dog) and some particular (Fido). The problem with this theory is that there are some words that refer to nothing empirical in the world (virtue and crime) and some words that refer to nothing that really exists in the world (unicorns and Hamlet). Where then do words for fictional objects and transcendental concepts come from? Saussure's explanation of language, as we'll see, is quite adequate for discussing real things in the world as well as fictional objects and abstract concepts; indeed, Saussure would explain everything that language can do.

The Sign   The sign is, for Saussure, the basic element of language. Meaning has always been explained in terms of the relationship between signs and their referents. In the nineteenth century an important figure for semiotics, Charles Sanders Peirce (pronounced 'purse'), the pragmatic philosopher, isolated three different types of sign.

The *symbolic* sign is like a word in so far as it refers by symbolising its referent. It doesn't have to look like it or have any natural relation at all. Thus the word 'cat' has no relation to that ginger monster that wails all night outside my apartment, but its owner knows what I'm talking about when I say, 'Your cat kept me awake all night.' A poetic symbol like the sun (which may stand for enlightenment and truth) has an obviously symbolic relation to what it means. But how do such relationships come about? Saussure will tell us.

The *indexical* sign is like a signpost or a finger pointing in a certain direction. The signpost to San Francisco or to 'Departures' may be accompanied by an arrow. The index of a book will have a list of alphabetically ordered words with page numbers after each of them. These signs play an indexical function (in this instance, as soon as you've looked one up you'll be back in the symbolic again).

The *iconic* sign refers to its object by actually resembling it and is thus more likely to be like a picture (as with a road sign). Cinema rhetoric often uses the shorthand that iconic signs provide. Most signs can be used in any or all three of these ways, often simultaneously. The key is to be able to isolate the different functions.

Saussure departs from all previous theories of meaning by discovering that language can be examined independently of its referents (that is, anything outside language that can be said to be what language refers to, like things, fictions and abstractions). This is because the sign contains both its signifying element (what you see or hear when you look at a written word or hear a spoken one) and its meaningful content. The sign cat must be understood as being made up of two aspects. The letters, which are anyway just marks – 'C' 'A' 'T' – combine to form a single word: cat. And simultaneously the meaning that is signified by this word enters into my thoughts (I cannot help understanding this). At first sight this is an odd way of thinking. The meaning of the word cat is not that ginger monster nor any of the actual feline beings that have existed nor any that one day surely will – a potential infinity of cats. The meaning of the word cat is its potential to be used (e.g. in the sentence 'Your cat kept me up all night.') And we need to able to use it potentially infinitely many times. So in some strict sense cat has no specific meaning at all, more like a kind of empty space into which certain images or concepts or events of usage can be spilled. For this reason Saussure was able to isolate language from any actual event of its being used to refer to things at all. This is because although the meaning of a word is determined to a certain extent in conventional use (if I'd said, 'Your snake kept me up', I'd have been in trouble), but there is always something undetermined, always something yet to be determined, about it.

Signifier/Signified So Saussure divides the sign into its two aspects. First there's the bit that you can see or hear. Actually you can imagine signs that are accessible to each of the senses. The laboratory technicians at Chanel, for instance, have an acute receptivity to the smallest nuanced difference between scents. In this case they are literally 'readers' or 'interpreters' of scent in so far as they are able to identify minute differences. So if you can see, hear, touch, taste or smell it you can probably interpret it and it is likely to have some meaning for you. Audible and visible signs have priority for Saussure because they are the types of sign that make up most of our known languages. Such signs are called 'verbal' signs (from the Latin *verba* meaning 'word'). The sensible part of a verbal sign (the part accessible to the senses) is the part you see or hear. This is its *signifier*. You can understand this much by looking at a word you don't understand; a word from a language you don't know, perhaps. All you get is its signifier. The following marks are the best approximation I can make to a word in an imaginary foreign language: *bluk*. It is a signifier. Already, though, notice that a certain amount of signification occurs – the foreignness is already part of its signifier and the fact that we recognize it as a combination of marks that can be repeated already presents us with a potential *signified*. And, most eerily, although we only saw the mark we simultaneously heard it in our heads, not actually but that part of our brain that listens out for sounds took one look at a non-existent word and heard something too. The *signified* is what these visible/audible aspects mean to us. Now we know very well that some marks mean very different things to different people at different times. The word 'cat' in my example means 'ginger monster' to me but to my neighbour it means cuddly old much-maligned softy who is only innocently going about its business. The signified is thus always something of an interpretation that is added to the signifier. Usually we individuals don't have to work too hard at interpreting signs. The groundwork has already been done, which is why 'cat' pretty much nearly always means what it means. One of the most influential aspects of Saussure's course is his explanation concerning that groundwork.

System and Utterance   There is no natural or necessary reason why the non-existent word *bluk* should sound the way it does. What we call phonemes (the elements of sound that make up words) correspond to the graphemes (elements of the written words) in no natural or necessary way. The correspondence has just come about over time and repeated usage and is constantly though imperceptibly changing. Yet literate speakers of a given language hear the correspondence *immediately*. (Now the invention of recorded sound is over a century old it might be fun to chart the changes, though, as we are just about to discover, it is entirely irrelevant.) That would be no big deal in itself perhaps (though I do find it eerie) if it were not for the fact that the meaning of words – the signifieds – attaches to their signifiers in just such an unreliable way. There is never a natural or necessary relationship between signifier and signified. Saussure says that the relationship is entirely arbitrary. So where does this meaning come from? How do signifieds and signifiers come together? Saussure tells us that we must get away from thinking about the changes that occur to languages through time. Before he arrived this is pretty much what language study was about: charting changes through time. Saussure calls this *diachronic* linguistics. Instead, he advises, we should focus our attention on what makes a language what it is at any given moment, forgetting about time altogether. He called this new linguistics, which he invented, *synchronic* linguistics. Synchronic linguistics studies what he calls *la langue* (which is French for 'language'). What he means by this is the language *system*. The word 'system', in this case, suggests an arrangement of interrelated elements and accounts for the way these elements relate to each other. The elements in Saussure's language system are signs. It is because of the specific ways in which these signs interrelate in the system that it is possible to say anything at all. When we do say anything it is an instance of what Saussure calls *parole* (French for 'speech'). An instance of parole can be called an *utterance*. An utterance is any meaningful event that has been made possible and governed to an extent by a pre-existing system of signs. There is virtually nothing in experience and certainly nothing meaningful that cannot be said to belong to one or more of these systems of signs. Let's look at some examples of types of utterance. The following are utterances: 'Your cat kept me up all night'; a sonnet by Shakespeare; Saussure's *Course in General Linguistics;* Beethoven's Fifth Symphony; my suit and tie; Alexander Pope's garden in Twickenham. As such there is in each case a specific system that underlies and to an extent governs the types of utterance that can be made. What is the specific mechanism that allows systems to operate in these ways?

Difference Up until now it might have been possible to understand the elements that make up this system, the signs themselves, as actually existing, perhaps even physical things. Get out your dictionary and there they will all be – a finite number, listed alphabetically and related to each other in definitive ways. Let's have a look at how this works with our most simple sign 'cat'. We look it up and find this:

> Etymology: Middle English, from Old English *catt*, probably from Late Latin *cattus, catta* cat. Date: before 12th century.
>
>   1 a: a carnivorous mammal (*Felis catus*) long domesticated as a pet and for catching rats and mice b: any of a family (*Felidae*) of carnivorous usually solitary and nocturnal mammals (as the domestic cat, lion, tiger, leopard, jaguar, cougar, wildcat, lynx, and cheetah).
>   2: a malicious woman.
>   3: a strong tackle used to hoist an anchor to the cathead of a ship.

Quite apart from the fact that the signifier appears to have three quite divergent signifieds (carnivorous mammal, malicious woman and strong tackle), we find that it belongs in a family and has already been opposed to its conventional sparring partner the mouse (as in Tom and Jerry). You wouldn't be that likely to call a malicious man a 'cat' (though who knows these days) either, so it seems as if some kind of gendering has gone on too. Furthermore, any worries about any of the words used to define cat can be solved by turning to their own entries in the same dictionary. If you were to be very pedantic and silly you might spend days following the trail of cross references. But these aspects are nothing to do with what holds the system together as a system. For that we must turn to something that it is not even possible to perceive and here we enter into the world of paradoxes. Saussure says that there are no actual positive existing terms in a language system – the dictionary must be an illusion then! Well, in some sense it is. Sure, the marks are there but our understanding and our impression of them are owed to something we cannot have an impression of at all. That something is *difference*. This is what Saussure says: 'A language is a system of differences with no positive terms.' We recognize the marks of a language because they are marks in distinction and different from each and all of the other marks in the system. In fact, we recognize marks as marks by virtue of the differences between marks rather than the marks themselves. You can see this easily with the fact that handwriting differences and quite stark differences in font on the word processor don't make any difference to the function of the mark itself – at best it is an aesthetic difference (not to say that that isn't important in its own right, of course). As far as their being marks of the language system is concerned, so long as a given mark isn't bent so far as to become a different one, that is, so long as they operate within the elastic range that difference allows, then we will recognize them in a positive way. All possible marks have their possibility thanks to their differences. But what is a difference? Ah! that is a tricky one. I've already shown that the signifier is the sensible part of a sign. And we know that its signified is not itself sensible. We might call it 'mental' or 'intelligible' as opposed to sensible. Now the trouble with difference is that it is neither sensible nor intelligible. Saussure had drawn a curious picture designating the two realms of the mental and the audible looking a little like a seascape with the sky above the horizon. Several vertical lines cut the picture into individual segments. He meant by this to demonstrate that neither sound nor thought has any meaning but is just a mass – a meaningless continuity – without the articulation into segments that language provides. These segments are the signs, the elements of a language system, which is all very pretty but how do you then picture the difference that makes it all possible? You can never actually see, hear, touch, taste or smell a difference. Sense is stuck in the world of impressions. But if we are asked to accept that differences are what make signs possible, that the signifiers cat, bat, rat, dog and mouse, have their distinctive qualities owing to their differences, then meaning can come into being for us only in the empty, imperceptible differences between signifiers. It is thus the system of differences that makes possible and *to a certain extent* governs meaningful experience.

'To a Certain Extent'   The earliest scholars working in the idiom of structuralism proceeded from the premise that all kinds of cultural activity could be analysed objectively on the model of the empirical sciences. The history of structuralism and semiotics shows two things in this respect. First, although the project turns out to be impossible in its ideal form, many otherwise inaccessible insights about cultural activity were made. And second, the reason for the impossibility of the structuralist project is contained in its premises from the beginning. So (1) structuralism was never able to achieve its most ideal aims but has always been very illuminating anyway; and (2) critical reading of the structuralist texts shows us why its task was impossible from the beginning. The reason is at first sight very trivial. The earliest structuralists were unable to take on board the importance and the difficulty of pinning down the category of *difference*. As I have already suggested, signifying activities are only ever determined by the systems that make them possible to an extent. This is because difference cannot be perceived, it determines nothing in a direct way, and as a principle it demands that there always was and always is something yet to be determined about any cultural activity whatsoever.

System and Difference   The scientific approach to a system would take for granted that the elements which make it up correspond to an organized and integrated unity (or totality), such that each element in the system can be located in its place on the web of relationships between elements. Even the subatomic universe has elements. Once it was thought that the atom was the smallest indivisible element. (As we all now know, by splitting the atom the human species discovered how to make its biggest explosion so far – another step towards its very own big bang.) But with Saussure's system the elements themselves are impossible to locate because, as he says (and I remind you), 'language is a system of differences with no positive terms.' A signifying system is made up of differences. This means that each element relates not only to all the other elements but to its own difference as well, and to this most pesky of signifiers, *difference* itself. The consequences are very far reaching but to start with we must consider this: if one element (a signifier) is related to another element (another signifier) through difference, then there is no hard and fast line that links the two. The linkage remains unstable and is subject at any given moment to the possibility of unpredictable change. In nineteenth-century Europe the signifier 'women' seems to have been attached to the signifiers 'passive' and 'weak' when applied in non-domestic contexts (in domestic contexts like the kitchen the reverse is true). The link was apparently inextricable, it seemed both necessary and natural. You have only to see any one of the recent mainstream cinematic releases to see that this link is now broken – any number of plucky post-feminist heroines characterize the stand-ard Hollywood narrative (e.g. *Ever After*). At least 100 years of movements associated with the liberation, separatism or equality of women have had some effect on what was once just one of the countless taken-for-granted attitudes that determine the way cultural relations are interpreted. The various ways in which these taken-for-granted aspects of culture have been questioned and even changed can help explain structuralism's failure to deal entirely objectively with its material. Yet we can also now see how structuralism's attempts to do so can contribute to our understanding of the arbitrariness of the link between signs like 'man' and 'woman'. Of course my example of the mainstream Hollywood narrative reveals something yet more disturbing. That is, even if apparently objectionable links can *to a certain extent* be dissolved, there seems to be no limits to the system's ability to reclaim them in some part of a tightly knit unity. It is OK for Cinderella to be plucky so long as the prince, who is her destiny in this particular myth, finds her attractive and they live happily ever after. Now the signifier 'women' is linked to 'strong' and 'active' in contexts beyond the domestic. Careful analysis might reveal that this change is in support of a particular ideological point of view. Such an analysis would still have recourse to many of the tried and tested methods of the structuralists.

Developments in Structuralism   Saussure's *Course* has had many dif-ferent kinds of influence on humanities scholarship in the twentieth century. He seems to have touched on so many different concerns that his influence is indicative of a fairly generalizable condition. Because his overt concern is language there have been some mistaken assumptions made about the impli-cations of structural linguistics. Benjamin Whorf, for instance, attempted to find a correlation between linguistic structures and cultural structures as if language itself determined cultural and even social experience. This attitude can be called linguisticism (the attempt to explain everything according to an understanding of language and its structures). Many trends after Saussure can be seen to be working on the assumption that there is no social or cultural experience outside the structures that language makes possible. In fact, as developments in linguistics show, what Saussure was interested in cannot be contained by the category language, despite his own assertions. By making his linguistics a general one, instead of an empirical one, he had to find his explanatory terms in phenomena that are not restricted to languages alone. If they apply to language, then, that just makes language one phenomenon among others that can be understood through structuralism. What then are the key explanatory terms of structuralism? Time for a summary and a little exercise.

An Exercise in Structuralism

SYNCHRONY/DIACHRONY   A distinction must be made between the way languages appear to us (as changing through time) and as they are at any given time (governed by systematic relations not affected by time passing). *Synchronic* linguistics is supposed to study the systematic aspects of language rather than the *diachronic* aspects. This will not be the only occasion where an attempt at a scientific understanding of something finds it convenient to discount time. We can learn a lesson here: ignore it at your peril.

SYSTEM/PROCESS   Structuralism assumes that for every process (an utterance, for instance) there is a system of underlying laws that govern it. The system arises contingently (there are no natural or necessary reasons for the relations within it to be as they are).

PARADIGM/SYNTAGM   Language can be analysed according to two different poles, or *axes*. On the *syntagmatic axis* we have the visible or audible utterance itself, e.g. 'the cat sat on the mat' (yes, I know, there's that pesky cat again). On the *paradigmatic axis* we have the way that our utterance remains tied to and governed by the system to which it belongs. 'Paradigm' comes from a Greek word, *paradeigma*, meaning 'example'. An utterance is an example of one of the uncountable possibilities that the system makes possible. I could for instance have said 'the dog sat on the mat'. This would have represented a slightly unexpected choice but a perfectly legitimate one. Try 'the log sat on the mat'. Notice that my examples relate to each other either according to their signifiers (dog and log) or according to their signifieds (cat and dog). The system into which the paradigmatic axis dips governs all possible relations between signifiers and signifieds. Poets, we notice, are often inclined to look out for the unlikely ones, for the more obvious your utterance is the more it will sound like a cliché (the moon in June) Roman Jakobson suggested that the functions of language can be understood according to the way the paradigmatic and syntagmatic axes of language interact. We'll have more on that later. For a graphic reminder watch this:

The cat sat on the mat.

> The dog sat on the mat.
> The log sat on the mat.

On the syntagmatic axis one of these sentences can be selected. One of the other two lying dormant on the paradigmatic axis can possibly be substituted for the first. If we put them all together (as I have) this projects aspects of the paradigmatic axis on to the syntagmatic axis. I thus draw attention to the systematic aspects of language. If you ignore this you might have an image of a cat, a dog and a log all sitting on a mat. Most texts can be read according to the way that systematic aspects are manifested on the syntagmatic axis (which is strictly all we see). Take the following poem by William Blake.

The Sick Rose

> O Rose, thou art sick!
> The invisible worm
> That flies in the night,
> In the howling storm,
>
> Has found out thy bed
> Of crimson joy;
> And his dark secret love
> Does thy life destroy.

The principles of selection and substitution allow us to draw up a provisional chart identifying aspects that are systematically linked to the rose and those that are systematically linked to the worm:

ROSE	WORM
	invisible
	that flies
	howling storm
thy bed	the night
crimson	dark
joy	love
life	destroy
	finding out
sick	

Remember that the structuralist is interested as much in what is not evident as what is. The gaps on the rose side can be filled in. Against 'invisible' we add 'visible'. Against 'flies' we add 'unmoving'. Against 'howling storm' we add 'calm'. And against 'finding out' we add 'being found out'. The whole thing adds up to an active yet invisible protagonist getting the blame for the sickness of a visible yet passive (and passionate) victim.

ROSE	WORM
PASSIVE	ACTIVE
visible	invisible
unmoving	that flies
calm	howling storm
thy bed	the night
crimson	dark
joy	love
life	destroy
being discovered	finding out
sick	*well*

Now we have a fairly thorough representation of the systematic aspects of this poem (it is an easy one to do because Blake is a good poet). Notice that we haven't concerned ourselves with the business of interpreting the poem. I could have said it is an allegory for syphilis. But what my analysis is teasing out are the conditions that make such allegorizing possible. Now look at something weird. The signifier (the visible part of the sign) could be placed on the left-hand side with the rose. The signified, on the other hand, could quite easily be placed on the right-hand side with the worm (which is invisible). We could then argue that the rose represents the poem 'The Sick Rose' and the worm represents the interpretation we give it (thus making it sick). However, notice too that the speaker (the one who says 'Oh Rose …') is the one who is really doing all this 'finding out' in so far as it is his (why did I gender the speaker?) interpretation of the rose's sickness (it was the invisible worm, I'm sure of it). A vicious cycle is in place. The speaker interprets the sickness of the rose as being caused by an invisible worm which we interpret as syphilis. Whatever the case the function of the invisible party remains enigmatic (a signified is always invisible – anything you put in its place will become yet another signifier). What makes all this speculation possible is the system of concepts that allows us to think in certain patterns. I interpreted the speaker as male not because I thought that he was Blake (in his typically lyric style). Because the rose is passive and lying in a crimson bed, and because love is in some sense implied, I am making a judgement based upon conventions and filling in yet more missing parts.

ROSE	WORM
PASSIVE	ACTIVE
visible	invisible
female	*male*
rose	*speaker*
signifier	*signified*
poem	*interpretation*

So, fundamentally, the structuralist sees nothing but signifiers and relations between signifiers. It takes a great deal of sophistication to see that the one thing that makes it all possible is always imperceptible. It is the absent signified that would ground the whole process if only it could be made visible without actually becoming just another signifier.

II Lévi-Strauss

Structural Linguistics and Anthropology Whatever interpretation we put on (or 'find out' in) 'The Sick Rose', we can see that it will have been possible owing to analogical structures. Roses become sick because some germ or bug infects them. People become sick when some germ or bug infects them. By extension we might find that societies become sick when some germ or bug (evil intentions) infects them. Our thinking about all kinds of things is infected too by structures and patterns that we find repeated in lots of different situations. The signified, that is the meaning, of anything seems to come out of a pre-existing system that makes it possible and governs it. Structural analysis thus aims to 'find out' the systems of thought that govern the ways we construct our world and interpret our experience. Structural analysis, however, as it was first set up, aimed to do this while remaining unaffected by social and/or cultural systems themselves. That is, they aimed for a purely scientific perspective that would not be governed or controlled by underlying structures. The most striking results in a field other than linguistics emerges with the work of the French anthropologist Claude Lévi-Strauss. He thought that linguistics was the first discipline among the humanities (or social sciences, as some parts of the humanities like to be known) to be established on purely scientific principles.

Necessary Laws In *Structural Anthropology* Lévi-Strauss writes: 'for the first time, a social science is able to formulate necessary relationships' (Lévi-Strauss 1968: 33). The most striking thing about that sentence is the characterization of the type of relationship structuralism is interested in. The laws it reaches for are the general ones (like scientific laws of gravity, say). Its laws must be necessary. A necessary law is a law that always applies whatever the situation. The basic criteria for a scientific analysis are as follows: a scientific analysis must be real, it must simplify and it must explain. Simple explanations from complex data ought to be able to lead to correct predictions regarding actual situations of the type being analysed. Lévi-Strauss took the example of structural linguistics and applied its method to the kind of relations that interest the anthropologist: kinship relations.

Kinship Relations Way back in ancient Greece Aristotle had made the famous statement '*Anthropos* is a political animal.' He had also pointed out that kinship begins with two parts in need of each other, the man and the woman. Right up until the emergence of structural anthropology, the structures of kinship were regarded as being determined by much the same simple unit that Aristotle had suggested, that is, the family. For instance A. R. Radcliffe-Brown in the 1930s had said that the unit of structure from which social relations are built up is the 'elementary family' consisting of 'a man and his wife and their child or children'. The *first order* of relation that is built from this unit is constituted by three types of social relationship, according to Radcliffe-Brown: 'that between parent and child, that between siblings, and that between husband and wife.' Beyond this first order is a *second order* of social relationships which connect different elementary units through a common member (uncles, aunts, cousins). From there any number, in principle uncountably many, of orders can be extrapolated. It is such a simple explanation and fits so well with common sense that it lasted as a convincing, hardly questionable account of social relations for thousands of years. However, Lévi-Strauss's application of the principles of structural linguistics produced quite a different picture of the underlying laws that govern kinship relations.

Second Order First On the basis of structural linguistics, Lévi-Strauss looked for the form of underlying relationships that could be said to apply to any group at all. That is, as a good scientist, he was looking for the 'essence of human kinship'. He found that what Radcliffe-Brown had called first order relationships (relationships within the elementary family group), were in fact a function of, and dependent upon, what Radcliffe-Brown had called second order relationships (those between families and involving a common member). In other words, kinship relations do not derive from the family unit with Mother and Father at its core. Rather they derive from systems that perpetuate themselves through specific forms of marriage. These specific forms, in terms of the given synchronic system, always precede the emergence of individual families. As Lévi-Strauss says: 'It is not the families (isolated terms) which are truly "elementary," but, rather, the relations between those terms.' There, he sounds just like Saussure talking about signs.

The Elementary Unit of Kinship   Lévi-Strauss, armed with the structural method, felt that he should be able to derive simple principles from an overabundance of apparently contradictory empirical data. Take a number of different types of social organization and you will have different systems of behaviour and attitude. There is nothing to explain the differences. The Trobriand Islanders of Melanesia tend to exhibit warm, open and friendly relations between fathers and sons but marked antagonism between nephews and maternal uncles. The Cherkess of the Caucasus, on the other hand, tend to show hostility between fathers and sons but a marked tendency for the maternal uncle to help his nephew and to give generous gifts. The former is characterized by a matrilinear descent, whereas the latter is characterized by patrilinear descent. But that is not the end of the story. In each case there corresponds a specific kind of relation between husbands and wives and brothers and sisters too. With the Trobriand the husbands and wives are intimate and open (like the fathers and sons) yet the relation between brother and sister is governed by a rigid and harsh taboo. On the contrary, in the Caucasus (where uncles and nephews have the special relationship), it is the brother and sister who tend to have reciprocal, warm and tender relations and the husband and wife who are joined antagonistically (the wife's brother often has to jump in to protect her from a beating by her husband). A pattern thus emerges. This is Lévi-Strauss's formulation: 'In both groups, the relation between maternal uncle and nephew is to the relation between brother and sister as the relation between father and son is to that between husband and wife. Thus if we know one pair of relations then it is always possible to infer the other' (Lévi-Strauss 1968: 42).

So the uncle's relationship to the nephew becomes the key to the most elementary structure of kinship and is thus the key to understanding any social organization that is governed by kinship. (Not all are. Modern post-industrial societies seem much more to be dominated by the logic of global commodity diversification, for instance, though the kinship relation is retained on the level of myth or ideology: the image of the family helps to sell breakfast cereal in a world where elementary family unity is actually less and less essential.) The formula, we should note immediately, is analogical. Analogy is a kind of logic that allows for the insertion of otherwise missing terms on the basis of presently known ones. The unknown can be derived from the known. If A is to B as C is to D and we know what A, B and C are, then we can infer D with no trouble. The only test of such a logic is empirical. Does it predict correctly? Lévi-Strauss found that in this case it did.

Uncles with Attitude   The starting point for his discovery was attitude. The key relations, as we have seen, concern the brother and sister, the husband and wife and the nephew and uncle. The attitude of the nephew and the uncle towards each other turned out to be the key for understanding the elementary unit of kinship for all social organizations that he looked into. The elementary unit is thus the structure that rests upon the four terms: brother, sister, father, son. One of the remarkable things about this is that attitude was and still is often thought of as an unimportant effect of the terms of social organization reflected in the psychological dimension, rather than a sign of the actual systems themselves. If a boy is antagonistic towards his father, perhaps it is a phase he is going through or something. Anyway, children are always like that, it is their response to authority. They'll grow out of it when they become fathers and start tormenting their own sons. This is partly because attitudes so often flare up as a result of non-institutionalized, diffuse psychological factors. However, once these are discounted then we find that attitude plays a fundamental role in the most elementary of institutional structures – the kinship relation. In other words what we often take to be the effects of individual emotional life turn out to be determined by structural laws that govern the organization of society generally. This is indeed a major break-through. However, it is very early days in the adventure of structuralism. Another significant gesture was Lévi-Strauss's turn towards the structural analysis of myth. Here we will see him adapting not only the structural method but also acting upon the strength of his findings regarding kinship. Most important is the analogical framework, which will allow him to suggest an ultimate equation. First, though, let's look at one or two objections that arise.

The Incest Taboo: Woman as Symbol of Exchange   The incest taboo, which for Lévi-Strauss was universal in all societies, is composed of a law: in human societies a man must always obtain a woman from another man (a daughter or a sister). The structure of the law implies an avuncular role from the very beginning. The maternal uncle is part of the structure even before, and independently of the fact of there being, any actual maternal uncle. What this means is that the relationship between the sexes is not symmetrical. You don't get women exchanging men anywhere, though you do get fictions in some societies that represent this as being the case. The woman is always that which is given in relations of exchange between men and she is thus the symbol of exchange for a system that functions only to perpetuate itself. Another analogy emerges: woman is to nature as man is to culture. If culture is regarded as the consequence of systems of social organization then woman stands symbolically for nature in a system of oppositions that seems to rise up spontaneously (remember the sick rose):

WOMAN	MAN
passive	active
visible	invisible
matter	form
sign	meaning
signifier	signified
moon	sun
left	right
dark	light

We could go on. These are famous and obvious. It is structuralism that provides the means to analyse these systems so thoroughly. A number of scholars in the last thirty years or so have very thoroughly interrogated both Lévi-Strauss's findings as well as his own preconceptions. This remains important when reading his work. But we must remember the principles upon which he started. This is not an empirical discovery. It is based not on experience but on structural analysis; the analysis of the relations between terms rather than the terms themselves. We are analysing a symbolic system rather than actual relations between particular men and women. Sure, the system determines to a large extent the way those relations might go and provides insight into them (and has considerable support in cultural history). But as a symbolic system it remains open to unpredictable change, as we have observed, and it is the nature both of the unpredictable element (i.e. it cannot be subjected to calculation) and the ways in which it can help effect desired changes that have been the concern of a great many of the critical discourses of the past thirty years. If woman really is a sign whose meaning is the system that governs her status in exchange, then her signified must remain open to a future that has in no way been completely determined (like the signified of any sign). In other words, the feminine is the name for that which cannot be named. This formulation will come back to haunt us.

The Structural Analysis of Myth Lévi-Strauss's method is encapsulated in a short yet justly famous article called 'The Structural Study of Myth', which was also published in the *Structural Anthropology* collection. It is worth returning to this article because both the strengths and weaknesses of the structuralist project are rather beautifully revealed there. He provides a concrete example to start with by analysing the well-known Oedipus myth of the ancient Greeks. We will have cause to return to this myth, but for now let's follow Lévi-Strauss as he lays its meaning bare. His purpose is to illustrate his technique, of course, so no definitive analysis is intended (that will be reserved for the group of myths he is actually going to go on to analyse in full).

On the model of language, he supposes that myth is formed of separable components or segments, minimal units of signifying material. In the same way that a verbal sign is composed of phonemes (a written sign by graphemes) a myth will be composed of *mythemes*. He then points out that, like language, there is a non-temporal (synchronic) aspect just as there is a temporal one (on the level of *parole*). It is the work of the analyst to lay out the structural conditions that underlie the myth – those that organize the mythemes. The sequence of events as they unfold in the story are treated as if they belong in columns so that repetitions of similar events or functions can be classed together independently of the chronological sequence. He uses an easy analogy (Lévi-Strauss 1968: 213):

> Say, for instance, we were confronted with a sequence of the type: 1, 2, 4, 7, 8, 2, 3, 4, 5, 6, 1, 4, 5, 7, 8, 1, 2, 5, 7, 3, 4, 5, 6, 8 ... the assignment being to put all the 1s together, all the 2s, the 3s, etc. The result is a chart:

1	2		4				
						7	8
	2	3	4	5		7	8
1			4	5		7	8
1	2			5		7	
		3	4	5	6		8

He then demonstrates the operation by trying it on the Oedipus myth. The significant events, as he takes them, are as follows:

1. Cadmos seeks his sister Europa, ravished by Zeus.
2. Cadmos kills a dragon.
3. The Spartoi fight and kill one another.
4. Labdacos, Laios' father comes in here and his name (meaning 'lame') will be significant.
5. Oedipus kills his father, Laios.
6. Significantly Laios means 'left-sided' (or lop-sided, limp on one side).
7. Oedipus goes on to kill the Sphinx.
8. Oedipus means 'swollen-foot'.

9. Then Oedipus marries his mother.

10. Later Oedipus' son Eteocles kills his brother Polynices.

11. And finally Antigone buries her brother, Polynices, against the prohibition of the state.

The chart (Lévi-Strauss 1968: 214) then looks like this:

Cadmos seeks his
sister Europa,
ravished by Zeus

                Cadmos kills
                the dragon

        The Spartoi
        kill one another

                        Labdacos = *lame* (?)

        Oedipus kills   Laios = *left-sided* (?)
        his father

                Oedipus kills
                the Sphinx

                        Oedipus = *swollen-foot* (?)

Oedipus marries
his mother, Jocasta

        Eteocles kills
        his brother

Antigone buries
her brother,
Polynices, despite
prohibition

Each column is now regarded as being a unit and can be read from left to right as if it was an orchestral score (the music analogy will continue to be popular among structural analysts). In this way, Lévi-Strauss tells us, we have the means of *understanding* the myth. This is his analysis of the first three columns: 'The first column has as its common feature the *overrating of blood relations*. The second column expresses the same thing, but inverted: *underrating of blood relations*. The third column refers to monsters being slain' (Lévi-Strauss 1968: 215).

Now it seems that the analysis has, like the study of kinship relations, a predictive power, that ought to be able to anticipate significance on the fourth column. The myth will provide its own context. One of the disputed aspects of the Oedipus myth concerns the fact that all the surnames in Oedipus's father-line have connotations that suggest difficulties in walking straight and standing upright. In mythological terms this relates to the third column in the following way:

> Column three refers to monsters. The dragon is a chthonian being [*chthon* = 'earth'; *chthonian* = 'of the underworld'] which has to be killed in order that mankind be born from the Earth; the sphinx is a monster unwilling to permit men to live. The last unit relates to the first one, which has to do with the *autochthonous origin* of mankind. Since the monsters are overcome by men, we may thus say that the common feature of the third column is *denial of the autochthonous origin of man*. (Lévi-Strauss 1968: 215)

By 'autochthonous' the anthropologist is referring to the belief that mankind is born from the Earth (literally, a native rooted in the Earth). Attacking and killing the chthonic monsters signifies a denial of mankind's autochthonous birth. The units in the fourth column, however, signify an affirmation of the belief in autochthonous birth, because of the persistent connotations of lameness and difficulty in walking upright. As anthropologists explain, in myth, chthonic people are generally represented as being lame. So the third and fourth columns represent a basic contradiction: (3) mankind is not autochthonous; (4) mankind *is* autochthonous. We know from the study of kinship what will happen next: (4) is to (3) as (1) is to (2). Thus two clear contradictions are rendered identical in analogy. As Lévi-Strauss puts it:

The overrating of blood relations is to the underrating of blood relations as the attempt to escape autochthony is to the impossibility to succeed in it' (Lévi-Strauss 1968: 216). This kind of correlation serves a purpose, according to the mythologist. It serves as a kind of tool that resolves contradictions on an ideological level. It displaces the original problem (born from one – the earth; or born from two – man and woman) on to a derivative one (born from different or born from the same). The myth thus maintains a cosmo-logical 'truth', according to which mankind is regarded as being rooted like a plant, say, but against all the evidence. The structural analysis of myth is, therefore, one example of the tendency among scientistic discourses to provide explanations of religion. This fact will get us into deep water as we proceed, so keep it in mind. We will ultimately have cause to subject it to a similar analysis (but then when will it end?).

The Algorithm of Myth   At the end of the same article Lévi-Strauss brings the structural analysis of myth to a speculative conclusion by devising a formula, as follows:

$$Fx \ (a): Fy \ (b) - Fx \ (b): Fa - 1 \ (y)$$

(a) and (b) are *values* and Fx and Fy *functions*. If, in the example of the Oedipus myth, (a) and (b) stand for types of kinship relation, then Fx stands for overvaluation while Fy stands for undervaluation. In the second part of the formula something interesting happens. In the second half of the equation (b) takes the place of (a) in the guise of the anti-autochthonous assertion and y, which now stands for the belief in autochthony, becomes a value in itself. (a), in turn, has become a function that surreptitiously links the kinship relation to the autochthonous belief. So the first two columns relate to each other in the same way as the third and fourth relate to each other. At the same time the fourth and the first relate to each other in the same way as the third and second (the autochthonous belief is to overvaluing kinship relations as the anti-autochthonous assertion is to undervaluing kinship relations). The contradiction is squared, thus preserving the mythical belief intact. We should now be able to see the extent of Lévi-Strauss's ambition in bringing scientific analysis to mythology. On one side you have the abstract simplicity of the algorithm, on the other the complex ideological sleight-of-hand of the myth. The relation is equivalent to a distinction that Lévi-Strauss draws out in his introduction to *Pensée Sauvage* (*The Savage Mind*). The distinction is between the maker of mythic narratives (on the model of the witch-doctor), on the one hand, and the technician of modern civilized cultures, on the other. He calls the creator of stories a *bricoleur* and dubs his craft *bricolage* in strict opposition to technical science. He says it is, rather, a 'science of the concrete'. The opposition between the abstract and the concrete will itself become problematic. But before we proceed it will be worth charting some of the grounds of language use.

III Jakobson

Two Types of Aphasia We can begin by being fairly schematic. The structural linguist Roman Jakobson made the discovery that aphasia, which describes a variety of problems with verbal expression, usually caused by brain damage, tends to involve one of two types of linguistic deficiency. A stroke victim, for instance, may have lost the full power of speech and is limited to certain kinds of verbal connection. The limitation tends to work in either one of two possible ways. The deficiency can be on the paradigmatic axis or the syntagmatic one. Let's go back to a simple example:

> The cat sat on the mat
> A dog stood on the carpet

The syntagmatic axis moves from left to right – across the sentence – so that the linguistic elements are related *contiguously*. They are all *present* and they are ordered according to grammatical construction, in Saussurian terms, as *parole*. The paradigmatic axis dips downwards into the *absent* pool of substitutions, similarities and differences available by virtue of *la langue*, the linguistic system. An utterance thus encodes meaning through *selection* from the paradigmatic axis and *combination* on the syntagmatic one. The two axes together thus allow addressees to understand an utterance by decoding the sentence on the combination axis with unconscious reference to the selection one. The sentence has selected 'cat' as a paradigm (perhaps) of four-legged mammals, 'sitting' as an example of posture (substituted for by 'standing' in the dog example), and 'the mat' as a place to rest, which might be substituted by sofa or bed, depending on the cat's inclination or its owner's tolerance. *The dog, standing* and *the carpet* are thus excluded from the first sentence (the cat cannot be a dog, you cannot both stand and sit at the same time). And any terms that can be substituted for 'cat' (pussy, feline mammal) or for 'sat' (crouched, reclined) are similarly excluded, because their addition would be superfluous to the sentence. We can illustrate the situation with the following schema:

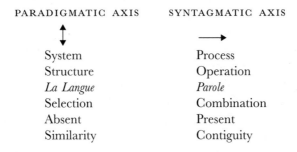

PARADIGMATIC AXIS	SYNTAGMATIC AXIS
System	Process
Structure	Operation
La Langue	*Parole*
Selection	Combination
Absent	Present
Similarity	Contiguity

Jakobson's discovery was that aphasia victims tend to have a language deficiency that corresponds to one or other of the two axes. So he called the deficiencies, respectively, the similarity disorder and the contiguity disorder. The following commentary is based upon Jakobson's 1956 paper, 'Two Aspects of Language and Two Types of Aphasic Disturbances' (Jakobson 1987: 115–33).

The Similarity Disorder   The similarity disorder restricts the victim's ability to select words from the paradigmatic axis. They cannot find words that exist as parts of the system, the dimension of the language universe that is at any given time absent from consciousness. We all have the ability to reach for more or less obscure elements of our vocabulary at any time, though we need not be conscious of these elements most of the time. But these aphasics have severely limited access to this fund and generally need some kind of prompt before they can say anything. For these patients, Jakobson says, 'context is the indispensable and decisive factor' (Jakobson 1987: 121). Context means two things here. First there is the context of situation, the immediate environment where there may indeed be a cat sitting on a mat. Second there is the verbal context, things that have just been said, as I say, 'the cat sat on the mat'. The important thing for victims of the similarity disorder is that, having lost the power to select from the pool of language, they rely on what is already present – the present context. They cannot *start* dialogues but they are able to continue or complete them after a fashion. Or they can come up with sentences that are at best the sequel of imagined previous utterances (i.e., 'it sits on the mat' as an answer to the imagined question, 'where is the cat?'). Specific nouns (cat, dog) tend to be dropped and more general ones, or catch-all nouns, take their place (so everything is a 'thing', as in the following imaginary example: 'The er … thing sat on the … er … thing').

Furthermore, once a picture of an object, or the word for an object, or even the object itself, is present, it is difficult for this kind of aphasic to find a similar or substitute expression (a name) for it. This is because a name has to be supplied from the pool of substitutions, access to which is restricted. So an actual cat sitting on a mat would already fulfil the selection demands of the sentence (i.e. it would be present). These patients may instead fill out their discourse with further contiguous material ('it catches mice/you do it to rest/ it's for covering floors'). Words no longer have a generic (paradigmatic) meaning for these patients, so verbal expressions tend to be strongly contextualized. A knife, in one of Jakobson's examples, may alternately be called, 'pencil-sharpener, apple-parer, bread-knife, knife-and-fork', and so on (Jakobson 1987: 122). What this means is that words on the contiguous axis are more bound by a given context and are thus less transferable to other contexts. You don't often read about people fighting with apple-parers or pencil-sharpeners.

Jakobson's paper is a good example of the ways in which damaged faculties can illuminate the actual functioning of the faculty itself. It is one of those situations where you need something to go wrong before you really understand how it works. What we learn here is that the total context (verbal and situational), which makes up the contiguous axis of the language universe, embodies something like the entire empirical field. This is shown by the inability of these patients to add anything that would be superfluous. Using the word 'cat' when faced with a picture of a cat would be the equivalent of using two nouns where one would do, 'the cat/the four-legged mammal sat on the mat'. The difficulty that the victims of a similarity disorder have reveals the dimension of instituted meaning negatively.

Related to these aspects of the substitution deficiency are two essential aspects of language, translation and metalanguage, both of which are compromised in aphasics with a similarity disorder. Bilingual or multi-lingual aphasics usually lose the ability to operate between different languages and they become monolingual.

Metalanguage Metalanguage means language on or about language. Without this ability to speak about language *in* language there'd be no linguistics at all. But the phenomena of metalinguistic usage are with us nearly all the time. I say, 'Do you know what I mean?' and, if the answer is, 'No, not really, I don't understand your use of …' I translate into another word or provide another description. If I hold up a pencil for an aphasic with a similarity disorder and ask, 'What is this?' the patient may not be able to find the right word. The reason that Jakobson gives for this is that most linguistic operations are condensed forms of a logic that the linguist can make explicit. So giving the name of an object is in fact acknowledging the use of a name in a specific code ('in our language it is called …') and it thus has a metalinguistic purpose. The full answer, taking the metalinguistic aspect into consideration, would be, according to Jakobson: 'In the code we use, the name of the indicated object is *pencil*' (Jakobson 1987: 124). A similarity disorder would restrict the speaker to forms like 'scribbler', depending on the context. Loss of the metalinguistic ability means that such aphasics cannot switch from a word to any of its synonyms nor to any words meaning the same thing in different languages.

Finally, in the dimension of figurative language, it should already be fairly clear that aphasics with a similarity disorder cannot use metaphor easily. A metaphor is a use of language where one term, a word or image, stands in for another; it is a kind of implicit simile. In our example, having noticed the cat's regal occupation of the centre of the mat, I might say: 'The queen sat on her throne.' It's a metaphor. That doesn't mean that the similarity disorder bars aphasics from figurative language. Figurative language operates on both axes. Rather, the similarity disorder restricts aphasics to metonymic operations, which are based upon contiguity rather than similarity. A *metonym* is a figure that substitutes an associated element, or even a part, for the whole. So, in Jakobson's example, '*fork* is substituted for *knife, table* for *lamp, smoke* for *pipe, eat* for *toaster*' (Jakobson 1987: 125). Words that often go together (knife and fork) can be substituted and, because a toaster produces toast, which can be eaten, the word 'eat' can be used instead of 'toaster'. In our example, the sentence produced through metonymy might be 'whiskers sits on the cat' (the metonymical 'cat' substituted for 'mat' because the example is so common).

The Contiguity Disorder   Aphasics with what Jakobson calls 'the op-posite' of the similarity disorder lose the ability to combine linguistic elements. Their grammar fails them and they can express only 'heaps' of words. The order of the words becomes chaotic and any words with purely grammatical functions (reference words such as 'he', 'she', 'it'; conjunctions such as 'and' and 'but'; articles such as 'a' and 'an') tend to drop out of the picture all together. These aphasics thus tend to sound infantile and can manage only very short sentences. They can indicate the name of something, perhaps, with some brief descriptive words, but little else. In severe cases sentences can be as short as a single word ('Cat'). On the level of word construction aphasics need to understand the word before they can utter it. 'A French aphasic recognised, understood, repeated, and spontaneously produced the word *café* (coffee) or *pavé* (roadway) but was unable to grasp, discern, or repeat such nonsensical sequences as *féca, faké, kéfa, pafé* (Jakobson 1987: 128). French speakers would not normally have a problem with these constructions. Because they are phonetically possible (like the English nonsense words 'kulb' and 'bluk'), a normal speaker can pronounce them, even perhaps accepting them as existing words that they do not know. We often find a similar situation with the game *Call My Bluff*, in which contestants on one team are given an obscure word and they take turns in convincing contestants on the other team that it means what they say. Only one gives the correct definition. The other team then has to guess which was the right one. An aphasic with a contiguity disorder would be utterly lost with *Call My Bluff*.

What distinguishes this type of aphasia from the first type is the depend-ence on the signified part of the sign. Where the first kind relied on *connections between signifiers* (on the syntagmatic axis), this type is reliant on *connections between signifiers and signified meaning* (on the paradigmatic axis). This, of course, is just what we'd have expected because the signified, as we have established, is always invisible, which is what allows for actual events of reference, when they occur (whether the referent is another word or a thing). The syntagmatic axis runs across the utterance and is dependent upon present context:

$$\text{Contiguity:}\quad S \to S \to S \to S \to S \to$$

The paradigmatic axis dips down into the absent pool of substitutions:

$$\text{Similarity:}\quad \frac{S}{(S)\downarrow}$$

So the two axes together make up the linguistic universe, just as Saussure had described it, with the utterance itself moving across in time whilst simul-taneously yet invisibly dipping down into the system of signs and thereby producing meaningful sentences:

Signified meaning: sd   sd   sd   sd   sd
Syntagmatic axis: Sr ↗   Sr ↗   Sr ↗   Sr ↗   Sr ↗
                ↕ →   ↕ →   ↕ →   ↕ →   ↕
Paradigmatic axis: (S)   (S)   (S)   (S)   (S)

    The signified (sd) is produced in the double action of contiguity (a combination of selected signifiers) and similarity (the system of possible substitutions). Without the system the line of contiguity would be made up of meaningless marks (imagine 'bluk tic ob fu lafe' or something) and signified meaning (sd) would not occur. It is very important to see here that the elements of signified meaning (sd) are not actually existing things but emerge negatively through the subtle exclusions that are the flip side of selection. We can see that two aspects are simultaneously necessary, as follows: (1) *context*, made up of present elements, which may or may not include actual cats, and (2) the *system*, comprising principles that govern the relations between absent elements. It is also very important not to try to define context too precisely, for the moment. For now it just means 'elements found next to each other' (contiguous and present). 'Elements' can be objects, words, pictures and, in general, observable marks of all kinds.

    I have included, in the following schema, suggestions as to some of the ways that the paradigmatic axis might make available certain kinds of signification. It is only schematic and there are many possibilities. Experiment with some of your own, but remember that any attempt to be too precise will tangle you in knots and controversies (but then you can institute your own school of linguistics!):

Syntagmatic axis:	the cat	→	sat on	→	the mat
Grammatical paradigm:	nouns		verbs		nouns
Generic paradigm:	mammals		postures		platforms
Substitutive paradigm:	dog		stood		sofa
Figurative paradigm:	queen		reclined		throne

Metaphor and Metonymy One of the most influential aspects of Jakobson's paper is his development of the wider implications of the two types of aphasia. As we have already seen, the two deficiencies imply recourse to two different types of figurative language, metaphor and metonymy. The two types of aphasia are polar opposites, yet there are many different varieties of aphasic disturbance, which all lie between the similarity disorder and the contiguity disorder. In the final section of his paper he suggests that a similar situation is the case for all discourse. According to a range of determining factors, which include history, culture, personality and psychology, we each tend to use these aspects of language with more or less emphasis on one or other of the two axes. This is observable in our own use of language and ultimately in our texts. Jakobson's text, for instance, clearly tends towards the paradigmatic axis, which is why I've found it useful in this section to come up with all those little schemata. Let's take a look at what we've ended up with:

PARADIGMATIC AXIS	SYNTAGMATIC AXIS
$\updownarrow$	$\longrightarrow$
System	Process
Structure	Operation
La Langue	*Parole*
Selection	Combination
Absent	Present
Similarity	Contiguity
Metaphor	Metonymy

The schema itself (with all its substitutions matched up on each axis) clearly owes its possibility to the paradigmatic axis. Jakobson, whose discourse resides largely in the metalinguistic universe, makes an ideal linguist (he was able to use a multitude of languages, in each of which he was fluent). The deficiencies of aphasics have thus allowed Jakobson to sharpen his understanding of the ways in which relatively unimpaired individuals operate in the world through language. At the extremes language fails altogether, so there needs to be at least some influence from each of the two axes. What is revealed is that most, *if not all*, discourses (from the arts to the sciences) can be understood in terms of rhetorical tendencies. If that is indeed so then knowledge itself is grounded in rhetoric. For we have learned that the syntagmatic axis (where context is the decisive factor) involves the whole empirical situation; that is, everything that is at any time present to my experience. Yet this 'whole' remains meaningless without its interaction with the paradigmatic axis, which provides resources for understanding and expression that are fundamentally the province of systems, institutions, laws, principles and rules of operation. Some of these principles are personal, habitual patterns, while others seem socially sanctioned and still others would seem to obey some more deeply inscribed necessity. Take the example of grammar. Some linguists have believed that there is at the most basic level a universal grammar that organizes the way all peoples speak. It seems that humans have the capacity to pick up particular grammars between certain ages, as those examples of children who have grown up among wolves or chickens show. If they have passed the age after which it is no longer possible to 'tune in' to a particular grammar they are confined to the languages of wolves or chickens (which we might think is a little limiting in a post-industrial world, but we'll come back to this issue). These children have to learn a 'national' dialect as a second language (French or English, for instance) by making translations between 'Wolf' or 'Chicken' and French or English. That's a lot of work on a rather limited paradigmatic pole. What seems more likely to be the case, then, is that there is no universal grammar, but a universal ability to pick up particular grammars, and that these grammars are grounded in historicity, their rhetorical evolution. In other words, speakers of languages are historical beings through and through.

The situation has been explored effectively in art criticism and literary theory, where Jakobson's paper has been particularly influential. Verbal works of fiction or poetry, as well as image-based artworks (painting, photography and film), can lay bare the rhetorical dimensions of representation. We must also take into consideration that these forms of what we call representation are also aspects that cannot be dissociated from the total context for addressees, readers, spectators and observers. They therefore contribute integrally to any given perception of reality. Thus if, as we have already established, all perception of reality is in some essential respects always interpretation of reality, then Jakobson's schemata may help us to understand the operation of these representations better.

The Map on the Wall I want to finish up by taking a short example of some modern literary writing. In this way we should see how a close analysis is capable of revealing the operation of rhetoric in texts, and we can interpret a particular text in terms of what it has to say itself about the rhetorical dimension. The example is from the British writer Henry Green's *Loving*, published in 1945 and written during the darkest days of the Second World War. The novel is set in (by then) postcolonial Ireland and the story takes place in a British castle called Kinalty, the home of a family (the Tennants who, as their name suggests, are not landed gentry but *nouveaux riches*) and their servants. The scene we are going to analyse concerns Charley Raunce, newly promoted to butler (following the previous butler Eldon's death) and the young Mrs Tennant (recently married to Jack Tennant, away at the war. Mrs Tennant has been having a secret affair with a local man, Captain Dermot Davenport of Clancarty castle, a few miles from Kinalty. We catch up with Raunce who, armed with the previous butler's notebooks, is investigating the castle for clues as to how he might make profitable use of the written remains of Eldon's knowledge:

What this forenoon halted Charley in the study while on his weekly round rewinding clocks was a reminder in the red notebook to charge 10s. 6d. for a new spring to the weathervane. This was fixed to the top of the tower and turned with a wind in the usual way. Where it differed from similar appliances was that Mr Tennant had had it connected to a pointer which was set to swing over a large map of the country round about elaborately painted over the mantelpiece. Raunce did not yet know how the thing worked. He stood and pondered and asked himself aloud where he could say he was going to fix replacements if she asked him.

This map was peculiar. For instance Kinalty Church was represented by a miniature painting of its tower and steeple while the Castle, which was set right in the centre, was a fair sized caricature in exaggerated gothic. There were no names against places.

As Charley stood there it so happened that the pointer was fixed unwavering ESE with the arrow tip exactly on Clancarty, Clancarty which was indicated by two nude figures male and female recumbent in gold crowns. For the artist had been told that the place was a home of the old kings.

Mrs Jack came in looking for a letter from Dermot. The carpets were so deep that Raunce did not hear her. He was staring. She noticed he seemed obsessed by the weathervane and turned to find what in particular held him.

When she saw and thought she knew she drew her breath with a hiss.

'Raunce,' she said and he had never heard her speak so sharp, 'what is it?'

He faced about, holding himself quite still.

'Why Madam I never heard you. The thing seems to have got stuck, Madam.'

'Stuck? What d'you mean stuck?'

'It does not seem to be revolving Madam and I'm sure the wind is not in that quarter.'

She reacted at once. She strode up to that arrow and gave it a wild tug presumably to drag the pointer away from those now disgusting people lying in a position which, only before she had known Dermot, she had once or twice laughed at to her husband. The arrow snapped off in her hand. The Vane up top might have been caught in a stiff breeze or something could have jammed it.

Charley knew nothing as yet about Clancarty. 'It's the spring Madam,' he said cheerful as he took the broken piece from her. 'You noticed the arm did not have any give Madam?'

'Oh get on with your work,' she said appearing to lose control and half ran out. Shaking his head, grumbling to himself, Raunce made his way upstairs. (Green 1978: 39–40)

Through the two characters, Mrs Tennant and Charley Raunce, we are treated to two different perspectives of a single situation, marked conspicuously by the different versions of their respective names (Mr Tennant, Mrs Jack –

wife of Jack Tennant – Charley or Raunce). For each of them, the empirical situation is significantly different, by virtue of the different interpretations they are constantly making, both of each other and of the situation itself. The dialogue is largely context-bound. What Mrs Tennant is doing is mistaking a metonymic relation (the pointer on the naked figures) for a paradigmatic (symbolic) message. She may believe that Raunce is attempting a little bit of subtle blackmail. Whatever, she cannot help but see the symbolism as pointing directly to her. Thus she inserts herself (and Dermot) symbolically into the position on the map beneath the pointer. In other words she mistakes a metonymic relation for a metaphorical one. Raunce, on the other hand, is positively *looking* for hidden significance, but rather literally. He wants to know where the 'clockwork' mechanism that connects the pointer to the vane is housed. Metaphorically he is looking for the hidden workings behind the empirical situation. As it happens, the pointer is jammed because a small mouse has its foot caught in one of the cogs. This could be another metaphorical hint for the reader, suggesting that the servants (the maids are often referred to as mice) are 'caught' in the workings of the house. But the *perspectives* are all important here. As such, perspective involves metonymic relations, relations of contiguity, of being proximal to, that is, being next to something or someone. Yet each perspective is related by some apparently meaningful interpretation of the situation, dipping into the pool of substitutable significations. There are many clues in the above passage. There is the map, first of all. There is a representation of the house and the country lying round about, in the house itself. A form of metaphorical centrism is implied here, especially with respect to the other key sites, which are partially drawn, or represented by metonyms, parts for the whole (the single steeple for the church). The map itself stands for the house, stubbornly remaining in the centre although doubly displaced (representing the English in an ex-colony). The map represents not by name (which would be the paradigm) but by caricature. However, the names themselves are less than paradigmatic, more metonymic in their slightly farcical suggestiveness. Kinalty, like a slightly disguised pun, forces the forms *kin* and *alty* together. *Kin* suggests the familiarity of kinship relations yet *alty* links to the alterity of otherness (same and different combined). Clancarty, on the other hand, gives us the more Celtic-sounding *clan*, putting it yet more clearly in the Irish camp. On the metaphorical level, what the map represents is the general picture of centric perspective broken up into metonymic part-relations, as if everyone has an imaginary map with their home in the centre and everything else represented partially round about. In this case the transcendental is nothing more than the personal matrix of selfish interests.

5 Derrida and Deconstruction

I The Text

In its most conventional and historical sense the word 'text' means: 'The actual words of a book, or poem, etc., either in their original form or any form they have been transmitted in or transmuted into: a book of such words: words set to music: the main body of matter in a book.' When we speak of a text in English studies we usually mean a particular bound and covered entity such as George Eliot's *Mill on the Floss* or Tennyson's *Poetic Works*.

Why does text come to mean the same as book? The word comes from the Latin *texere*, which means 'to weave'. And 'text' still has that meaning for us. We say textile, which is 'woven' or 'capable of being woven' or, as a noun, 'a woven fabric', a textile. So when we use the word 'texture' we might mean one of a number of things: 'something woven', or 'a web'; we might mean a certain manner of weaving or simply of connecting; the disposition of the parts of a body; or 'a structural impression' which might come about through a way of combining parts of a whole, as in music, art or writing; or, finally, it could mean the quality conveyed to the senses by woven fabrics.

Clearly the use of the word 'text' to describe a book is possible on the model of weaving, which, we might assume is appropriate to a certain way of thinking about books, about the way they have been put together, about the way writing is woven into text from the material or the fabric of our language. After all this, imagine my disappointment at finding the definition for textual-criticism as 'critical study directed towards determining the true reading of a text'.

The true reading? Isn't it as if the truth had got lost on the way to becoming a text? As if it was the job of the critic to find it again by reading. Does this make the text just a vehicle for delivering meaning or a coat that needed to be taken off? Well, this model of the text is as old as our history and our language opposes it systematically to all the things it might represent, such as life, the world, the real, anything it refers to, the mind, consciousness, personal or shared experience. The best text would be one that conveyed the most accurate impressions of these things. The trouble with the text is that it might not convey the *right* impression, the *true* impression, and it might therefore be misleading. A rhetorical frontier has been drawn between the *truth* of things and the *text*. According to this historical prejudice: the text is on the outside, the truth of things is hidden away on the inside. However, according to the same logic, the truth of things remains hidden inside only because it is essentially outside the text, in some far off yonder. Once again we are bound by the rhetorical distinction between the empirical (the text) and the transcendental (its meaning or truth). This, of course, does not fit the facts. But it does indicate a pervasive and history-bound prejudice, which for centuries has been instrumental in the way people have thought.

Deconstruction shakes up a concept like 'text' in a way that provokes questions about the borders, the frontiers, the edges or the limits that have been drawn to mark out its place in the history of concepts. Meanings take on their identity, they come to mean what they mean, by just such a marking out of frontiers, opposing concepts to each other, defining terms by their differences. So deconstructive reading begins by asking, 'What are the borders? What are the limits? And how do they come about?' This is the question that Jacques Derrida asks in his article 'Living on/Borderlines'. What are the borderlines of a text? How do they come about?

We fail to read a text at all if we jump straight in from out of nowhere proclaiming our opinions and making rash generalizations. The text is woven from the same system as the one we each inhabit, the system of concepts that allows us to think the things we do. So the text, and any given text, demands that we read it first of all in terms of the historical and rhetorical conventions that allow us to understand it, and which, by and large, allow us to agree, more or less, on what it means.

Derrida's Work   Derrida's work consists in *readings* of other texts. The problem of reading Derrida just *is* the problem of reading. Geoff Bennington gives the following account of why his introduction to Derrida's work ('Derrida-base') is from the beginning and always caught up with the problem of reading (while at the same time mentioning many of Derrida's key topics):

> *All* the questions to which this type of book must habitually presuppose replies, around for instance the practice of quotation, the relationship between commentary and interpretation, the identification and delimitation of a corpus or a work, the respect owed to the singularity or the event of a work in its idiom, its signature, its date and its context, without simply making them into examples or cases ... are *already* put to us by the texts we have to read, not as

preliminary or marginal to the true work of thought, but as this work itself in its most pressing and formidable aspects. (Bennington and Derrida 1993: 9–10)

We cannot first solve the problem of *how* to read Derrida and then read him. The problems of reading and of reading protocols are already the whole problem. Bennington also tells us that 'only Derrida can give us the means to understand this situation' (Bennington and Derrida 1993: 8). Why, then, am I introducing Derrida through the writing of his representative? The answer lies in a certain concept of repetition. A repetition must be more or less the same as what it repeats but it cannot be identical. My reading of Bennington's reading of Derrida's reading of the metaphysical tradition's reading of … constitutes a series of non-identical repetitions of the same text. In Derrida it is in this same repetition, this 'repetition of the same', that there is the possibility of something new (what he will call an invention of the other). The following sections are intended to clarify these points by subtly repeating them in slightly differing contexts.

Presence and Absence The metaphysical tradition (or philosophy) can be characterized by two basic desires or trends, admittedly manifested in various different forms. As we have seen in other sections, there is a consistent desire to reconstruct the transcendental realm, which is otherwise radically absent. The lost origin of our finite or fallen state drives us continuously to reconstruct our beginnings. Second, the ideal of *presence* turns up everywhere. All aspects of experience and/or existence are relegated to a moment called the present. But the ideal of presence always implies more than one moment:

1. Presence, we assume, describes an original state, a state that must have come first. As I gaze out into the world I can say the world is present to my observing eye. If that is the case, then my observing consciousness must be present to my own self-reflection. It thus follows that 'meaning', in its most pure sense, as conscious thought, must be present to me as I gaze out on to the world. Presence is, therefore, the main predicate for a text's meaning (its sense or its reference), despite the fact that this meaning is always absent and in need of reconstruction through reading or interpretation.

2. For this reason, a second moment of presence invades consciousness as *absence* – the disappearance of the world behind the veils of language, consciousness going astray, the reign of death, non-sense. In this way gaps, absences and deficiencies of all imaginable kinds are subordinate to a principle of *presence*. Is it possible to imagine an absence without reference to the principle of presence? It would be a radical absence, something always and from the beginning absent, missing, lost to experience. If there was such an absence, how could we glimpse it?

3. We glimpse it between repetitions as their repeatability. If the present moment can be repeated (i.e. remembered) then, preceding the present moment is the possibility of its being repeated in memory (i.e. memory itself as repeatability). So memory precedes and exceeds the present moment, which we will have remembered. Memory, as traditional accounts make clear, gets associated with death and the memorializing of the dead, or mourning, in a way that gets us back, always and from the beginning, to the second moment (absence).

Derrida's much-cited statement, 'there is nothing outside the text', suggests an absence that has never been, nor could ever be, present. This is what we must try to think with regard to the sign, and with the notion of text.

1. The sign is irreducibly secondary. It always refers to something else. Sometimes the something else that a sign refers to is actually itself (e.g. this sign here) but this doesn't mean that the sign's meaning (its reference to itself by virtue of its sense–sign = signifying unit) is primary. What is primary is the signifying aspect of it. The *sign* comes before its referent (*sign*) in so far as this sign means this sign. And that, of course, is secondary. It also illustrates that signs are necessarily always divided. Their principle is the repeatability that allows them apparently to jump out of themselves to refer back. However, in the repetition the sign is irremediably changed. It is no longer the sign it was. Disconcertingly, this kind of punning cannot be dismissed as a kind of sophistic rhetorical game. Or rather, it *can* be dismissed. But the principle of your ability to dismiss it (your ability to ignore basic rhetorical processes and pass over them in silence) is in fact the same principle that allows meaning to arise in the first place, cancelling out the rhetorical dimension, the secondary text (vehicle or coat).

2. So the sign *is* at the beginning. We never arrive at a meaning independently of some aspect of text, through which we must pass before cancelling it out as unwanted rhetoric (vehicle or coat). Therefore there is no beginning.

The Way We Think   We can understand how deconstruction operates if we examine Jacques Derrida's reading of Lévi-Strauss, which is exemplary. A much-republished essay from 1968, called 'Structure, Sign and Play in the Discourse of the Human Sciences', has contributed to a widespread understanding of Derrida as a key 'poststructuralist' thinker. Derrida's writing has certainly contributed to the critical revision of structuralism that has occurred over the years, but his own work is more wide ranging than the term 'poststructuralism' suggests.

In *The Savage Mind* Lévi-Strauss had made the following statement: 'Science as a whole is based on the distinction between the contingent and the necessary, this being also what distinguishes event and structure' (Lévi-Strauss 1966: 21). Derrida begins 'Structure, Sign and Play' with the following observation: 'Perhaps something has occurred in the history of the concept of structure that could be called an "event", if this loaded word did not entail a meaning which it is precisely the function of structural – or structuralist – thought to reduce or suspect' (Derrida 1980: 278). So Derrida begins by drawing attention to the popularity of structuralism (in the 1960s) as an *event* in the history of the concept of structure. But the meaning of the word event is something that structuralism would need to contain as an element within a structure or at least exhaustively determined by a structure. In the same way that science must contain all contingencies (chances, accidents and secondary causes) within the thought of what is necessary, all events should be contained as parts of a comprehensive structure. The reference is to the structuralist model that contrasts *La Langue* (the system or structure) to *parole* (the event of speech or the utterance). So, strictly speaking, and according to Lévi-Strauss, the concept 'event' is opposed to the concept 'structure'. Once again the model is a version of transcendental/empirical difference.

The logic is as follows: the event of structuralism is a 'rupture' in so far as the break between classical thinking in the human sciences and structuralism is like an overturning of old ways of thinking by new ones. But the concept of structure is itself a classical concept and its meaning belongs to ordinary ways of speaking. Furthermore, its meaning is something like 'that which determines and makes possible all events'. The concepts 'event' and 'structure' must have been determined by the field that structuralism sets out to explore and explain, that is, structure (rather than event).

Episteme

An *episteme* is an ancient Greek term denoting the field of scientific knowledge. Scientific knowledge is necessary knowledge and best characterized by the cool rational certainty of mathematics. Derrida accepts the more elaborate meaning of *episteme*, which refers to the age of western science and philosophy that extends – in some fits and starts – from the Greeks to the late twentieth century (three thousand-odd years). The word *episteme* thus refers to the fact that the concepts we use have a historicity (the condition of being historical) and belong to a system of thinking that is at least three thousand years old. This is the system that structuralism hopes to overturn.

Structure   The classical concept of structure has what Derrida calls a 'contradictory coherence'. In other words it is coherent only while it is suppressing a contradiction on which it is based. A structure is an organization (like a literary text for instance) and takes the form of a law or institution. Structures of this kind are always *instituted*, which means that an establishment through inclusions, exclusions and various means of cancelling out contradictions has been necessary from (or at) the beginning. Beginnings of this kind, which are not really beginnings at all but modifications, are often conveniently forgotten or shrouded in mystery.

All notions of structure have a centre – a point of presence, as Derrida puts it – a place where the structure originates. Thus any organized thing must have a point that can be regarded as its centre, and which limits the *play* that structures may be subject to. With a text any number of possible readings, based upon the substitutions that the language of literature particularly suggest, can be limited and qualified by the notion of its centre. Typical concepts of centre in literary criticism, for instance, would include the 'author', the 'historical context', the 'reader', the 'ideology' of a 'political economy', each of which provides a ground outside the text for limiting interpretation. The centre is in each case unique. It is a place where substitutions are no longer possible and in fact it escapes structurality (i.e. the author of the text is outside the structure of the text itself). So the centre is not in the centre. The centre is outside the structure. This is why the coherence of the concept of structure is contradictory. It rests upon a paradox.

Play   Derrida here borrows a notion from psychoanalysis – *desire* – suggesting that the fact of a contradiction indicates a semi-repressed desire. Anxiety is caused by a desire that is unacceptable. In the case of the concept of structure the desire is for 'immobility' beyond the reach of play. An origin or an end beyond the play of a structure has throughout the history of this concept (and all other metaphysical concepts) been mythologized as a point of full presence beyond play. Play (in all its senses, e.g. games, alternative to work, elasticity, gap between word and thing, word and meaning, wordplay) puts off full presence (e.g. of the world to my senses) in order for me to get a sense of the fact that it is there – even if not fully present. My access to the world is an access to traces of a world, in the same way that my access to a text is to the traces that the writer has left for me to decipher. *The* trace (an original and permanently necessary absence) cannot of course be made present to my senses but without it there'd be nothing of the world for me. The only way to master the anxiety about this absent outside is to hide the contradiction involved in saying that the centre of a structure is outside the structure. The ancient Greeks used the word *arche* for origin and an end was called a *telos*. From these words we derive *archaeology* (which digs back to the beginnings of man) and *teleology* (which dreams of a final purpose to all this scattered and contingent life). Scientists think that without teleology science would mean nothing. That is, all these facts must add up to something one day; they must have a final purpose that right now we cannot even guess at. However, this belief, which a scientist holds as strongly as the pre-Socratic Greeks held to their belief in Zeus, has neither justification nor support in the facts themselves. It is just a dream. No one ever knows what is to come.

Philosophy demands that its concepts have single naked positive meanings beyond the play of substitutions (metaphors and metonymies) that are possible for all concepts, as elements of a structure. If the sun can stand for the truth of reason then where does the play of possible substitutions end? As we saw with Plato we never actually reach the end. This single (unique) meaning must therefore be outside the structure itself (and outside the text – whether the text is literary, mythological, philosophical or scientific). But all the names for the centre (God, Man, History, the Subject, Mind) are themselves subject to *play* because they must each be thought of as absolutely unique when in fact they are historically *substituted* for one another. In order for the concept of an author to limit the play of the text an attempt must be made to play down or efface the influence on interpretation that the reader, or the historical and ideological context, has upon it. The centre is itself a concept among the concepts that it would limit from outside.

The Way of the Text   Derrida names three influential authors who have each been seen as challenging the history of metaphysics: Friedrich Nietzsche, Sigmund Freud and Martin Heidegger. But he points out that the tools they use for the destruction of the history of metaphysics are themselves derived from the concepts of that history. Anyone who tries to 'step outside' philosophy is trapped in a circle:

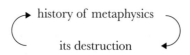

history of metaphysics

its destruction

No language is absolutely foreign to it. So all criticism slips into the form that it is contesting. Absolute foreignness (alterity, exteriority or, more colloquially, the other, the outside) can never be made present to sensible or intellectual intuition. But without this absent aspect we'd have no presence or absence at all. The tendency is to name or otherwise characterize this outsideness that gives origin, meaning and purpose to everything. But whatever the privileged term is called it must remain an outsider (infinite, necessary and missing from the beginning) or always come like a Messiah or Mr Right.

Structuralism, on the other hand – and here is its radical promise – appears to operate without a privileged term that belongs outside the structure itself (unlike other forms of theory/philosophy). Structuralism says that there is no outside to the structure. However, its privileged term – *the sign* – is a metaphysical concept. For metaphysics 'Sign' always means 'sign of … (something)'. Thus a *signifier* always has a *signified*. They are related in the same way that the 'sensible' is related to the 'intelligible'. One is 'visible' while the other is 'invisible' (and supposedly immortal). The sign, in other words, is always reduced by metaphysical thinking to the 'content' it signifies. Structuralism, against this (classical) conception, *begins* with the concept of the sign in an attempt to put the system, in which the opposition sign/content (signifier/signified) functions, into question. In other words, Lévi-Strauss *uses* the concepts of metaphysics without subscribing to their 'truth value'. They function as signs only without a grounding centre outside the structure (of historical concepts).

Bricoleur and Engineer

One would therefore be led to think that structuralism has made a breakthrough by giving up on the thought of the eternal outside. However, Derrida's reading of Lévi-Strauss reveals that such a thought remains a central part of his thinking. Lévi-Strauss contrasts the primitive science, the science of the concrete, with modern technical science (the science of the conceptual) by making an analogy on the basis of the difference between engineering and what he calls *bricolage*. *Bricolage* is a skill that involves using bits of whatever is to be found and recombining them to create something new. In French the word is used to describe the very skilful professional DIY expert. Lévi-Strauss suggests that the model of the *bricoleur* is a good way of characterizing the primitive scientist (medicine-men) as well as the one who makes up the mythological narratives (the story-teller). He says: 'the elements which the "bricoleur" collects and uses are "pre-constrained" like the constitutive units of myth, the possible combinations of which are restricted by the fact that they are drawn from the language where they already possess a sense which sets a limit on the freedom of manoeuvre' (Lévi-Strauss 1966: 19). Doesn't this sound like the structure (i.e. the language system) out of which the utterance must be drawn? Nevertheless, Lévi-Strauss still finds something to contrast the *bricoleur* to: 'The engineer questions the universe, while the *bricoleur* addresses himself to a collection of oddments left over from human endeavours, that is, only a sub-set of the culture' (19). Yes, the engineer, who questions the universe, who is, according to Lévi-Strauss, 'always trying to make his way out of and go beyond the constraints imposed by a particular state of civilization', can be contrasted to the *bricoleur*, in so far as the latter 'by inclination or necessity always remains within them' (19). Lévi-Strauss makes the opposition even clearer by saying that the engineer works by means of concepts and the *bricoleur* by means of signs. You should already be able to see the trap he has (amazingly) fallen into here. How could a structuralist have considered a concept as being separable from a sign – or thought the sign without the concept? Derrida's answer is the one we all ought to be able to have given by now. He says:

> If one calls *bricolage* the necessity of borrowing one's concepts from the text of a heritage that is more or less coherent or ruined, it must be said that every discourse is *bricoleur*. The engineer, whom Levi-Strauss opposes to the *bricoleur*, should be the one to construct the totality of his language, syntax, and lexicon. In this sense the engineer is a myth. A subject who supposedly would be the absolute origin of his own discourse [...] would be the creator of the verb, the verb itself. [Listen for the echo: *in the beginning was the verb.*] The notion of the *bricoleur* who supposedly breaks with all forms of *bricolage* is therefore a theological idea; and since Lévi-Strauss tells us elsewhere that *bricolage* is mythopoetic, the odds are that the engineer is a myth produced by the *bricoleur*. (Derrida 1980: 285)

There are many implications that would have to be drawn from this statement – concerning the discourse of ethnology (the anthropologist's mythopoetic *bricolage*), the inability to get outside the text of metaphysical oppositions and so on – but one thing must be made clear at this stage. Derrida is not saying that we are all doomed to mythopoetic recombination. Here and elsewhere he continues to affirm the locus previously reserved for *the truth* but this is now to be thought of as the necessary alterity (otherness, outsideness, absence) of the trace. One of the terms he applies to his reading of the ethnologist's paradox is *supplement*. This has to be understood in a special way, but once this special way has been grasped it will provide access to many other aspects of Derrida's writing strategies.

Supplementarity   What is at stake here is the question of totalization. In common with the natural sciences the assumption is that the field of enquiry is complete in itself and it is the task of knowledge gradually to cover the entire field. That is, we don't know everything yet but it is just a matter of time before the scientist reveals it. In the physical sciences the drive for what is called a theory of everything (the TOE) is one symptom of the desire for totalization. The idea is that everything (the totality of Being) ought one day to be part of a complete knowledge with nothing escaping (no particular finite thing). However, the dream is always just that, a dream, as certain demonstrable conditions show. These conditions are revealed in the para-doxical patterns of philosophical and scientific thought. Derrida uses the term 'supplement' to elaborate the paradox at the heart (the centre) of what was once known as the human sciences. Lévi-Strauss often affirms the lack of totalization in ethnology but sometimes he sees the project as just useless and at others as impossible. For Derrida this indicates two different kinds of implicit thesis about the field in question. By 'implicit' I mean that Lévi-Strauss is not aware – probably could not be aware – of the paradoxical double-bind that he is operating within. It is Derrida's intention to draw out the nature of this double-bind. There is no question about the fact that there are insurmountable limits to totalization. The difference concerns the way the limits are conceived. Lévi-Strauss provides an example of how there are two mutually exclusive interpretations of the way in which the 'human' sphere eludes totalization.

1. The world (of people, texts, histories, subjects, particular individuals) contains a richness and variety that cannot be reduced to any attempts at totalization (the language of theory). There *is more than one can say*. There is no theoretical language rich or dense enough to capture the finite world of rich particularity. This is a clue to the endless searching through the variations of particular myths that so much of Levi-Strauss's work involves. It is the struc-tural essence that underlies each variant that he is interested in.

2. On the other hand, it is the character of the field itself (and not its contents) that excludes totalization: it is a finite field of infinite *substitutions*, and the centre is missing (there is no centre). Instead of a centre there is the play of substitutions. The reference to 'something missing' (rather than the more popular reference to play) is crucial for an understanding of the kind of intervention that Derrida is making. He puts it like this:

> But nontotalisation can also be determined in another way: no longer from the standpoint of a concept of finitude as relegation to the empirical, but from the standpoint of the concept of *play*. If totalisation no longer has any meaning, it is not because the infiniteness of a field cannot be covered by a finite glance or a finite discourse, but because the nature of the field – that is language, and a finite language – excludes totalisation. This field is in effect that of *play*, that is to say, a field of infinite substitutions only because it is finite, that is to say, because instead of being an inexhaustible field, as in the classical hypothesis, instead of being too large, there is something missing from it: a centre which arrests and grounds the play of substitutions. (Derrida 1980: 289)

What this means is that totalization is impossible not because of our finitude (we are finite beings limited by space, time and language, such that we'll never be able to embrace the infinite totality of the universe), but because of unpresentable absence at the very core of experience. In an earlier article on the French philosopher Emmanuel Levinas, Derrida has already marked out the form of the paradox he is teasing out in this reading of Lévi-Strauss. The paradox concerns the difference between our old friends the empirical and the transcendental. These two terms, roughly charting the distinction between scientific (finite, empirical) discourses and religious and/or meta-physical (transcendental) ones, are complements of each other in so far as the one attempts to supplement what is deficient in the other (reciprocally). My finite empirical knowledge is deficient in what I cannot know of the infinite. My transcendental concepts are deficient in terms of what they cannot make into objects of empirical knowledge (totality, infinity, God). It will turn out that these two deficiencies are the same. We'll call it 'difference' for now and locate it as the difference between the empirical and the transcendental.

Radical Empiricism   In the article on Levinas, Derrida affirms what in Levinas seems to be reducible to neither empirical nor transcendental deter-minations of experience. The determination in Levinas seems to be something like a radical empiricism, in which notions such as exteriority, infinity, alterity and the other (names for things that could never be the objects of experience) are privileged. What Derrida says is this:

> By radicalizing the theme of the infinite exteriority of the other, Levinas thereby assumes the aim which has more or less secretly animated all the philosophical gestures which have been called empiricisms in the history of philosophy.
>
> [And a little later:] Empiricism has always been determined by philosophy, from Plato to Husserl, as *nonphilosophy*: as the philosophical pretension to non-philosophy, the inability to justify oneself, to come to one's own aid as speech. (Derrida 1980: 152)

An empiricism establishes knowledge on the basis of experience alone; including the sensible experiences gained through sight, hearing, touch, taste and smell (this is perhaps more the case in France than in Anglo-American traditions but when the point has been made that will be irrelevant). If you are a philosopher, on the other hand, knowledge will have been achieved through some dialectical relationship between experience and theory – determinations of thought, reason, concepts, ideas, *ratio*, spirit, and who knows what else. What Derrida affirms in Levinas is his 'radical empiricism':

The experience of the other (of the infinite) is irreducible, and is therefore [quoting Levinas now] 'the experience par excellence.' And, concerning death which is indeed its irreducible resource, Levinas speaks of 'an empiricism which is in no way a positivism.' But can one speak of an *experience* of the other or of difference? Has not the concept of experience always been determined by the metaphysics of presence? Is not experience always the encountering of an irreducible presence, the perception of a phenomenality? (Derrida 1980: 152)

An experience of the infinitely other is what causes the metaphysics of presence (experience considered as a clouded present that needs to be cleared by rational or empirical means) to crack wide open. 'Nothing can so profoundly solicit ['shake the structure of'] the Greek Logos – philosophy – than this irruption of the totally-other; and nothing can to such an extent reawaken the logos to its origin as to its mortality, its other' (Derrida 1980: 152). It is actually quite funny (without letting go of the seriousness of the argument, of course) to see how an article in 1964 which shows that Emmanuel Levinas, the philosopher of infinity and the absolute other, is an empiricist, might have stirred up the intellectual world a little. Well, the fact is, difference and the other are neither sensible nor intelligible (nor are they either just words or concepts). You cannot see a difference per se (nor taste one). You cannot think a difference per se. If you are serious about calling the experience of difference an experience, then you have to go beyond both empiricism and metaphysics. The empiricality of the trace or mark (like written marks, which are a kind of paradigm in Derrida's work) cannot be reduced to sensible or intelligible experience. There is now a different concept of experience altogether.

So Derrida says that Empiricism is the name that metaphysics gives to the pure thought of pure difference. Pure difference, however, could never be the object of a perception. That's why empiricism is a transcendental mediation, like all metaphysics. What in experience could you definitively claim was other, alterity, future as such? All you have is a horizon (the Greek words *horizen* and *horos*, become through a series of transmutations the Hegelian *Begriff*, or philosophical concept). The present (and its self-presence) seems always to have been already mediated anyway – that just is experience – experience mediates the pure thought and pure difference (or would do if there was any), but is there any? Philosophy corresponds to the dream of a univocal concept while empiricism corresponds to the dream of the absolutely idiosyncratic and infinitely plural world of things and objects. As philosophy since Hegel has known, they're the same thing.

'Something Missing'   We have already seen how language functions by virtue of the fact that the signifying element (called *signifier*) relates to its *signified* by way of a perpetually undetermined aspect, an absent trace, which allows the fleeting and transient phenomenon called *reference* to occur. I refer to this table here by virtue of what remains undetermined in the word 'table'. (You'll have to take my word for the fact that there is actually a table here that I'm pointing to, that is after all what language makes possible, whether or not there is an actual table – anyway what do you think my computer is sitting on?) The difference between the word and the thing necessarily involves a gap – this is *play* – which, as we will go on to see, involves both differentiality (the condition for there being differences) and repeatability – the condition according to which a sign can signify again and again and again, each time in a different context, potentially infinitely. Derrida's formulation reveals a solution to the age-old problem of the relation between the finite and the infinite too. The finite field (of theory, knowledge and experience generally) is finite owing to the absent, unpresentable 'something missing' that leaves it groundless. For this same reason it is infinite too. A sign is always a substitution for another sign, with no anchoring point, except the 'something missing', the differentiality and infinite repeatability of the always absent trace.

What is perhaps not clear from the 'Structure, Sign and Play' article, which is specifically concerned with Lévi-Strauss and the analysis of myth, is that the formulation does not only concern language. The total field (the world) is replaced by a signifying structure (signs) in the same way that one sign replaces another (cat = *chat* = feline mammal). The singular condition that allows us to represent the world to ourselves at all is the absent trace, the gap between word and thing, the differences between signs and so on. Our experience of presence is mediated by an absence that we can never experience as such. This is the crucial limitation to science and to knowledge generally. However, once the nature of the limitation has been recognized a new implication can be affirmed. If a sign is produced as an attempt to make up for a deficiency in the field (the 'something missing' of one-to-one representation, the gap between sign and thing), then the addition of the sign is in fact the production of a new signifying structure that cannot itself be reduced to that which it is supposed to signify. Another way of putting this would be to point out that structuralism doesn't simply discover underlying structures; rather, it adds more signifying structure. The pattern follows what Derrida calls *supplementarity*.

The *supplement* must be thought of as having two mutually exclusive meanings: (1) it is a *replacement* (e.g. replacing the absent centre); and (2) it is an *addition,* adding something new to the structure itself.

The point is, for Derrida, that there is a remainder (an excess) of significa-tion always remaining 'unsignified' (a lack of signification) which allows new readings in new contexts. So Derrida comes down neither on the side of 'structure', nor on the side of 'play', but locates at the absent centre a process that he names *différance*.

II *Différance*

The Same   The easiest way into an understanding of *différance* is (paradoxically) through the concept of the *same*. The notion of the same concerns a problem with identity, ideality and concept. In an article called 'Plato's Pharmacy', from *Disseminations*, Derrida provides a commentary on the law that governs the truth of the *eidos* (Plato's word for the idea). If this reading concerns the specifically Socratic version of the law (from *The Crito*), it can none the less easily be generalized. According to *The Crito* the most worthy object of the philosophical dialogue is:

> The truth of *eidos* as that which is identical to itself, always the same as itself and always simple, *eidos*, undecomposable, invariable. The *eidos* is that which can always be repeated as *the same*. The ideality and invisibility of the *eidos* are its power-to-be-repeated. Now, law is always a law of repetition, and repetition is always submission to a law. (Derrida 1980: 125)

A bit later on it turns out that this law of repetition (already paradoxical in the last sentence) involves a double participation in which the two parts (e.g. body and soul) are related to each other not through their being separate but by the one referring back to the other as a repetition of the same. This is a law that governs the relationship between writing and idea: 'This double participation, once again, does not mix together two previously separate elements; it refers back to a *same* that is not the identical, to the common element or medium of any dissociation' (Derrida 1980: 127).

The law can be outlined as follows: if there is repetition there is sameness, and there is only repetition if it is of the same, but the repetition of the same can never be identical. This dissociation of the same from itself is the principle that governs the identity of the idea (its ideality and invisibility). The idea must be able to be repeated in order for it always to be the same idea. But the principle and the medium of this dissociation and repetition of the same just is writing. (Which is why Derrida is led to call everything by the paradoxical formulation *arche-writing*). Elsewhere, in 'Signature, Event, Context' and in *Mes Chances* particularly, the law of repetition is developed as the iterability of the written mark. The identifiability of the mark in its repetition and its differentiality is what allows it to hop about from context to context (in fact condemns it to perpetual hopping about). So the *same* in Derrida is a combination of identity and difference governed by a simultaneous repeatability and differentiality.

Différance *Différance* is a term that Derrida coins on the basis of a pun that the French language makes possible. An understanding of this term is helpful because it can explain a lot about Derrida's apparently 'mischievous' playing with language and ideas. I put 'mischievous' in quotation marks because many people have misunderstood the powerful implications of his witty strategy. The pun is possible because in French the word *différer* can mean either to differ or to defer, depending on context.

1. *Différence*
2. *Déférence*
} to differ from something and to defer full identity and presence

If I was comparing two different objects of the same generic type (this hat is different from this one) I'd use *différer* just as I would if I was putting off an appointment (let's defer it until a time when we'll both be free). The one, take note, implies spatiality (difference) while the other implies temporality (deferral). What Derrida is asking us to do is to combine both, normally mutually exclusive, meanings in the one new term *différance*. (Because the term has passed into the English language, at least in theoretical registers, I'll not be maintaining the italicized and accented French form from now on). The pun involves the use of the little letter *a*. The French *différence* might mean either difference or deferral. Derrida's new term, spelt with an 'a' instead of an 'e', should be taken to mean both difference and deferral simultaneously. The first part of the pun we can call the performative, or auto-referential, aspect. What this means is that by both differing from itself (it means two different things at once) and deferring until infinity any final meaning (it cannot at any one time mean both differ and defer) the word itself is a performance of its meaning. Differance just is what differance means. The second part of the pun involves the fact that Derrida's misspelling is only noticeable when the word is written. Saying *différence* and *différance* makes no difference (sorry!) in French. It is pronounced the same way with or without the alteration. What this brings to our attention is the difference between phoneme (audible mark) and grapheme (written, visible mark) and a certain imperceptibility of this particular difference. It is this imperceptible difference that Derrida is using in the 'Différance' article to draw our attention to the permanently absent, inaudible and invisible trace.

So we can say that 'differance' is the word that Derrida coins to describe and perform the way in which any single meaning of a concept or text arises only by the effacement of other possible meanings, which are themselves only deferred, left over, for their possible activation in other contexts. 'Differance' thus both describes and performs the situation, or the conditions, under which all identities and meanings can occur, so that any text can be repeated in an infinite number of possible contexts for an infinite number of potential but undetermined addressees. It is a powerful modification of the ordinary notions of identity and difference. We need to explore this logic further.

Difference a Priori   Let me put the implications of the differance argument into a formulation: it is possible to speak of things, words and concepts because it is not possible to present the absence that differance (which is supposedly neither a word nor a concept) designates. Absence = difference a priori = the condition of being different of all possible differences. I called this, under the rubric of the *same*, differentiality. Derrida claims that this is not the same as the differences between letters. It is not the same as the difference between grapheme and phoneme. Nor is it the difference between word and concept. Rather, he says that it is the vehicle of all those differences. But because such an a priori difference/absence can be named only by a word that is itself subject to the effects of differentiality that it is trying to name, then differance is precisely both a word and concept designating its own condition of possibility (and impossibility).

When reading Derrida it is useful to get a sense early on of what he is trying to say. The first thing to come to terms with is the fact that what he is trying to say cannot in any ordinary sense be said. To say the unsayable is impossible. However, the general message is that without this missing unsayable thing there would be nothing to say at all ever and no possibility of saying it anyway. This is the possibility that Derrida calls (with characteristic perversity but also for very good historical reasons) *writing*.

A Commentary on 'Différance'   The following paragraphs present a commentary and a reading of the opening remarks to the essay just called 'Différance'. Here's a clue: unless you can see that there is something permanently and necessarily missing from your understanding, you'll be missing something important. If you need something to hold on to you could do worse than think through the implications of what Derrida has to say for the concept of identity. Identity is conventionally opposed to the concept of difference. But the opposition can take contrasting forms. Identity can be considered as an essential and integrated unity (my identity involves my name, my status, my hair colour and the number of my fingers, among many other things). The idea of a unity broken into differences is one possible traditional idea. Another one would be the idea of an identity that could be contrasted to other identities as its differences (and for which it too would be different). I am different from my colleagues, my students, my family and friends and my enemies. Any notion of difference (whether subordinated to unity or subordinated to identity) is always a difference subordinated, in fact, to some notion of presence (present at the origin or a present identity). Even the notion of an absent presence (someone or something was indeed here once but now they are gone) is subordinated to the concept of presence (if only the having been or will one day be – in the case of the Messiah and Mr or Mrs Right). The whole notion of Being is in fact subordinated to the concept of presence. What has been, is now, or will one day be present adds up to Being as a whole, according to the traditional assumptions. The arguments concerning Derrida's made-up word 'differance' show, however, that without a notion of absolute absence – a negative that must be logically prior to any presence whatsoever (like God, certainly, but nothing actually) – there would be neither presence nor absence as we experience them. It is easy to demonstrate with language, but the implications reach far into the ethical, political and practical realms of intellectual life.

As we have seen, the identity that is made possible by differance (as repeatability and differentiality combined) is the same but not identical. Neither repeatability nor differentiality can be made present to thought or to senses. Differentiality does not simply mean differentiation, which is easy to think. The absent insignificant trace is the mark of a difference a priori. Difference before unity, before identity. Unless we can learn to read the necessity of this a priori absent, insignificant difference, Derrida's writing will remain bewildering. But this is not because Derrida is a muddled writer. On the contrary, each sentence illustrates, through a witty play with the French word *différer*, a silent, insignificant, non-existent, unnoticeable aspect that none the less makes it possible to play in the first place. Without this ( ) it will turn out that nothing could have been possible in the first place. In other words, what differance names are the conditions that make it possible to play with French words like *différence* (or any word at all and thus any concept). The first full paragraph alone systematically sets out the main aspects of the argument. The paper was originally given as a talk and the relation between talking (phonemic sounds) and writing (graphematic marks) is a key one for the argument. In the spoken version of the paper Derrida begins by promising to speak of something: 'I will speak, then, of a letter, the first one, if we are to believe the alphabet and most of the speculations that have concerned themselves with it.' The first letter of the alphabet, the letter 'a' and the *alpha* of the Greeks, has a special place in the tradition. It is supposed to be the original letter of writing, the first written mark. What luck that it is this letter that performs the punning effect that Derrida has found! This is an important point: it is just luck and not anything grand or mysterious. At this stage we should be aware that this something (the letter 'a') might be more obscure than we'd have imagined. Surely it is the most obvious and evident thing, a simple letter. But consider this: are we talking about the sound we make when voicing the letter 'a' or are we talking about the visible inscription of the mark? They are two quite different things as we know and related to each other only by virtue of deep-seated historical and conventional usage (repetition). The relation has chance at its basis. Yet Derrida's promise is to speak (in phonemes) about a written letter (a grapheme).

Have a look at the next sentence:

> I will speak, therefore, of the letter *a*, this initial letter which it has apparently been necessary to insinuate, here and there, into the writing of the word 'difference'; and to do so in the course of a writing on writing, and also of a writing within writing whose different trajectories thereby find themselves, at certain very determined points, intersecting with a kind of gross spelling mistake, a lapse in the discipline and law which regulate writing and keep it seemly. (Derrida 1988: 3)

This sentence is yet more systematic in its idiomatic French of course but differance also names the possibility of this less than perfect translation. This sentence which begins by promising speech on writing goes on in its main clause to set out what is at stake. This is important and each section of 'Différance' will return to it. It is the relationship between at least two forces that will later on come to characterize a *play of forces* (a writing on writing and a writing within writing). On the one hand there is a writing that regulates and on the other there is a writing (a writing that is both on and in writing) that apparently capitalizes on the possibility of accidents (lapses, mistakes). 'Différance' represents this play in its insinuation of the letter 'a' where it does not belong. The naughty 'a' is a meeting point between two forces: a writing that regulates through the application of discipline, law and convention and a writing that reveals the accidental, the chance, the mistake, as a necessary possibility (for all writing whatsoever). This possibility is undoubtedly one of the key aspects. The next sentence is as follows:

> One can always, *de facto* or *de jure*, erase or reduce this lapse in spelling, and find it (according to situations to be analyzed each time, although amounting to the same), grave or unseemly, that is, to follow the most ingenuous hypothesis, amusing. (Derrida 1988: 3)

What is always possible? Correction or trivialization (especially in this case!). It is after all just a joke. No good trying to make a mystery of this little letter. It just happens to be the first letter of the alphabet. All the different effects of the play on *différer* are just accidental. They are trivial. It is always possible to correct the mistake or to laugh it off as a joke. Notice the parenthesis has already introduced the topic of the *same* as differences in repetition, all the finite particulars adding up incessantly to repetitions of each other. Is this what is so scandalous about differance? There is nothing special or important about it at all. It is a jokey play with language. It names nothing but the possibility of jokey plays with language. But this possibility, as Derrida hints in the next sentence, in its silence and its trivial insignificance, just is possibility. Let's take another look:

> Thus, even if one seeks to pass over such an infraction in silence [notice the parodic repetition of Wittgenstein], the interest that one takes in it can be recognized and situated in advance as prescribed by the mute irony, the inaudible misplacement, of this literal permutation. (Derrida 1988: 3)

Let's reconstitute the sentence that this last sentence ironically inscribes within itself: 'what we cannot speak about we must pass over in silence.' The famous and often quoted final proposition from Wittgenstein's *Tractatus*. It's a joke again, of course, and refers us to the first words of the talk (repeated again at the start of the paragraph). 'I will speak …', but that which Derrida will speak about cannot be spoken. It is the mute 'a' that occurs only for vision as an *accidental* effect of the graphematic mark (but not the phonetic one). I will speak about what we cannot speak about. But that is not just a joke; that is the topic of the essay and the aspect of it that we still find Derrida worrying away at in much more recent works. The word-concept 'differance' is an attempt to reveal the kind of thing that is made possible by what cannot be spoken about.

A little later, Derrida anticipates an objection. Let's have a look at the summing up section of the paragraph preceding 'it will be objected':

> The play of difference, which, as Saussure reminded us, is the condition for the possibility and functioning of every sign, is in itself a silent play. Inaudible is the difference between two phonemes which alone permits them to be and to operate as such. The inaudible opens up the apprehension of two present phonemes such as they present themselves. If there is no purely phonetic writing, it is that there is no purely phonetic *phone*. The difference which establishes phonemes and lets them be heard remains in and of itself inaudible, in every sense of the word. (Derrida 1988: 5)

Phonemes operate as differentiated sounds because of an inaudible element that comes between them as the difference between them. The difference is inaudible (no possibility of anybody ever hearing it). What Derrida is trying to do here is to draw attention to the function of the inaudible as difference and to show why the inaudible difference that makes it possible to distinguish between two different sounds cannot be reduced to any present sound whatsoever. This inaudible difference must be possible a priori as the possibility of all the empirical differences, the apparent differences between sensible experiences of sound. Derrida's proof of this is rather simple. When you write phonetically you must incorporate lots of marks (e.g. punctuation) that are not phonetic. These are graphic (and we are back with the difference between phoneme and grapheme). That is precisely the concern of the potential objection. Let's have a look:

> It will be objected, for the same reasons, that graphic difference itself vanishes into the night, can never be sensed as a full term, but rather extends an invisible relationship, the mark of an inapparent relationship between two spectacles. (Derrida 1988: 5)

Derrida has just about reached the point where he has said everything he needs to say. The graphic play does, certainly, act as a kind of revenge against the primacy of speech in all those texts he has already looked at. But the implications are greater. Speech is not now to be simply replaced by writing (sound is not going to simply be replaced by graphic marks). No. Difference eludes both hearing and vision. No one has ever been able to see or to hear a difference as such. The objection – 'but writing depends on invisible differences too' – in fact anticipates by repeating a generally acknowledged truism about writing in so far as it pertains to speech too (which even then in the 1960s was not generally acknowledged). Derrida is not privileging writing now over speech but showing that the conditions that apply to the one apply to the other just as much. As we're just about to find out, furthermore, the conditions in question constitute the very relationship between speech and writing per se.

So here is the argument so far. Differance, with its peculiar, inaudible, illegal 'a', refers us to that which cannot be spoken; inaudible difference as such without which there would be no differences for our experience (and no spoken language). But for all the reasons that have been given it will be objected that this applies to graphic difference too. Well yes it does:

> Doubtless. But, from this point of view, that the difference marked in the differ( )nce between the *e* and the *a* eludes both vision and hearing perhaps happily suggests that here we must be permitted to refer to an order which no longer belongs to sensibility. (Derrida 1988: 5)

It is the inaudible. It is the blank. This is what differance is about. It is about nothing else. But at this stage the stakes are in one move raised (a move *almost* identical to what has just gone before):

> But neither can it belong to intelligibility, to the ideality which is not fortuitously affiliated with the objectivity of *theorein* or understanding. Here, therefore, we must let ourselves refer to an order that resists the opposition, one of the founding oppositions of philosophy, between the sensible and the intelligible. (Derrida 1988: 5)

The move that disrupts the stable hierarchy of speech and writing is now repeated in a way that disrupts the hierarchy of ideality and sensibility. What this means is that the inaudible aspect that makes speech possible and its relation to the invisible aspect that makes writing possible is the same as the invisible/inaudible aspect that makes perceptions and conceptions (intuitions, images, ideas and thoughts) possible too. A series of affiliations are evoked, which repeat another series:

concept/word   sound/vision
mind/body   speech/writing
intelligible/sensible   phoneme/grapheme
signified/signifier   form/matter

The translator Alan Bass adds a footnote here that may be a little misleading, which just shows how difficult it is to get this stuff across. He says:

> A play of words has been lost in translation here, a loss that makes this sentence difficult to understand. In the previous sentence Derrida says that the difference between the *e* and the *a* of difference/differance can neither be seen nor heard. It is not a sensible – that is, relating to the senses – difference. But, he goes on to explain, neither is this an intelligible difference, for the very names by which we conceive of objective intelligibility are already in complicity with sensibility. *Theorein* – the Greek origin of 'theory' – literally means 'to look at,' to see; and the word that Derrida uses for 'understanding' here is *entendement*, the noun form of *entendre*, to hear. (Derrida 1988: 5 f.n.)

The reason this may not necessarily be helpful is that it suggests the order of differance (inaudible, invisible difference) cannot be intelligible *because of* these untranslatable semantic or literal affiliations (theory = seeing/understanding = hearing). Derrida's point is in fact much more devastating. The 'order that resists these oppositions' does so because 'it transports them'. Differance is the possibility of the affiliation. It refers to that which is neither sensible nor intelligible because (1) it cannot be seen or heard (or tasted or smelled or felt); and (2) it cannot be thought, understood, theorized, made the object of an empirical science, or analysed either. But you would have no sensible experience and no thought whatsoever without the differentiating differance that can be neither sensed nor thought. That's the argument. And we're only on the third page.

To sum up: there are always at least two writings, one within and on the other. The one regulates, disciplines and forces its way by convention and rule. The other plays, gives rise to mistakes, accidents, jokes, puns and witty manipulations. The absent ( ) of Differ( )nce reveals that the possibility of the latter is necessary for the former. A correction, a trivialization, a passing by in silence is always possible in the face of such accidents basically because such accidents (and such silences) must always be possible.

The order of this differ( )nce is inaudible, invisible, unthinkable but its effects are always on each occasion among us. Traditionally this order would be something like God. But differance is an example of these necessary effects and does not itself escape them. Is Derrida replacing the divine being (or just Being as opposed to beings) with the possibility of accidents? Could be. But then *everything* changes. There is an unthinkable, invisible, inaudible trace without which there would be no differentiation. That is the argument. Differance attempts to think it, to make it visible, something that one can hear. And it fails to do this. But its failure does illustrate its necessity. It's a paradoxical ground in the necessary possibility of failure.

What to Look for   In the 'Différance' essay there is a series of repetitions each involving the following characteristics:

PERFORMANCE   Differance performs the effects it designates. The word-concept that explains the possibility of all words-concepts cannot escape the effects it designates. Theological word/concepts, on the other hand, are supposed to be able to escape the effects that they make possible. Differance is a self-dramatization.

DELAY   After-effects that must be presupposed not before the discourse as such but as after-effect that retrospectively has to be presupposed. A secondariness that then has to be presupposed as being necessary a priori, that is before any postulated beginning. The 'thing' (concept, referent) precedes the sign. But the differentiality and repeatability of the sign precedes the presence of the 'thing' (concept, referent).

REPETITIONS OF THE SAME   Couples of a certain kind (body/soul, word/concept, grapheme/phoneme, signifier/signified) generally have hanging off them a third, hardly significant, aspect, that is as it were added to the binary coupling but which turns out to be the very principle of the coupling itself (in this instance, *writing*). The formula is as follows: (concept + speech) + writing = writing + writing (governed by repeatability and differentiality). The secondariness of writing is as it were doubly secondary (tertiary?).

THE LAW OF REPETITION You know this one.

III Exemplification

Deconstruction *Deconstruction* is the term that has been used to describe Derrida's 'method'. If we accept this provisionally as an acceptable usage (we will qualify it later), we must take note of some important features. Like all Derrida's terms it has two mutually exclusive (and contradictory) meanings: to destroy/construct. Deconstruction does intuitively sound like a form of destruction, of taking apart, perhaps, of undoing some construction. Many people have agreed that some deconstruction (thought of in this way) was necessary. The totalitarian projects of western metaphysics, the ethical, aesthetic, epistemological projects of post-Enlightenment science, the imperialism of European countries as they carved out their empires throughout the colonized world, the great patriarchal domination over women – all of these structures and institutions, people agree, need to be taken down to their foundations in order to expose their contradictory logic. But now, the argument goes, we need some reconstruction. We need to put things together again in some new, more democratic order. However, this consoling sense of reconstruction is anathema to any rigorous sense of deconstruction. Deconstruction actually names the impossibility of setting up 'perfect' or 'ideal' structures. That which cannot be presented for conception or perception takes its determination from things like the future and from the radical alterity of the other (which in its permanent absence guarantees the particularity of all of us finite particulars). No law could be set up to take that into its consideration – that is the very condition of the law. Deconstruction does indicate a certain amount of what Derrida calls 'de-sedimentation', which would imply undoing the work of sedimentation, the consolidation that occurs with systems of thought. But this is not simply with the aim of destroying the systems or ensembles in question. Rather, deconstruction implies reconstituting them according to the conditions (previously hidden or made mysterious) of their institution. In giving an account of his use of the word 'deconstruction' Derrida gives the following explanation: 'The undoing, decomposing, and desedimenting of structures, in a certain sense more historical than the structuralist movement it called into question, was not a negative operation. Rather than destroying it was also necessary to understand how an "ensemble" was constituted and to reconstruct it to this end.' So deconstruction names something rather more powerful than simply undoing. It names the conditions according to which it is possible for events to occur and for institutions to be constituted. We saw at the beginning of this chapter that Derrida seized upon the word 'event' in the work of Lévi-Strauss and his reading of Lévi-Strauss affirms the radical alterity, the 'something missing', that Lévi-Strauss's peculiar ethnology allows us to read. In other words, in order for structuralism to have been an event at all (something surprising, unpredictable, that eludes the conceptions of existing orders), it was necessary to find this 'negative' space. There is no escape from the 'odds and ends' (as Lévi-Strauss puts it) that make up a cultural inheritance and, more determinedly, the historicity of metaphysical oppositions, but we can open up this space (alterity, futurity, negativity) in such a way that an event is welcomed and the law, the institution, the structure, the whole conceptual apparatus, undergoes a change. So deconstruction is never the closing down of one institution in order to set up another in its place. Rather it is the persistent opening up of institutions to their own alterity, towards which they are hopefully forced to adapt. Deconstruction names the conditions upon which it is possible for things to change. If there is a strategy, or a method, to deconstruction then it would involve opening boundaries up to an alterity – almost literally making a negative space – that welcomes the surprise of future events. It makes or allows things to happen. The triumphal part of the structuralist project, hinting at its escape from the bounds of metaphysical thought, is treated with extreme vigilance by Derrida for, as we have seen, the metaphysics tends to rush back in just when you're least expecting it (like the engineer-god as origin of his own language). What kind of term can replace the recourse to metaphysical concepts? Can you have theory, or even thought, without concepts? As we have suggested, the notion of alterity, the other, that 'something missing,' which is obviously not a concept, can none the less act against the solidifying or sedimenting of dogmatic thought.

Alterity and Writing   Alterity is still quite a trendy word in critical discourse but not one that is always well understood. This is not because it is particularly difficult to understand – it is not a complex concept in the theoretical sense – it is just that it is supposed to designate a structural condition that cannot in itself be understood. Alterity designates nothing real or actual, but as a condition we could not do without it. It is a necessary condition. In the first instance it is a necessary condition for what we experience in the most basic sense as writing. Let's stop and have a look at the word first. It's not yet in every English dictionary, but there is a word that seems to provide its root: *alter*.

We get the word 'alter' from the Middle English, and that comes from Middle French, *alterer*, and from medieval Latin *alterare*, and that has passed over from the Latin *alter* meaning 'other' (of two), as in 'this one and the other one'; akin to Latin *alius*, meaning 'other'. When I take on an alias I assume a different identity.

Current transitive senses are: (1) to make different without changing into something else; (2) castrate; spay. The intransitive sense is: to become different.

Thus alterity, which takes all of the above into consideration (as well, please note, as the possibility of these permutations in etymological passage), is the condition of otherness, difference, or change. Words ending in –ity or –ability usually designate conditions that can be grasped only in terms of the effects they describe and are supposed to make possible. So we know that texts are translatable because we have translations and can speak in more than one language. We also know that pure or simple or literal translation is strictly impossible. Translatability is implicated in that impossibility (because a pure or literal translation would be literally 'the same' in the sense of being 'identical'). So translation implies as a basic condition of possibility, a certain notion of altered-ness; the translation will be different or in some way changed from its pre-translation form. Alterity doesn't just mean 'other', then, in the Latin sense (e.g. this burger is nicer than the other one), which would imply a contrast between two actual discrete entities. Rather, it designates the conditions upon which different discrete entities can be compared and contrasted at all. One of the basic conditions of a text (of any kind) is, then, that it can be translated into different languages (languages that its author, for instance, may not know). The text is permanently affected by this alterity, which in other sections we've isolated as 'something missing' of its complete meaning (thus enabling further contexts and translations). It takes up the space of the otherwise absent referent, and/or sense (or signified if you are still attached to Saussure). It gestures forwards to the future of randomly determined addressees, and backwards to the absent origin of the text – in so far as such an origin would be in some sense (yet to be determined) 'outside the text'. Alterity can also be considered in this way as the always-not-yet-determined sense of a text. The fact is, of course, that texts usually have both a sense and can be attributed with a referent (even a fictional one). But this is only because of their essential alterity – leaving those possibilities open. So when Saussure tells us that 'language is a system of differences with no positive terms', what he implies without actually being explicit about it is that language relies, as one of its most basic conditions of possibility, on a certain alterity – a structure that grants difference to its entities, the individual signs.

Repetition and Writing   Unlike Saussure, Derrida focuses on this sense of alterity in its relation to repetition. In Derrida the senses of alterity and repeatability are combined to form the notion of *iterability*. *Iterum* (likewise in Latin), which generally composes the central moment in analogical constructions, also means altered. It signifies the combination of a repetition (which implies sameness) and difference (which implies alteration). A repetition is an altered version of that which it repeats. Another one of the main conditions for our basic sense of writing is that it be composed of repeatable marks. A written mark must always be identifiable as such. Sometimes cloud formations or rock formations look as if they are composed of repeatable marks. But for something to be considered as writing we must be able to recognize the marks (re-cognize/re-mark). The same, rather obviously – yet the implications of this are profound – must be the case for that which the marks signify as sense, signified, referent or whatever, as and when a mark actually does signify something definite. The definite meaning is provisional and, again rather obviously, made possible only by the fact that the mark of its meaning be repeatable. The consequence is that the meaning, as a repetition of whatever minimal sense it always has, is in fact a usually slight but potentially quite extreme alteration of what it means in other repetitions, other incarnations. So, you see, deconstruction would not concern simply all the different interpretations that clever readers can manipulate by critical reading but, perhaps more than that, it concerns the *minimal ideality* of signs and texts; that which makes more or less repeatable meanings possible. The name he gives for that possibility is iterability. A minimal ideality ensures that a text maintains a singularity that contests any attempt to subsume it as an example. Literary texts more than any other kind draw attention to this; George Eliot's *Mill on the Floss* would not be adequately described as an 'example of the nineteenth-century novel'.

Superfluity and Writing   Writing always seems to be added. I have a thought. I write it down. My thought has thus acquired a vehicle that allows it to roam from its starting point to some other time and place, to you perhaps, who are now free to take it over. However, that starting point would remain first of all a silence, a nothing, if I didn't find some way to express it. Thus the expression, which is added to the thought, is not only superfluous; it is also in some sense necessary. Let's stop and think about that. I'm using writing now a little more in Derrida's extended sense in so far as he has shown that all language functions on the same conditions as writing does (iterability). So by speaking the thought I'm repeating it in a perhaps rather different form than the one it started in. By writing it down I repeat it again. But then the thought too must have emerged on the same conditions as the spoken and the written word, the conditions of iterability. It must have been repeatable (if I have repeated it in some form) from the beginning. So the superfluous parts of expression turn out to be the necessary (essential) parts of the expression.

Alterity and Transcendence   I have already pointed out that iterability, as the double action of repeatability and alterity, cannot be considered as anything actual or real. Yet the very nature of alterity as a condition suggests, even conjures up, the thought of the transcendental reality, the fabulous yonder of much religious thought. Iterability implies or suggests or evokes a past (the original before repetition) that never was and is already on the way to a future that is also nothing actual (rather obviously but against ideas of predestination etc.), but which structures the experience of the present. This is why Derrida's concepts are, as he says, quasi-transcendental. That is, they are not to be taken as actually transcendental but they do indicate that all thought and action must pass through an apparently transcendental alterity in order to have been possible in the first place.

Writing and Interpretation   Language is one of the phenomena that Derrida attempts to generalize by the term '*arche-writing*'. *Arche* is the Greek word for origin or beginning. It is one phenomenon among others where marks, interpretations and meanings of all kinds, as well as actions and the experience of things in the world generally would constitute other phenomena. So, for Derrida, there is an originary writing (on the model of certain essential predicates attached to writing in the ordinary sense) without which there'd be no phenomena for us at all. Because language functions according to the conditions of its possibility – that is, *arche-* or originary-writing – then it is easy to see why writing is open to often similar though never identical interpretations. The very concept of interpretation already assumes this. It has always been well known that interpretation involves seeing a text differently. That is why there have been numerous attempts to close down the possibilities, that is, to legislate over interpretations. Sometimes these legislations are explicit (e.g. with certain types of biblical or religious text exegesis) and, at other times, they are internalized rules or laws like implicit assumptions, the things we always take for granted as 'natural' or as being 'common sense' yet are thoroughly institutionalized. They are like a kind of framework that we use to contain a picture but without actually seeing the framework itself. When you look at the frame you no longer see the picture in any natural-feeling way (which spoils things for lots of people). Derrida is permanently focused on the hinges of the frames. This is just a metaphor but it is a metaphor for the possibility of metaphor in general too. Most frameworks of knowledge and understanding function on the principles that allow the literary text and figurative expressions to function as well. So if we want to concentrate on the openness to interpretations of texts we must also acknowledge the institutions that have deeply, historically, already imposed powerful interpretative strategies upon our everyday reading practices. In other words this 'openness' is hard to achieve (despite appearances) as most people tend to read the same text under the institutionalized illusion of humanistic or democratic differences of interpretation, which is not at all the point. All interpretations, whatsoever, are overdetermined by multiple causes, never fully controllable or systematizable. A responsible reading would acknowledge this beginning in overdetermination as a basic starting point. It leads to slow and patient readings and a range of self-reflexive considerations about reading protocols, assumptions and presuppositions, which certain aspects of all texts, by the very fact of their being texts, escape, contest, resist and subvert.

Transcendental Contraband   The only proof of a text is one that can be grounded in a certain notion of text. In other words all appeals to textual truth that gesture beyond the text itself must assert a transcendental origin, system, pattern, cause or whatever. A transcendental system is one in which at least one key concept in that system cannot be explained within the system itself. Derrida calls this 'transcendental contraband'. It can take numerous forms: the empirical, the context, the divine, the mathematical, history, authorship, the work. These have all, as has been voluminously documented, been used as anchor or centre for various modes of textual interpretation. But they ground interpretation each time in an unverifiable assumption determined only within a system, as its outside. The notion of text – in Derrida's expanded sense, that is, meaning not only language but all of what we call experience (and 'experience' is one of those transcendental contrabands too) – can be relied upon as a ground because of its quasi-transcendental properties. It always refers beyond what it is but never to anything actual or real or asserted to be actual or real even though supposedly existing in some 'fabulous yonder'. What is essential for a text to be a text is that it always remains undetermined with regard to what we might call its future contexts. Thus the predicates of writing include repeatability and that sameness or minimal identity that Derrida calls difference. They stand as verifiable conditions of a general textuality, according to which each text has a certain singularity also, its minimal identity in repetition that cannot be compromised by any institution, interpretation or law of any kind, but which also stands as an example of what makes laws possible in the first place. What in principle must remain absent is anything that would aim to complete or to close, even implicitly, that potential space. What was always traditionally perceived as a deficiency (the problem of interpretable texts or situations, the problem of justice and law, for instance) could never be 'made good'. Derrida mobilizes this apparent deficiency as an impossibility to be affirmed. It is that which makes provisional justice and interpretations of all kinds possible at all. So it is demonstrable that the transcendental opening is nothing transcendental but a necessary 'something missing' that allows interpretations and experiences of what is to come. By 'demonstrable' I mean grounded in demonstrable aspects of texts and textuality. So a deconstructive reading might read according to the conditions of possibility for reading as opposed to some extra-textual interpretive motive that can always be put up against others.

Derrida works within and upon a tradition, several traditions in fact, which he repeats in certain ways. These traditions provide the vocabulary and terminology that we find stretched beyond their limits in Derrida's texts. It is important to understand the double-bind of responsibility that his texts consistently present. A reading could hardly be considered responsible unless it could: (1) regard the text in its full complexity, even to the extent of the *regressus ad infinitum* (if you consider everything that must be considered in order to provide a truly responsible reading of a text, you will never be finished); and (2) respond to what is exorbitant in it – the beyond of interpretation that makes interpretation both necessary and possible – though impossible according to criterion (1), with an exorbitance that goes beyond the text, that reads what is missing in it, its inadequacy, its 'something missing', in a way that maintains the sense of that 'something missing'. In other words, a responsible reading should fail resolutely and exorbitantly to complete a text by interpretation.

There have throughout the long history of written texts (i.e. all of history) been consistent attempts to fix or to pin down meanings against the evident fact that texts tend to be interpreted in different ways. In the past this evident fact was more proof of the fallen nature of 'Man' and the imperfect nature of finite mortal existence. The fact had correspondences in politics, ethics and epistemology (knowledge) as well as in ontology (the enquiry into the basic grounds of being). Derrida points out that language is the way it is because that is the way that it works, as part of a system of powers or forces that produce the phenomena that are seen to be limitations on it (finite and translatable language). These limitations (no perfect translation, no simple interpretation) are the resources by which language works. The perfect and the simple turn out to be myths based on the failure to understand why language works in that way. Why should such a failure to understand come about? It is probably – but here we are speculating– an anxiety about finitude and death. If language is the way it is (blocking us from its dreamed of transcendental attributes against which language acts as a limitation), then it must be considered as just one example of many such systems. The whole dreamed up transcendental realm of perfection, eternity, infinity, omniscience, omnipotence, essence of existence, transcendental cause functions on behalf of the refusal to grasp the most basic facts of finite existence – that finitude positively produces the 'something missing' as an inherent structural component of experience. It is a limitation that produces what is limited (the dream of a perfect knowledge or a perfect morality).

Exemplification So the non-present space of possibility cannot *ever* be made present as such – otherwise nothing would happen. But deconstruction has become a kind of strategy (or a number of strategies occurring among many domains and dimensions) for outlining such a space. At this stage we must return to the issue of exemplification. How does it work? How does deconstruction change things?

There are two ways in which a text can exemplify deconstruction. Both cases may be understood if we shift our focus to the level of address.

> Standard Communication Model:
> Addresser   →   Message   →   Addressee

A text would need to be considered not simply as a message alone, standing independently of the level of address (someone addresses a message to someone else). Rather, the level of address is a major component of the message. A message can be regarded both at the level of *statement* (it says something) and at the level of *enunciation* (someone addresses someone else). Most messages have both sense (they mean something) and a plane of reference (they refer to some specific thing). At the level of address (or enunciation) a text can be analysed in its self-referential aspects, as referring to itself. Some texts do this in obvious ways. The mainstream cinema release *Mrs Doubtfire* is an interesting instance of self-conscious auto-referentiality. The story is, at the level of its *statement*, a sentimental tale of a father (Robin Williams) who would do anything to carry on seeing his three children after having been estranged from them following his divorce. He takes on the persona of a female housekeeper/ governess/childminder, heavily yet convincingly disguised in professional costume and make-up, and gets the job. In the meantime he works lugging canisters of film for a TV company, though he gets a break when the company director overhears him rehearsing his ideas for an informative yet entertaining children's show. He is eventually found out in his Mrs Doubtfire guise while attempting to play both roles (housekeeper at one table and aspiring TV actor at another during a restaurant farce). So he loses access to the children but gains a job as a TV presenter in his Mrs Doubtfire role. Needless to say he eventually returns to the kids in the role of their father as a full-time carer. The cinema rhetoric is fairly dancing all this time and issues of cross-dressing, gender and sexuality, the roles of mothers and fathers and so on, intrude constantly. It comes together at the level of enunciation, the level of address. The lingering shots of the entertainment world, his gay brother and friend who labour to produce his Doubtfire persona, the quickfire wit of Williams in all his personae, all serve to draw attention to the fact that this is about show business and thus the address is at all times an appeal to the audience on behalf of the product itself, that is, entertainment. The Doubtfire character (1) succeeds (where husband and wife failed) to produce fulfilled children who improve steadily at school; and (2) his programme is responsibly educational as well as being entertaining. These dramatic presentations draw attention to the responsible yet entertaining role of the media in relation to their spectators (the children). It is a message that builds in an evaluation of itself. It also, in grounding the absent *real* as the father beneath the disguise, appeals to a transcendental concept of truth but only in so far as it is contained in the form of the product, that is, theatrical entertaining fiction. The false persona and the real father are one and the same thing, a responsible and entertaining parent. In this sense we should be able to see that the text attempts to legislate, in its own way, over its own conditions (of production and reception). However, the 'something missing' intervenes when we see that the film operates as a consistent claim to responsibility only by inscribing its addressee – the spectator – as passive child, at the mercy of good or bad parents.

In this case a message attempts to legislate over its own conditions. In the second kind we would witness a message that is *responsible* to its own conditions (the alterity of origins and addressees). In each case the message can be said to *exemplify* its own condition, its own laws and the rules of its constitution. In the first case the constitution can be deconstructed (and there's barely a text that cannot). In the second case we should be able to see, at the level of enunciation, that the text is already so constituted as to exemplify its conditions of construction. It would in that case simulate a presentation of its own singularity, the alterity of its origin and the alterity of its addressee, with no appeal to a transcendental concept that would otherwise ground it.

This logic is intricately related to the 'ideal objects' like literature and the artwork, where the *examples* each tend towards a powerful singularity. In the case of literature this singularity is so powerful that it allows Derrida to formulate the questions and, thus, the laws that govern iterable singularities (the laws that govern the iterability of singularities generally – which is already a paradox). In an interview with Derek Attridge, first published in *Acts of Literature*, Derrida says:

> What is fascinating is perhaps the event of a singularity powerful enough to formalize the questions and theoretical laws concerning it. [He comes back to the word *power* later in the interview]. The 'power' that language is capable of, the power that *there is*, as language or as writing, is that a singular mark should also be repeatable, iterable, as mark. It then begins to differ from itself sufficiently to become exemplary and thus involve a certain generality. This economy of exemplary iterability is of itself formalizing. It also formalizes or condenses history. (Attridge 1992: 42–3)

A text by Shakespeare or Joyce is a powerful condensation of history (i.e. an example on the paradigmatic axis) but it is also an absolutely singular event. There is an absolutely singular and untranslatable uniqueness, which because it is iterable as such, 'both does and does not form part of the marked set'. The implications of this fact are directed here to science. In learning to understand these laws (which may be something like learning to read Derrida's texts), we ought to recognize that their formalization can never be finished, brought to an end, closed down or completed. He points out that 'to insist on this paradox is not an antiscientific gesture'. It is done in the name of a kind of science that would refuse to ignore the paradoxes of its own common sense or reason.

6 Psychoanalysis

I Freud and the Dream-work

Psychoanalysis and Critical Theory Critical Theory aims for an untiring vigilance against the sedimentation of thought. The notion of the unconscious has been powerful in this respect. We have seen how structuralism claims to gain access to otherwise unconscious systems of production (the production of meanings and the production of social relations). Deconstruction is an affirmation of what cannot be known or even perceived. Much of what goes on in systems of language and thought compares in apparently very precise ways with Sigmund Freud's account of unconscious psychic systems. The work of a French psychoanalyst, Jacques Lacan, has been a key influence on the development of critical psychoanalytic theory. His most famous move was to marry psychoanalysis with structural linguistics. Both Lacan and Freud have come under powerful critical review and the institutions of psychoanalysis are in constant turmoil, despite the calm exterior that they present as clinical and therapeutic professions. Psychoanalysis none the less remains an important discourse, not least for the controversies it provokes. The following sections are designed to allow some initial exploration into the field.

In this section we explore Freud's notion of the unconscious and, in the next section, we'll see what happens when psychoanalysis and structural linguistics come together. In the last section we will go on to a critical reading of Melanie Klein's 'object-relations theory', which though overshadowed by Lacanian trends has recently been reassessed both for its contribution to analytical thought and for its tempestuous history as the British School of Psychoanalysis.

The Unconscious since Freud The concept of 'the unconscious' did not begin with Sigmund Freud who, between 1893 with his *Studies on Hysteria* and 1938 with his last work, almost single-handedly invented and then developed the historical and cultural phenomenon known as psychoanalysis.

What is new with Freud is the way in which the concept of the unconscious comes to be the focus for a range of influential and effective resources for treating problems of at once a clinical, a philosophical and a cultural character. The concept as it stands is hardly promising. The prefix *un-*, meaning 'not', suggests a negative definition: without consciousness, not aware, not self-conscious. Yet, as with many words that begin with this prefix, the word 'unconscious' is very much more than a mere negation (compare it with, say, 'unkind', which generally means 'cruel'). But by saying this I still leave room for misunderstanding. Since Freud, the concept of the unconscious is often thought to denote a deep inaccessible level of the psyche in which reside impulses and memories that have been repressed. This sense leaves open the possibility of treating the unconscious as if it were a cave, dark and inaccessible but a place nevertheless, full of fearful things. Or, less mythically perhaps, it is regarded as the dark end of a scale, the other end of which corresponds to the clear light of consciousness (back to the negative definition). Neither of these interpretations is adequate for Freud's use of the notion. For him, the relationship between the unconscious and consciousness is the result of mental work that is characteristic of all psychic life, and neither of these concepts can be explained without reference to it. What is new with Freud is the consistent attention that he pays to the processes that characterize psychic life.

Every aspect of psychic life for Freud is at least *double*. For this reason psychoanalysis tends to focus on the borders, frontiers and fissures, the spaces of difference where relatively clearly bounded areas, such as the one hypothesized between conscious and unconscious psychic life, begin. It is common to suppose that consciousness refers to the state in which we have thoughts and wishes, make decisions, form intentions and so on, while the unconscious remains (always necessarily) the province of the unknown. But it is more accurate to see that, for Freud, thoughts, wishes and decisions *become* conscious by virtue of a tension between two unconscious agencies. The first corresponds to the simplest notion of instinct, an essentially neurological drive, the purpose of which is to reduce what Freud calls *unlust*, in English, un-pleasure. Unpleasure is caused by any form of excitation, whether internally produced (anger or hunger) or externally (noise or pain). The impulse to reduce this unpleasure can therefore be thought of as the most basic instinct, simply, the drive for pleasure, or the *pleasure principle*. The drive for pleasure is always a defence against stimulation and the aim is always to reduce it to as low a level as possible, ideally, altogether. The second agency, which Freud would come to call the *reality principle*, is also a defence mechanism but this time the aim is to temper the force of the first one. We can easily see that the desire for immediate gratification, not tempered by any kind of caution or principle of delay, might itself be extremely dangerous to a vulnerable organism. The baby's scream seems to be saying, 'I must eat and I must eat *now*.' But as the baby grows older and becomes a child, eventually an adult, the immediacy of the demand is tempered and the desire becomes less urgent. In humans of course the desire – sometimes even in adults expressed with something like this infantile urgency – is always operative. Adult life thus seems very often to be a series of detours, delays or carefully constructed secondary roads back towards an initial desire for peace and tranquillity. Once again the theory of these psychic forces seems grounded in a pattern, or structure, that corresponds roughly to the traditional distinction between the empirical (conscious awareness) and the transcendental, the structures that give meaning to our experience, however obscure those structures might be. So the basic idea is by no means new. It is at base another narrative of false or deceived consciousness. The two agencies were later in Freud's career given the titles *id* (the drive for pleasure) and *super-ego* (a sort of internalized moral law). Between these two powerful forces lies the result of their engagement, the *ego*, which is a kind of compromise formation in the basic pattern of the personality. The ego serves both the desires of the id and the policing control of the super-ego, both of which might be thought of as forces of desire and as internalized components of an individual's character. The id, Freud thought, represents eternally desiring mankind, while the super-ego represents the interests of civilization, carrying the laws that bond society and representing, in the first instance, the infant's chief experience of loving authorities, the parents. Language, culture, institutions of all kinds, are thus implicated in and internalized as a basic component of personality. So the ego is the site of the compromise between unfulfilled desires on the one hand (id) and social relations on the other (super-ego).

Freud began as a neurologist in the nineteenth century. An early insight was gained while observing the work of a French neurologist Jean-Martin Charcot, who was experimenting with hypnotherapy as a means of curing hysteria. Under hypnosis the hysteric would have symptoms both produced and removed through the hypnotic suggestion of the doctor. Symptoms of hysteria were then, as they had been for thousands of years, associated with the female (the word hysteria comes from the ancient Greek *hysteron* which means uterus or womb). Though hysteria has no traceable physical or biological cause, one would always have been found among the repertoire of ills associated with the feminine (everything from lack of children to witchcraft depending on historical context). In the nineteenth century the standard prejudice about women's weak physical disposition – so fragile, always getting ill – would regularly be drafted in. Symptoms included various forms of paralysis, speech disorders, nervous tics and muteness as well as obsessions and phobias. Even the inability to get up in the morning, a kind of chronic lethargy, would be regarded as hysterical. What Freud noticed during the hypnotherapy sessions was that the patients exhibited two quite distinct types of behaviour. The first type was socially sanctioned: the patients were polite and comported themselves more or less as middle-class women in the nineteenth century would have been expected to, ignoring the unfortunate symptoms. But Freud saw that the second kind of behaviour, if it was not ignored, resembled a kind of alternative, antisocial communication. He saw that with the hysterical symptom, 'the body joins in the conversation'. He came eventually to important conclusions. The first was that there is a kind of censoring force in psychic life that *represses* the instinctual drives. Repression is the word he used for the way a particular kind of wish or desire has been found unacceptable and thus pushed away from consciousness, to be buried unconsciously. The thought, for instance, 'I am sexually attracted to my best friend's lover', might be censored or otherwise disguised, for being morally unacceptable – all without my knowing. Often, however, the repression is not completely successful, so the repressed wish returns in some alternative form (the return of the repressed), as a hysterical symptom. Some specific symptoms particularly emphasize the antisocial aspects of the repressed wish, as the victim is compelled to snore loudly, fart, stick out the tongue or otherwise make rude noises and gestures. Symptoms are, thus, substitutions, in which one type of expression replaces another. A successful repression would involve a fully socialized substitution, of course. My desire for my friend's lover might be replaced by a desire for an object that bears some resemblance to her. The resemblance should not be too strong, of course; that would be too much of a give-away. It would preferably be accidental; for instance, a similar piece of clothing worn on a particular night might do the trick. This transferring of desire from object to object is an extreme form of neurosis and it can some-times border on psychosis. But desire does seem to operate through these forms of sly substitution, which as we shall see become very complex. So much so that the slightly parodic example, 'I am sexually attracted to my best friend's lover' (sounds like Elvis Presley), would probably already have been a substitution for a yet more obscure expression, and so on.

Another thing that Freud discovered early on was that hysteria is not confined to women. Everyone is more or less hysterical. With its special repertoire of conventions and social prejudice, the nineteenth century seems to have been particularly hard on women whose wishes may have been impos-sibly compromised by social expectations. One of the first great rows that Freud provoked concerned the discovery of male hysterics. Freud began with the hypnotherapy treatment but soon gave it up, as he found that stress-free conversation was more effective – hence psychoanalysis becomes known as 'the talking cure'. But he discovered early on that the most secure route to the discovery and interpretation of the processes of the unconscious could be made by way of dreams, a kind of symptom that nobody fails to produce.

Dreams There has never been any real doubt, except among the institutions of empirical science, that dreams encode some significant material (omens about relations or even the future, for instance, if not about the secrets of the dreamer's personality). It is often assumed that the process of dreaming involves a kind of encryption of significant material which requires specialized interpretation or analysis. In *The Interpretation of Dreams* Freud points out that there is no scientific method in existence that can help in the analysis of dreams. For the scientist, dreams are not mental acts but purely somatic, physical processes. Freud thus leaves the scientific view to one side and, as so often, looks for clues in the popular views about dreams. In popular accounts, dreams are either symbols of a hidden content or they are coded, with each image standing for a fixed meaning. As a result, there are two different methods of interpreting dreams among the popular accounts. Either they are regarded as symbolic, such that the whole content of a dream is replaced by another more intelligible but analogous content, or they are regarded as a form of code. With the decoding method each sign or image in the dream can be translated according to a pre-established dream dictionary. If, for instance, a dream features the images of a letter and a funeral, the dream dictionary might translate the letter as a sign for trouble and the funeral as a sign for marriage. The dream can then be interpreted as a warning against a possible imminent marriage. So from the earliest days the phenomenon of trope substitution was always assumed to be part of dreaming. There are problems for each method, however, corresponding to the basic rhetorical problem of allegorical or analogical doubling. How can you guarantee the security of the suggested substitution? The dream is normally full of unintelligible and contradictory aspects, which would have to go without interpretation if you were using the symbolism method. In the case of decoding there is no way to be sure that the fixed code or key is right for each element. To help solve the problems, Freud puts the two methods together. The decoding method can supplement the symbolic method because it can focus on individual fragments thus contributing, bit by bit, to the overall picture. Freud's *Dreambook* develops an uneasy alliance between stock symbols (e.g. the notorious phallic shapes, towers and cigars for the male and dips, valleys and containers for the female) and a more intuitive, questing, interpretative method that must rely on an analyst's skill for identifying what is pertinent to a particular case. The dream is considered as a special type of symptom (common to all of us), which can be interpreted with help from word-associations during a psychoanalytic session (determined by personal, individual circumstances).

Interpretation Freud's description of how he prepares his patient for dream analysis once again shows the relation of the critical or judgmental side of the psyche to social relations. What is crucial is that there must be a suspension of the 'critical' faculties, what he calls 'a relaxation of the gates of reason'. The rational, judging, organizing side of the personality is given a rest so that the pleasure-seeking side of the personality can come up with associations that the rational side would not normally have sanctioned.

The interpretation then follows these three steps:

- The dream is cut up into pieces and the series of associations belonging to each piece can be considered as 'background thoughts'.
- The elements making up the background thoughts to each piece of the dream can be related to each other under the assumption that the meaning of the dream is of a composite character.
- Like decoding, the details can be interpreted; like symbolism, a dream can be regarded as a distorted version of a coherent psychic formation of unconscious thoughts.

In this way Freud was able to show that ideas which once would have been regarded as involuntary – just popping into your head as if from nowhere – can in fact be regarded as voluntary but from an agency of the psyche that is literally not conscious. His findings also lead him to a famous conclusion: 'a dream is the secret fulfilment of a wish that has been repressed.' Freud suggests that there are two psychic agencies (currents or systems) at work: 'One of these forces constructs the wish which is expressed by the dream, while the other exercises a censorship upon this dream-wish and, by use of that censorship, forcibly brings about a distortion in the expression of the wish.' The dream represents a series of limitations, distortions, defences and disguises, which are the consequence of a repression on the agency of wish creation, that is, on desire, the force of the drive for pleasure. They are like two forces. One creates wishes; the other represses them. The compromise between these two forces is typified by our contradictory dreamscapes.

The Dream-work

Now that analysts have become reconciled to replacing the manifest dream by the meaning revealed by its interpretation, many of them have become guilty of falling into another confusion which they cling to with equal obstinacy. They seek to find the essence of dreams in their latent content and in so doing they overlook the distinction between the latent dream-thoughts and the dream-work. At bottom dreams are nothing other than a particular form of thinking, made possible by the conditions of the state of sleep. It is the dream-work that creates that form, and it alone is the essence of dreaming – the explanation of its peculiar nature. (Freud, *The Interpretation of Dreams*, footnote added in 1925)

In this footnote, added twenty-five years after the original publication of *The Interpretation of Dreams*, Freud is drawing attention to two kinds of mistake that analysts make when interpreting dreams. The first (typical of the earlier days) is to attribute too much importance to the manifest content of dreams, to make too much of what is obvious. The dream is a *disguise*, so that interpretation must dig beneath the manifest content to its symbolic core. However, the other mistake (more typical of later analysis) is to jump too quickly to some latent content not visible on the surface but lurking below like the monster from the black lagoon. The point is to see the dream not simply in terms of either its manifest or its latent content. Rather it is to understand the *processes* by which the dream comes into being. That is, the analysis of dreams must come to grips with what Freud calls 'the dream-work'. Analysis is thus concerned with process, rather than content, as it is the process that reveals the workings of the unconscious. Freud locates four main aspects to the dream-work, the means by which the hidden wish becomes expressed. These four aspects account for how wishes and desires become structured and organized unconsciously.

The Four Aspects of the Dream-work

1. Condensation: condenses many different ideas into one.
2. Displacement: replaces a latent element by a well-concealed allusion to it, so the psychical emphasis is shifted from an important element to a relatively trivial one.
3. Considerations of representability (or 'figurability'): transforms thoughts into visual elements ('I was in a tower above the audience' might mean 'I towered above the audience intellectually').
4. Secondary revision: makes something whole and more or less coherent out of the distorted product of the dream-work.

These aspects of the dream-work transform a latent (unconscious) set of thoughts into the manifest content (the dream), which is a disguised version of those thoughts.

1. CONDENSATION (VERDICHTUNG) In a footnote to his often rather dream-like poem, *The Waste Land,* T. S. Eliot describes the role of the 'character' Tiresias. This is what he says:

> Tiresias, although a mere spectator and not indeed a 'character', is yet the most important personage in the poem, uniting all the rest. Just as the one-eyed merchant, seller of currants, melts into the Phoenician Sailor, and the latter is not wholly distinct from Ferdinand Prince of Naples, so all the women are one woman, and the two sexes meet in Tiresias.

The way Eliot describes these characters as melting into each other, and the role of Tiresias as the one who unites all the rest, is directly reminiscent of the way Freud describes the work of condensation. It is, in fact, exactly the situation we find in dreams. The remark about all the women being one woman seems to me to correspond suspiciously closely to Freud's example of one of his own dreams that he uses in order to explain how condensation works. The dream is quite famous because it is the one he analyses as 'a specimen dream' in *The Dream Book* and it has become known as 'the dream of Irma's injection'. This is what he says about it:

> The principle figure in the dream-content was my patient Irma. She appeared with the features which were hers in real life, and thus, in the first instance, represented herself. But the position in which I examined her by the window was derived from someone else, the lady for whom, as the dream-thoughts showed, I wanted to exchange my patient. In so far as Irma appeared to have a diphtheritic membrane, which recalled my anxiety about my eldest daughter, she stood for that child and, behind her, through her possession of the same name as my daughter, was hidden the figure of my patient who succumbed to poisoning [...] she turned into another lady whom I had once examined, and, through the same connection, to my wife. (Freud 1976: 399)

So Freud's explanation of the work of condensation shows that a single figure can be turned into a collective image, combining often contradictory elements. 'Irma became the representative of all these other figures which had been sacrificed to the work of condensation' (Freud 1976: 399–400). It thus turns out that the manifest content of a dream is smaller than the latent one; it is a kind of abbreviated translation, much like Eliot's *Waste Land*, which was severely cut before publication. The unifying image (Tiresias or Irma) represents one of the points of intersection for many otherwise hidden associative chains.

Condensation is brought about by latent elements that have something in common being combined and fused into a single unity in the manifest dream. Freud points out that the process is like constructing a new concept out of something that various people, things and places have in common. The new temporary concept has this common element as its nucleus. It is like a creation of the imagination that can combine things that do not normally belong together into a strange new unity. Freud says that the 'creative' imagination cannot invent anything; it can only combine components that are strange to one another. The dream-work puts thoughts ('which may be objectionable and unacceptable, but which are correctly constructed and expressed') into another form. But he contrasts condensation ('this rendering into another script or language') to translation in the following way:

TRANSLATION	CONDENSATION
A translation normally endeavours to preserve the distinctions made in the text and particularly to keep things that are similar separate.	The dream-work tries to condense two different thoughts by seeking out an ambiguous word in which the two thoughts may come together.

The distinction is extremely important. As we have seen, Jakobson's distinction between the paradigmatic and syntagmatic axes suggests that translation occurs on the paradigmatic axis, substituting words in one language for words in another. Condensation, on the other hand, seems to squash the elements together, thus disguising distinctions by containing them all in a single ambiguous image. Imagine a translation of a long novel of 400 pages by a highly condensed prose poem of maybe forty or less. By condensation, many quite different latent trains of thought can be combined in one manifest dream. But no simple relation will remain between the elements in the latent and the manifest dream. It is not a word-for-word or a sign-for-sign translation. In addition to the metaphorical structure of substitution, reminiscent of Jakobson's paradigmatic axis, we must include a powerful simplifying of complex signifying material, demanding an equivalent labour of unfolding on the part of the interpreter. Instead of simply substituting image for image, the dream-work squashes them all together as a composite usually under a rather minor (i.e. less significant) member of the group.

2. DISPLACEMENT (VERSCHIEBUNG)

Dream-censorship only gains its end if it succeeds in making it impossible to find the path back from the allusion to the genuine thing. (Freud, *Introductory Lectures on Psychoanalysis*)

Those elements that stand out in the manifest content (the dream itself) are usually not important with respect to the dream-thoughts (the distorted wish). The essence of the dream-thoughts need not be represented in the dream at all. *Displacement* refers to the fact that an idea's emphasis, or its interest, or its intensity, is liable to be detached from it and to be passed on to other ideas, which were originally of little intensity but which are related to the first idea by a chain of associations. The energy runs along pathways allowed by censorship.

We do not need a similarity of subject matter to make the kind of allusion that displacements follow. Allusions replace the original idea by unusual external associations such as similarity of sound, verbal ambiguity, and so on. The allusions used in displacements are connected with the elements they replace by the most external and remote relations and are therefore not always intelligible as such. When they are undone, Freud says, 'their interpretation gives the impression of being a bad joke or of an arbitrary and forced explanation dragged in by the hair of its head'. The allusions that facilitate displacements are like metonymic tropes, opportunistic with regard to accidental or proximal factors, making it all the more difficult to retrace the route back to the site of the worrying intensity. They operate a little like cockney rhyming slang. This coded use of English may have first been developed by criminals or inmates of prisons in an attempt to disguise what they were saying to each other when in earshot of prison guards or, outside the prison, when in the earshot of the newly instituted Peelers (the prototype police force). The unconscious too is in its own way speaking in a disguised way in an attempt to evade the notice of the law. It is a little like a secret code, using English words that have no obvious relation to the words actually meant. There are two steps in the creation of a cockney substitution. First you take a pair of associated words (e.g. fish-hook), where the second word rhymes with the word you intend to say (e.g. book). Then you use the first word of the associated pair to indicate the word you originally intended to say ('fish' can be used to mean 'book'). As always on the metonymic axis context is everything, so some creative inference is demanded of the addressee. Take the following phrase: ' 'Allo, me old china – wot say we pop round the Jack.' This would mean: 'Hello, my old mate [china-plate], what do you say we pop around to the bar [Jack-Tar].' The word for 'wife' is often 'trouble' (from 'trouble-and-strife') and the 'kids' are 'teapots' (from teapot-lids). It sounds silly, which is just as well, for that is exactly how an unconscious displacement should sound, once you've unravelled it. The silliness is part of the disguise. A friend once reported a dream in which she was at her workplace and met a fireman in the passageway where they began to kiss passionately. I suggested that it may have meant that she unconsciously desired to have an affair with one of her colleagues, whose name was Sam, on the basis of the arbitrary connection *Fireman Sam*, a popular children's TV show. The fireman in the dream looked nothing like Sam, of course, and she flatly denied this. Not long after, however, the two did go out on a few dates (though the romance failed to develop). None of this would count as psychoanalysis as such, but it does point to the ways in which the dream-work functions through the substitution of tropes and to how our emotional lives are to an incalculable extent determined in similar ways.

Freud, in his *Introductory Lectures,* uses an anecdote to call up the way displacement produces the effect of 'going astray': 'There was a blacksmith in a village who had committed a capital offence. The court decided that the crime must be punished; but as the blacksmith was the only one in the village and was indispensable, and as on the other hand there were three tailors living there, one of them was hanged instead' (Freud 1973: 209).

This story suggests that because there are enough tailors for the loss of one to be a relatively minor disaster for the villagers, one of the tailors can act as a replacement – a scapegoat substitute – for the only blacksmith, a person who, owing to his singularity, would be severely missed. Displacement works in an analogous way. The thought that the displacement escapes can be substituted for by any number of relatively unimportant yet numerous alternatives. Displacement, though difficult to track, is grasped because of what Freud calls *overdetermination* – a term with an interesting history.

Overdetermination describes Freud's unconscious as a 'thought factory' on the analogy of an inexhaustibly productive team of weavers, the shuttle flying *over* here and *over* there.

Freud was by no means the first neurologist to refer to the fact that symptoms appear to have multiple causation. He does seem to be one of the few in the late nineteenth century to be making claims such that multiple causation is the rule rather than the interesting exception. In *Studies on Hysteria* he points out that:

> There is in principle no difference between the symptom's appearing in a temporary way after its first provoking cause and its being latent from the first. Indeed in the great majority of instances we find that a first trauma has left

no symptom behind, while a later trauma of the same kind produces a symptom, and yet the latter could not have come into existence without the co-operation of the earlier provoking cause; nor can it be cleared up without taking all the provoking causes into account. (Freud 1974: 245–6)

Overdetermination refers to all the provoking causes of a hysterical symptom. There is a reference here to what Freud called *Nachträglichkeit* (deferred action), by which a cause or provocation seems to be activated after the event, strengthened by a lesser, though similar, event that occurs later – and which seems rather profoundly to suggest a notion of time not subordinated to the present. The loss of a loved one might be traumatic and perhaps not fully recognized, yet the subsequent loss of a trivial possession might provoke the severest grief, perhaps reactivating the original provocation under the sign of the lesser tragedy.

The pattern is as follows: a trauma may have little or no effect at first, yet a later trauma of a similar kind provokes a symptom by triggering off the provocation of the earlier trauma as well, a process that is continued repeatedly. It is also the pattern of the *repetition compulsion*, according to which a person is compelled to repeat situations that are harmful or distressing.

Later in *Studies on Hysteria* it is Joseph Breuer who first writes the actual word, although he does attribute it to Freud: 'Such symptoms are invariably "overdetermined", to use Freud's expression.' The word is *überdeterminiert*. When Freud employs a similar term at around this time it is *überbestimmt* (emphasizing the multiple causation as provocation). In the *Dreambook* the notion is pretty much taken for granted. A parenthesis explains to the reader why it is possible to have more than one interpretation of a dream: 'The two interpretations are not mutually contradictory, but cover the same ground; they are a good instance of the fact that dreams, like all other psychological structures, regularly have more than one meaning.' The notion of meaning here should be referred to the notion of 'provoking cause'. But later he defines it in a famous statement derived from Goethe's *Faust*. Analysing a dream (his own) in which 'botanical' is a nodal point (of condensations) he says: 'Here we find ourselves in a factory of thought where, as in the Weaver's masterpiece:

> A thousand threads one treadle throws,
> Where fly the shuttles hither and thither [*herüber hinüber*],
> Unseen the threads are knit together,
> And an infinite combination grows.
>
> (Trans. B. Taylor).

The factory of thought, or the textile, is explained thus: 'The explanation of this fundamental fact can also be put another way: each of the elements of the dream's content turns out to have been "overdetermined" – to have been represented in the dream-thoughts many times over.' In other words, a plural and busy production team – actively producing, causing, provoking symptoms (like dreams and puns and jokes) ad infinitum – overdetermines the textile unconscious.

The other two functions of the dream-work can be summarized quite succinctly.

3. CONSIDERATIONS OF REPRESENTABILITY Freud says, 'Considerations of representability consists in transforming thoughts into visual images. They comprise the essence of the formation of dreams [...] The dream-work reduces the content of the dream-thoughts to its raw material of objects and activities.' For instance, nonsense and absurdity are meaningful in dreams. They mean 'this is nonsense' or 'it is absurd that', etc. If I had dreamed that a close colleague, whom I greatly admire but with whom I sometimes compete, was talking gobbledegook – nonsense language – I might have to face the fact that the dream was aiming to satisfy a rather unpleasant wish that my colleague talks nonsense. That is, his lectures are not lucid and his articles are half-baked – though that last one might have involved him taking uncooked bread from an oven, when in fact his work is excellent and clear.

4. SECONDARY REVISION Secondary revision refers to the ways in which the dream-work will utilize aspects of coherent narrative to help disguise the fact that there are contradictions – the film-like sequences (often taken straight out of part of the waking day) are patched in to get away from the otherwise contradictory material. In other words, it is a *second order* of disguise. The first order disguises the wish (displacement and condensation), the second order disguises the obviousness of the disguise. It is manifested in waking life by our failure, for instance, to catch all the typographic and spelling errors when we read through our own work; secondary revision will convince us that the errors are just not there.

Kettle Logic Freud shows how a dream might offer contradictory statements that none the less make the same plea. The combinations of condensation, displacement, figuration and secondary revision result in a kind of contradictory text, a text that makes too many contradictory claims towards the same purpose. He says that it is like

the defence put forward by the man who was charged by one of his neighbours with having given him back a borrowed kettle in a damaged condition. The defendant asserted, first, that he had given it back undamaged; secondly that the kettle had a hole in it when he borrowed it; and, thirdly, that he never borrowed a kettle from his neighbour at all. So much the better if only a single one of these three lines of defence were to be accepted as valid the man would have to be acquitted. (Freud 1976: 197)

For psychoanalytical interpretation it is not the contradictory argument that is interesting; it is the existence of a desire that the contradictory statements reveal. This aspect of psychoanalytic theory has been most influential outside psychoanalytical institutions. Apparently irrational attitudes or theories, including inconsistencies and contradictions, can be read as possibly serving some function other than the one intended. A contradiction need not mean the simple downfall of a point of view or a theory. Rather it might always lead back to a deeper, or somewhat hidden, determination. Michel Foucault's argument about the European prison service since the nineteenth century, published in *Discipline and Punish*, can be seen to be operating on the supposition that an apparently inefficient and contradictory institution in fact serves a function other than the ones it was explicitly set up to serve.

While Foucault doesn't openly acknowledge the influence of Freud in his argument, and is strictly opposed to the influence of the institution especially in its function as normalizing production of power/knowledge, his argument does illustrate Freud's 'kettle logic' rather neatly and in a way that can show how institutions might also be said to embody unconscious processes. Consistently, the complaints made about the prison service – that inmates gathered together are more likely to foster criminal intentions and ideologies among themselves, that the prison does not punish criminals enough, that prison actually produces recidivism and so on – have not dimmed throughout the prison's history. Foucault notes that the responses to these complaints are, increasingly, more of the same (fast-growing prison services around the world). So his hypothesis is that the prison has not failed at all. Rather it serves a function quite other than the ones it was overtly set up to serve (punishment, rehabilitation, decreased recidivism and so on). The team of pathologists, the officers, psychologists, educators, parole officers function covertly – as a kind of institutional unconscious – to pathologize crime as a way of simultaneously legitimizing the law in general, enforced by modes of disciplinarity and surveillance. It is then possible to generalize the various modes of disciplinarity (standardization, normativity, regimen, examination and surveillance) as the discursive modes of modern existence.

II Lacan, Freud and Sexuality

Lacan and Language Jacques Lacan was a French psychoanalyst who from 1953 until 1980, in addition to his own clinical practice, gave regular seminars in Paris to an audience sometimes amounting to 800, many of whom were distinguished intellectuals in their own right. Lacan's influence over the last twenty years or so on nearly all humanities disciplines cannot be doubted. His influence has been especially marked in literary criticism, film theory, art history and theory, continental philosophy and in some areas of social and political thought. Several schools of psychoanalysis have split off from his own, sometimes with intense bitterness, but otherwise his relation to established psychoanalytic institutions is strained, to say the least. His theory is by his own account a development of systematic readings of Freud's works, and in fact his seminars, many of which are available in transcriptions, are each based around particular texts by Freud. But many other influences are apparent, including surrealism, continental philosophy and structural linguistics, which provides much of his vocabulary if not his theoretical base. He uses other sciences such as biology, optics, mathematics and physics more for their metaphorical resources rather than any objective principles. This is an important point: Lacan follows Freud in making use of analogies to explain otherwise un-explainable things, so in this respect we can see that psychoanalysis shares some similar characteristics with literature and art generally. It is an insistence on the rhetorical dimension underlying human experience. Lacan's writings provide the clearest example of this aspect of psychoanalysis, so much so that, according to Lacan, literature and psychoanalysis are merely two different types of discourse with the same aims – that is, to expose the discursive dimension of knowledge, power and social relations.

The Unconscious is the Discourse of the Other According to Lacan, the human subject is always split between a conscious side, a mind that is accessible, and an unconscious side, a series of drives and forces that remain inaccessible. The cost of human 'knowledge' is that these drives must remain unknown. What is most basic to each human entity is what is most alien. This ($\cancel{S}$) is the symbol that Lacan uses to figure the subject in its division. We are what we are on the basis of something that we experience to be missing from us – our understanding of the other – that is the other side of the split out of which our unconscious must emerge. Because we experience this 'something missing' as a lack we desire to close it, to fill it in, to replace it with something. Lacan calls this lack *desire*. Desire is what cannot be satisfied even when our demands are met. All our needs are at once converted into desires that cannot be satisfactorily fulfilled. This is why sexuality cannot be considered as the result of a need. The unconscious manifests itself by the way it insists on filling the 'gap' that has been left by the very thing the subject feels is lacking in him or her, that is the unconscious! (The unconscious attempts to fill in the gap caused by the unconscious.)

The Unconscious is Structured like a Language   Lacan borrows some ideas of linguistics that Freud did not have access to. As we have seen, Saussure showed that a sign is not necessarily something that connects a word or name to a thing, but is in fact something that connects a sound or image to a concept. The sound or image is called a signifier. The concept is called a signified. Meaning is produced not only by the relationship between the signifier and the signified but also, crucially, by the position of the signifiers in relation to other signifiers (in a given context). When Saussure's theory is put together with Freud's it is not difficult to see that the movement of the signifiers that generate meaning must remain fundamentally unconscious. Meaning may have a place only in what Lacan calls 'the signifying chain'. So the signifier has primacy over the signified, which means that meaning is generated not by the normal meaning of a word but by the place the word has in a signifying chain.

Metaphor and Metonymy   These two axes of language – substitution and displacement – correspond to the working of the unconscious. Metonymy, which carries language along its syntagmatic axis, corresponds to the *displacement* of desire that characterizes the dream-work in Freud. Metaphor, on the other hand, corresponds to the *paradigmatic* axis, the axis of substitution and, therefore, corresponds to that aspect of *condensation* whereby different figures can be substituted or are condensed into one through an overdetermined nodal point.

Compare Freud's distinction to Saussure's formulation:

Signified	Conscious
Signifier	Unconscious

A Brief Reminder

Metaphor: substitutes a word for another word.
Metonymy: involves a linear form of displacement.

Lacan turns the formulation on its head:

$$\frac{Sr}{Sd}$$

Henceforth the unconscious, sexuality and fantasy can be pictured as the signifier over the signified. The unconscious is constituted in the same way as our intrinsic ability to speak. Desire is left always unsatisfied and is either displaced from signifier to signifier or it is substituted for (one signifier for another) and the whole process makes up a 'chain of signifiers', which remains unconscious but which, like the unconscious, leaves traces of itself, traces which may be read.

Metonymy follows the horizontal line of signifiers which never cross the bar (of repression) that leads to the signified and to signification. Just as desire is always deferred from one object to the next, so the signifier suspends signification while following the horizontal chain. Each signifier that fails to cross the bar has exactly the same meaning. It signifies lack (desire).

Metaphor is placed in a vertical relation. One signifier can substitute as the signified for another signifier. 'Crossing the bar' is really the action of one signifier becoming signified by taking the place reserved for the signified itself – the bar allows the substitution of one signifier for another:

$$\frac{Sr}{Sd} \searrow \frac{S}{Sr}$$

Sexuality and Sexual Difference   One of the most controversial contributions of psychoanalysis has been on the issue of sexuality and sexual difference. Most famously Freud introduced a new definition of sexuality. We need first to look at the more traditional one (which still has adherents today) and then examine the nature of the Freudian definition. The terms on which sexuality is usually defined turn on the relation between notions of normality and notions of perversity. Freud was at his most controversial when he stated that he had discovered a form of sexuality present in infants. At this stage the infant expresses his or her sexuality *polymorphously* (taking many forms); that is, with no particular fixed object or aim, just a kind of indulgent pleasure. The meaning of this pleasure is then presented back to the adolescent in a kind of *deferred action* in which primal fantasies are given a more fixed shape (helped along by the notorious Oedipus complex) with a socially sanctioned object type and a useful aim in reproduction.

Freud's *Three Essays on Sexuality* can be a frustrating read, with its delays and detours and often inconclusive observations. Perhaps because of this, however, it remains one of the key books on sexuality and sexual difference both within and outside the institution of psychoanalysis. There are two striking aspects to Freud's work on sexuality. The first involves his use of the mainstream professional views of his time. He doesn't simply critique these or oppose them and he doesn't even try to produce a convincing alternative vocabulary to talk about these issues. So his quite stark departure from mainstream knowledge is made within the terms and the frameworks of that knowledge itself, which is why the standard oppositions such as normal and perverse, masculine and feminine, remain part of the vocabulary. However, the system governing the meanings of that vocabulary is both subverted and transformed in Freud's text. The second aspect involves his use of evidence in relation to the professional views. Basically he employs the same hypothetical framework but transforms it through his rigorous and tenacious insistence on the evidence – what happens to the theory when one confronts it with these facts? The theory changes. *Perversity*, which was once a category for sexuality *gone wrong*,

---

Deferred Action

Nachträglichkeit describes the ways in which an infantile experience that is either incomprehensible or traumatic is nevertheless somehow retained by memory unconsciously and reactivated at a later time in a different context. The notion comes from an early stage in Freud's speculations and was used to explain the mechanism of hysteria, in which a traumatic early experience is reactivated in terms of a less traumatic later provocation. He sometimes explains this with the mildly comic story of a young man infatuated with women. 'A young man who was a great admirer of feminine beauty was talking once of the good-looking wet nurse who had suckled him when he was a baby. "I'm sorry", he remarked, "that I didn't make a better use of my opportunity"' (Freud 1976: 295). This is not, of course, an example of deferred action, but it does illustrate the notion by emphasizing an inability at the early stage to understand or to act at all on experiences, which are retrospectively activated in later life. Freud's commentators have found the notion more useful than he evidently did, in so far as the rhetorical aspect has become much more obvious. Signification involves the constant reactivation of significant material in new and unpredictable contexts, which thus produces new significance and new meanings.

a perversion of normal sexuality (like fetishism, same-sex desire, bestiality, even masturbation), becomes the general condition of all sexuality per se. *Normal desire,* on the contrary, which had an extremely narrow definition supported (as it still is) by everyday common-sense assumptions, is now understood as being one of the numerous contingent possibilities of a general perversity. Thus Freud appears to be saying extremely odd things in a rather traditional language. *In* that language, that framework, that vocabulary, however, Freud's theories remain the ones that work.

Freud describes the psychoanalytic theory of sexuality in the following way:

> Psychoanalysis considers that a choice of object independently of its sex – freedom to range equally over male and female objects – as it is found in childhood, in primitive states of society and early periods of history, is the original basis from which, as a result of restriction in one direction or the other, both the normal and the inverted types develop. Thus from the point of view of psychoanalysis the exclusive sexual interest felt by men for women is also a problem that needs elucidating and is not a self-evident fact based on an attraction that is ultimately of a chemical nature. (Freud 1977a: 57)

In other words, the normal assumption is that normal sexuality involves an exclusive sexual interest felt by men for women. Both the implicit one-way sign (men → women) and the exclusive nature of the interest are present in the traditional notions. Of course it is obvious that sexual interest ranges all over the place and that women fancy other people as much as men do. But for the traditional views these would have been problems. For Freud, that is no less true, but for him the normal version is also a problem and has no clear explanation. For him the evidence shows that sexuality is grounded in a condition where there is no pre-existing object and no defined aim. The pleasure principle is unscrupulous.

Some rudimentary definitions of sexuality don't much help. The standard definitions of sexuality grow out of husbandry. 'Sexuality' has the following related meanings: the condition of being sexed; being male or female; having sexual characteristics; feelings or desires to a specified degree (over-, under-, etc.); the condition of having a sex. Thus the sexuality of someone (their being one or other of the sexes) is extended also to signify behavioural characteristics. You might begin to expect certain types of behaviour from one or the other sex and you can justly express shock or concern when people behave outside those norms. So what is a sex? The dictionary tells us that 'sex' is that by which an animal or plant is male or female; the quality of being male or female; either of the divisions according to this, or its members collectively;

the whole domain connected with this distinction. (In so far as I am sexed, my sex is male; I share this quality with the whole of the male sex; but I share the quality of being sexed with the entire human race as well as the animal and plant kingdoms.) It seems that we are not going to get very far without encountering some aspect of our universally shared sexual difference. This is all very well if you are breeding chicks or growing violets. In that case the distinctions have a practical and functional purpose. This is the female and this is the male. Put them together in these particular ways and they will produce. In so far as people reproduce in these ways too, a kind of loose analogy emerges, conferring specific meaning upon each relation that may or may not have a sexual aspect (in the biological sense). The idea that biology is at the root of human sexual relations, and thus explains human sexuality, is at best grounded in the loosest of analogies. Psychoanalysis has played an important role in helping to undo these narrow and ungrounded assumptions. Along the way it has revealed a tangle of problems.

Psychoanalysis, without departing from the traditional vocabulary, develops an extended and transformed understanding of the concept of sexuality. Before Freud, sexuality was most likely to be defined as an instinct with a predetermined object and aim. The object was a member of the opposite sex. The aim was for union of the genital organs in coitus. The sole function was considered to be reproduction. Any kind of sexuality or sexual behaviour that does not aim for reproduction is considered to be perverse. Again, the influence from cultivation and husbandry is clear. What is the good of a stud that won't mount the mare? But psychoanalysis questions the notion of perversity.

Freud takes one of the most influential and highly respected authorities on the matter, Krafft-Ebing, as an example of the normative explanation:

> During the time of maturation of physical processes in the reproductive glands, desires arise in the consciousness of the individual, which have for their purpose the perpetuation of the species (sexual instinct) [...] with opportunity for the natural satisfaction of the sexual instinct, every expression of it that does not correspond with the purpose of nature, i.e. propagation – must be regarded as perverse. (Krafft-Ebing 1965:)

According to this view, nature somehow makes itself felt in the consciousness of the mature adult, in the form of a conscious desire to mate with a member of the opposite sex. Nature, in this sense, is simply the need for the reproduction of the race (that peculiarly nineteenth-century notion of evolution is evident here). The only 'natural' satisfaction of this itch, this desire, would be subordinated to the purposes of nature. Anything that does not obviously lead to reproduction is not natural ('it's not *natural!*'), because it would be a perversion of nature's aim. As usual with scientific views of this time, purpose itself, the Greek *telos*, is the unanalysed aspect underlying these assumptions. Krafft-Ebing, it is important to remember, is merely representing the popular views in scientific discourse.

Freud responds explicitly to these views at the beginning of his 'Three Essays on Sexuality':

> Popular opinion has quite definite ideas about the nature and characteristics of this sexual instinct. It is generally understood to be absent in childhood, to set in at the time of puberty in connection with the process of coming to maturity and to be revealed in the manifestations of an irresistible attraction exercised by one sex upon the other; while its aim is presumed to be sexual union [...] We have every reason to believe, however, that these views give a very false picture of the true situation. If we look into them more closely we shall find that they contain a number of errors, inaccuracies and hasty conclusions. (Freud 1997a: 45)

In the 'Three Essays' Freud doesn't substitute a new theory for the old ones. Rather, he extends and transforms the popular and scientific notions of sexuality by correcting the errors, clarifying the inaccuracies and rethinking the hasty conclusions that make up what he calls the 'false picture'. A new picture thus emerges out of the ruins of a now transformed vocabulary.

Evidence against Normativity

- The distinction between the normal and the perverse is riddled with overlaps.
- A great diversity of sexual 'perversion' not only exists but is common.
- This diversity involves not only the choice of sexual object but also the type of activity used to obtain satisfaction.
- In the popular view, the 'normal' type of sexual activity involves only coitus between members of the opposite sexes with the aim of reproduction.
- The 'normal' and the 'perverse', however, are not so easily separated.
- For instance, the usual form of satisfaction may become temporarily impossible, so a 'perverse' satisfaction may replace it. And the sort of foreplay leading up to normal sexual behaviour is usually also found leading up to perverse types as well.

The evidence against holding to the false picture is available in everyday life. Freud also draws explicitly from his fund of analytic experience, in many cases with distressed men and women of the inherently conservative European bourgeoisie, who had never been able to voice their discomfort about their own apparently perverse desires. The distinction between normal and perverse is so riddled with overlaps that it is impossible to extricate the two. There are numerous perversions and they are common (though not explicitly talked about in Freud's time). Not only are there numerous varieties of different object but also there are uncountable and creative methods for achieving satisfaction. On the model of *means* and *ends*, the normal view holds that sexuality manifests in activities designed to achieve the aim of reproduction. The *end* is reproduction; the *method* is union of the male and female genitals. However, in Freud's experiences with his patients, the methods often overlap between the normal and perverse. In other words, very similar kinds of activities occur whether there is an obviously reproductive function or not. Men and women will have 'sex' in all kinds of ways *including* 'normal' coitus. The ends are as various as the means. Furthermore, same-sex relations, as well as masturbation and the fantasies of all kinds that accompany it, each exhibit similar routes to satisfaction, in terms for instance of flirting and foreplay. Even a comfortably heterosexual couple will use a creative variety of methods, including coitus, to achieve satisfaction. So what is consistent in all this is not the function of reproduction at all but the function of satisfaction. Thus the reproductive teleology has no ground in evidence at all.

Freud often found that repressed wishes and desires are of a sexual kind and that the repressed wish in these cases is a perverse sexual wish. He concluded that the so-called normal types of behaviour belong with the forces of rational and socially acceptable convention defensive of the desiring and creative agency. In other words, the normative version of sexuality is socially rather than biologically determined. There is a biological difference but – like all difference – it is meaningful only in terms of the institutions that organize experience in specific ways. And we are back in the rhetorical dimension. The libido is thus a kind of undetermined force that becomes bound by the various kinds of restriction, paradigmatically the Oedipus complex, that represent the institutions of culture and society.

Oedipus Freud was struck by the similarity between the myth of Oedipus and his own discoveries of unconscious processes. The myth is most clearly dramatized in the plays of Sophocles (who was a contemporary of Socrates). In Sophocles' drama the unfolding of the tragedy involves Oedipus' gradual discovery of his own guilt. He discovers that he has in ignorance killed his father and that the woman he loves and has married is his mother. As a consequence of his discovery he blinds himself and exiles himself from his home. In fulfilling the oracle that begins the story he fails to escape his predestined fate. This is Freud's explanation: 'It is the fate of all of us, perhaps, to direct our first sexual impulse towards our mother and our first hatred and our first murderous wish against our father' (Freud 1976: 364). Freud argues that the power of this artwork lies in the ability of the poet to force us into a transferred recognition of what he calls 'our own inner minds'. Those same impulses (to patricide and incest with the mother) are still lurking yet 'suppressed' within all of us. Oedipus' unconscious guilt (which is literal – he is not at first conscious of his guilt) stands figuratively for our own unconscious guilt. 'Like Oedipus, we live in ignorance of these wishes, repugnant to morality, which have been forced upon us by Nature, and after their revelation we may all of us well seek to close our eyes to the scene of our childhood' (365). This last sentence has many resonances. Freud points out in a footnote to a later edition that it is this part of his theory that has provoked the most embittered denials, fiercest opposition and the most amusing distortions (100 years later we are often led to suspect that this is still the case). Thus the blinding scene is a metaphorical indication of the vicious resistance to the insights that psychoanalysis offers. Freud also, significantly, likens not the myth itself but the action of the play to the processes of psychoanalysis. He says that it 'consists in nothing other than the processes of revealing, with cunning delays and ever-mounting excitement – a process that can be likened to the

---

The Phylogenetic Hypothesis

Freud returned many times to the question of innate disposition and perhaps the most outrageous, yet most consistently held, version is the hypothesis of *phylogenesis*, which follows a somewhat Darwinian trend. Here, at its most extreme, the argument suggests that in human prehistory a great tribal father was actually killed by the jealous horde and that all of us are born with traces of this prehistorical guilt carried through the genetic *phylum* (like hair colour in the chromosomes). One thing is constant here. There is a constitutional *anxiety* (the Danish philosopher Søren Kierkegaard had in the previous century coined the phrase 'anxiety over nothing') that is related unconsciously to a desire for the death of the father and a desire for union with the mother.

work of a psycho-analysis' (363). It places Freud firmly within the canon of arguments about false consciousness (along with Plato, Descartes, Marx and Wittgenstein). But, we need to ask, what is the so-called 'Nature' that the Oedipus myth actually represents (the truth behind the false and blinded consciousness). Freud's use of the word 'Nature' in fact already illustrates how he is replacing the traditional biological ground of sexuality (the cultivation/ husbandry ground) with an alternative in the Oedipus complex.

Sexual Difference It is Freud's account of the Oedipus complex and its modes of resolution that really grounds the psychoanalytic theory of sexual difference. As such the theory is diagnostic only in so far as it attempts to lay bare the underlying structures that lead to certain tendencies in the relations between people. Unlike the traditional notions there is no sense of what men and women should or should not be like, how they should live in terms of their sexual differentiation. It attempts, instead, to find out how people come to be as they actually are in the first place.

In classical psychoanalysis the father represents a third term that must break the imagined dyadic unit of mother and child. Until the 'father' inter-rupts it, the mother–child unit – a perfect self-contained dyad – is asocial. The father stands for social symbolization. In terms of this structure the distinction between men and women exists but it has meaning only sym-bolically. Lacan provides the following witty diagram, based upon the story of a boy and a girl on a train who, on arriving at a station, see this sign:

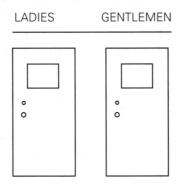

The boy exclaims, 'We are at Gentlemen.' The girl responds by saying, 'No we're not, we're at Ladies.' The two doors indicate the ways in which boys and girls are given the choice of two alternatives – each of which has intractable meaning in terms of the other – as to where each is in the social topography. The doors are themselves just signifiers as are the different sexes.

Sex (male and female) is always subject to identifications, which tell me who I am in terms of my gender. In traditional terms *sex* would be the *empirical* dimension of sexuality and *gender* would be the *transcendental* structure or system that gives *sex* its meaning. As we have already indicated, however, the distinction between the empirical and the transcendental is already extremely problematic, so we are going to have to find some way of dealing with the *difference* itself.

Lacan's version of the triangulated Oedipus complex (mother–child–father) combines Freud's theory with structural linguistics, developed as we have seen particularly from the theories of Saussure, Lévi-Strauss and Jakobson. The relationship between the child and mother is imagined in the infant's unconscious as something that was once self-contained and entirely satisfying but has since been broken up. The post-break-up (which is a psychoanalytic version of the fall from grace, mankind now banished from its eternal Garden of Eden) is in fact the child's beginning. Its prehistory is nothing but an imaginary desire. In other words, the child's experience begins with a feeling of something having been lost. The symbol of this loss is like a third term that has come between the mother and the child – the father who (in a literal version) comes home from work at the end of an otherwise perfect day ordering his dinner and smelling of pipe smoke and the intrusive outside. Lacan calls this 'third term' the *symbolic* because it 'symbolizes' all relations. Freud had called this third term 'the father', perhaps because of the specific nature of his own upbringing, his dreams, and the dreams of most of his patients (who were mostly bourgeois Europeans). But the father is just a symbol too (anything can represent it). Symbolization works because we make imaginary identifications, which are based upon proximity and immediate experience (the contiguous axis, or *metonymy*). What we imagine to be the case is always to be understood symbolically and that makes it seem real (the paradigmatic axis, or *metaphor*). Symbolization thus acts as an introduction to the world that is at the same time an introduction of lack. The introduction of a meaningful element disrupts the perfect unity of the imaginary relation, which has the sense of a perfect unity only by virtue of the meaningful element that excludes perfection. The experience of lack is therefore the very thing that gives us the sense that there was something to lack in the first place – it gives meaning to my partial relations and opens my experience to the other – which, of course, I cannot experience at all. The *real* in Lacan's theory is a *plenum*. A *plenum* is something complete in itself, so full that nothing need be added to it. However, because experience is determined by the relation between the symbolic and the imaginary (Lacan's complicated version of the transcendental and the empirical), the *plenum* is figured only as an impossible outside. It can therefore appear as a horrifying mysterious thing (enter the house of horror) that sometimes threatens to break open the illusion (our social reality) brought about by the symbolization of our imaginary desires.

Lacan was so taken by the similarities between Freud's theory of the unconscious and structural linguistics that he was able to come up with some fairly systematic concordances. At the risk of over-schematizing (which Lacan attempted to resist, though his theory encourages it) we might chart them in the following way:

SYMBOLIC	IMAGINARY	REAL
Father	Mother	All
Paradigm	Syntagm	The Impossible
Metaphor	Metonymy	Literal language
Condensation	Displacement	Death
Relation to the Other	Relation to the object	No relation

Under the Symbolic we find the system of differences between signifiers that determines their meanings, which Lacan relates to the metaphorical dimension of figurative language (*this* stands in for *that* and excludes it). He felt that Freud's explanation of the dream-work allied metaphor to the process of condensation (which puts different images together under the single sign of a metaphorical nodal point). Under the Imaginary we find proximal identifications that indicate the relations of individual desire, which Lacan relates to the metonymic dimension of figurative language (*this* stands in a proximal and inclusive relation to *that*). He felt that Freud's explanation of the dream-work allied the movement of metonymy to the process of displacement (which in a disguised way displaces from an object of immense intensity to an object of relatively trivial significance). Metonymy tends to exclude the meaningful aspect of language for the sake of being-next-to while metaphor privileges the meaningful aspect of proximal signs, giving them meaning, thrusting signification underneath them, under the symbolic 'cut' of the bar between signifier and signified in Saussure's diagram of the sign.

$$\frac{S}{S} \searrow \frac{S}{S}$$

Under Real, in contradistinction to these runaway overdetermined signs, lies the impossible experience of the *plenum*. The real stands for literal meaning (as opposed to literal uses of meaning, which are always possible). In so far as no experience of the real is possible (experience is the consequence of the interaction between imaginary identifications and symbolic signification) it stands for the *impossible*. The ideal, beyond signification, which stands in for the fact that there *is* no real relation, is the non-relational possibility itself, or just death. We can fairly clearly see, I think, that relations of any kind are possible only through certain kinds of signification. In terms of desire, the proximal relation (I just want to get next to you) blots out signified meaning in favour of contiguous relation (pure chance in its extreme form, which is a little disconcerting for those who are waiting for Mr Right). This is perhaps best experienced as a kind of *jouissance* (the French term denotes ecstatic enjoyment) or *petit-mort* ('little death', a colloquialism for orgasm). In terms of the symbolic, relations are overdetermined by many permutations of social identification, including gender, class, position, status. Anything like a real relation is of course impossible, as is a pure symbolic or pure imaginary relation. Everything seems to appropriate bits of everything else like a per-petually shifting system of parasites with no non-parasitical host. Everything to a certain extent depends upon something of its others.

As far as the Oedipal triangle is concerned it is possible to map a Lacanian triangle over a Freudian one, in the following way:

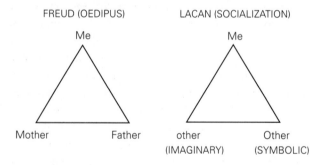

Cinema: Pleasure and Drive

> I think of cinemas, panoramic sleights
> With multitudes bent towards some flashing scene
> Never disclosed, but hastened to again,
> Foretold to other eyes on the same screen
>
> (Hart Crane)

Why do people read fiction, go to the cinema, and watch TV? What is pleasure? The classical psychoanalytic arguments assume that dreams, fan-tasies and fictions each have their source in (perhaps) unconscious desires.

THE DRIVE FOR PLEASURE The notion of *drive* (both verb and noun) is closely related in psychoanalytic theory to the notion of *instinct*. But use of the term 'drive' helps to get away from certain tendencies that view instinctual responses as fundamentally somatic or biological. Freud distinguishes between instinct (German: *instinkt*) and drive (German: *Trieb*) in the following way:

> An instinct [*Trieb*] appears to us as a concept on the frontier between the mental and the somatic, as the psychical representative of the stimuli origina-ting from within the organism and reaching the mind, as a measure of the demand made upon the mind for work in consequence of its connection with the body. (Freud 1977b: 118)

The separation of body and mind in representation, memory, symbol or signifier is thus a function of drive. A drive is an instinct in so far as it is attached to an idea and manifested as an affective state (or feeling). In traditional views the instinct – e.g. the sexual instinct – was characterized by an inbuilt object, aim and function (member of the opposite sex, coitus, reproduction). It is now well known that Sigmund Freud's refutation of this assumption led to his notion of polymorphous perversity, that is, aimless heterogeneous drives that pursue only pleasure for its own sake. What, then, is *pleasure*? An idea or image in its repeatability as a signifier (the image of the breast for an infant) becomes pleasurable or distressing in its own right. The repeatability of signifying marks puts the pleasures of the body in touch with social systems of signification.

For Freud, the drive for pleasure has a simple aim in the reduction of what he calls *unlust* or 'unpleasure'. The infant is driven by its responses to stimula-tion, which it experiences as pain or at least discomfort. In an early formulation he makes a well-known theoretical distinction between the *pleasure* and the *reality* principles. The pleasure principle aims for immediate gratification. The reality principle gradually involves the internalization of a delaying mechanism that gradually lessens the need. The reality principle is a kind of survival mechanism. What Freud calls the *primary processes* produce a kind of discharge that is dangerous if unchecked and so *secondary processes* such as repression, delay, deferment, put obstacles in its way.

PRIMARY PROCESSES	SECONDARY PROCESSES
Pleasure	Reality
Displacement	Repression
Condensation	Detour/delay
Immediate gratification	Deferment of Gratification

In a later (1921) text called *Beyond the Pleasure Principle*, Freud gives an account of the Fort/Da game, in which Freud's young nephew, mourning the prolonged absences of his mother, repeatedly throws a cotton reel on a string outside and back into his cot. The game serves several possible functions:

(1) It may stand for the leaving of the mother and simulates her return so it could act as a straightforward wish fulfilment fantasy.

(2) More determinedly the game may symbolize the omnipotent desire of the infant who now in the fantasy controls the coming and going of the mother.

(3) More disturbingly, the phenomenon can be allied to similar symptoms that manifest masochistic desires, extending even, for Freud, to the popularity of distressing dramatic tragedies (like *Oedipus*, of course). The continued 'playing out' of the distressing event of the mother's absence cannot be explained purely by recourse to wish fulfilment and a disturbing *repetition compulsion* becomes the focus of Freud's discussion.

The compulsion to repeat describes the neurotic repetition of actions that cause pain or misery or discomfort. He writes:

> We come across people all of whose human relationships have the same outcome: such as the benefactor who is abandoned in anger after a time by each of his *protégés*, however much they may otherwise differ from one another, and who thus seems doomed to taste all the bitterness of ingratitude; or the man whose friendships all end in betrayal by his friend; or the man who time after time in the course of his life raises someone else into a position of great private or public authority and then, after a certain interval, himself upsets that authority and replaces him by a new one; or, again, the lover each of whose love affairs with a woman passes through the same phases and reaches the same conclusion. (Freud 1977b: 292)

It is the active behaviour of the person concerned that (however little consciousness there is about this) produces this 'perpetual recurrence of the same thing'. It is caused by what Freud assumes at this stage is an essential character trait, which is compelled to find expression in a repetition of the same experiences. The hypothesis of the *death drive* (which aims for absolute reduction of excitation as return to the inorganic state) follows, and the strangest of all dialectics emerges, that between life and death. The most consistent (and therefore complex) reading of this strange double is that of Jacques Derrida (who also finds that Freud's own accounts of the unconscious require incessant recourse to scriptural metaphors). Geoff Bennington's account of Derrida's account of Freud's account of the formulation follows:

> The primary processes seek discharge, pleasure, at whatever cost, scorning any consideration of the system's survival. The secondary processes bind them. Discharge, absolute unbinding, would be immediate death, but total binding,

non-mobility, asphyxiating compression, would be death too. So the apparatus must protect itself from its own life pleasure (die a little) and protect itself against too much protection to live (a little). There is no life before this compromise. (Bennington and Derrida 1993: 138)

In Bennington's reading, the pleasure principle cannot be opposed to the reality principle. The latter serves the former: 'pleasure is in the end nothing other than the passage of its own detour through reality, and it thus never arrives at its purity, which would again be death' (Bennington and Derrida 1993: 139). As a kind of *différance* the relation is that of the *same*, or the structure of the non-identical same, called life-death in reference to Freud or just *archewriting*, the structure of repeatability and difference, iterability and its alterity.

The Ring   The recent Japanese film *The Ring*, like so much contemporary cinema, clearly thematizes aspects of media representation but, unlike the obsessive auto-referentiality of most mainstream American cinema, *The Ring* has managed to maintain the inextricable relation between death and representation as the condition of representation itself. Representation and death go together in this remarkable film, which might at first sight have Heidegger and Derrida in mind throughout.

A woman, who is incidentally the manager of a media production company, discovers a video of a ghostly broadcast, which has apparently caused the death of a number of people including a young relative. The deaths have something to do with a ghost story told among the children of a certain region, whereby one stumbles on the broadcast late at night or watches it on a video copy, after which the phone rings. A week later the viewer dies. Having seen it for herself she then shows her ex-husband and makes him a copy, which they watch several times together, using the clues – the signs on the video, which include an image of a woman brushing her hair in a mirror (the camera mysteriously missing from the picture); writing that trembles and moves on its support; crawling men and women; and a scene apparently fixed upon a raised well-like object apparently in a yard – to discover its origin, now convinced that their own time is running out. They trace it back to the murder by her father of a girl with powerful psychic powers and who is now claiming the souls of those who watch her mysterious broadcasts and videos. In a scene near the end we watch as the ex-husband watches a video/broadcast of the girl crawling out of the well and then out of the television set to scare him to death (don't laugh). The only way, it turns out, of surviving the curse is to make a copy of the video and show it to someone else (who then must do the same if he/she is also not to die within a week of viewing).

The most frightening aspect of this, in some senses classic, ghost story is the fact that the ghost, because it is a media image, is seen on screen unmediated; the media image rather than representing the ghost just is the ghost. It is the first ghost in cinema that cinema has been able to represent as it is in itself. The variety of forms of distancing thus comes into focus in a peculiar way. The tele-function or distancing function of tele-kinesis, tele-pathy, tele-phony, tele-vision, tele-photo-graphy produces a powerful condensation, such that each time the tele-event plays a similar (ghostly) function to the others. The message seems to be this: you will die but you can put off your death by circulating the broadcast in repetition among others. Your life depends on the continued circulation of the broadcast, which simultaneously signals your impending death. It powerfully evokes 'life-death' in the form of the media image.

III The Return to Melanie Klein

Acquiring Knowledge   The work of Melanie Klein not only reveals one hypothetical source of the ambivalent attitude towards the other, but it also refers us back to the question of the difficult relation between a self and its outside. Klein came to England in the late 1920s and helped to found what is now known as the Object-Relations school of psychoanalysis. She presided over the British school and her work on child analysis is now legendary. Klein describes the earliest stages of infantile psychic life in terms of a successful completion of development through certain *positions*. A position for Klein describes a set of psychic functions that correspond to a given phase of development, always appearing during the first year of life, but which are present at all times thereafter and can be reactivated at any time. There are two major positions. The *paranoid-schizoid* position occurs at the earliest phase of development and it is characterized by the relation to part objects (parts of the mother etc.), the prevalence of splitting in the ego and in the object, and paranoid anxiety. The *depressive* position is ushered in when the infant recognizes the mother as a whole object. It is a constellation of object-relations and anxieties characterized by the infant's experience of attacking an ambivalently loved mother and losing her as an external and internal object. The experience, according to Klein, gives rise to pain, guilt and feelings of loss. For either paranoid-schizoid (PS) or depressive (D) identification to occur, two processes are needed. On the one hand an object is *introjected* into the ego, which then identifies with some or all of the object's characteristics. On the other hand the *projection* of parts of the self into an object results in the object being perceived as having the characteristics of the projected part of the self, which also results in an identification. For instance, in PS the ego will split the object into an ideal satisfying part, and a persecuting part, in order to achieve an at least partial identification with a good object. The result of this defence mechanism, which is essentially a denial of persecution, may be that the ego is itself split into two so that identifications can be made with a persecuting part object that can then be projected outwards. But the projection is now in danger of infecting the good object, threatening to destroy it, or provoking the possibility of retribution.

In her 1940 paper, 'Mourning and its Relation to Manic Depressive States', Klein describes the depressive position as a process of early 'reality testing' and argues that this is a prototypical form of what will later become the process of mourning (Klein 1998b: 344). She writes:

> The object which is being mourned is the mother's breast and all that the breast and milk have come to stand for in the infant's mind: namely, love, goodness and security. All these are felt by the baby to be lost, and lost as a result of his uncontrollable greedy and destructive phantasies and impulses against his mother's breasts. (Klein 1998b: 345)

So for Klein the earliest active relation to reality, to the outside, begins with an awareness of our own uncontrollable greed and an inconsolable sorrow for a plenitude we feel we have destroyed. What really distinguishes Klein's theory is her notion of *phantasy* describing the arena in which these processes are played out. For the child the outside world is nothing more than a series of images and passing forms that are used to characterize an inner world of phantasies. The form of the mother, for instance, is 'doubled' and 'undergoes alterations' as it is internalized (Klein 1998b: 346). In this way, external reality can be *read* so long as the forms of the outside world can be 'fitted into the patterns provided by the psychic [inner] reality which prevails at the time' (347). Klein's work can thus be read as entering into disputes concerning epistemology, particularly where her account of the process of reality-testing is given in terms of an acquisition of knowledge: 'In the process of acquiring knowledge, every new piece of experience has to be fitted into the patterns provided by the psychic reality which prevails at the time; whilst the psychic reality of the child is gradually influenced by every step in his progressive knowledge of external reality' (374).

It is important to recognize that the child's use of *external* reality is never anything more than an attempt better to understand *inner* psychic reality. Reality is itself understood in terms of the doubling bifurcation of images. So there is, in effect, nothing but unconscious phantasy, on the one hand, and the forms and images that flit across the perceptual screen, on the other. This argument reinforces the sense, which we have already noted, that psychoanalysis remains within the structures defined by the difference between the empirical and transcendental. The difference is now understood in terms of the difference between external form and internal phantasy. Jacqueline Rose argues that it lies at the heart of what is most controversial in Klein, both within and beyond psychoanalytic institutions. The implications are philosophical and concern the status of traditional notions of truth and certainty themselves. What Rose suggests is that Klein's development of Freudian psychoanalysis loosens up the scientific, objective notion of truth, which inevitably informs Freud's discourse (though as we have seen Freud himself has gone some considerable way in shaking up these notions). With Klein, truth 'does not belong to an order of scientifically verifiable knowledge' (Rose 1979: 147); but rather Klein's notion of truth at the very least puts the possibility of any objective truth in suspense. Donald Meltzer describes the philosophical problem like this: 'It requires an immense shift in one's view of the world to think that the outside world is essentially meaningless and unknowable, that one perceives the form but must attribute the meaning' Meltzer 1978: (86).

So in Klein's version of reality objective truth is suspended, debarred from any epistemological privilege and thus held in an indeterminate state. A kind of radical form of expectation that defers knowledge also informs knowledge. It excites a desire that cannot be fulfilled for a kind of knowledge that cannot be presented as such. This 'attribution of meaning', then, as an inevitable element in the formative process of psychic development, cannot but be a kind of hypothesizing about a reality that is never itself presentable as such. The only clues available for the acquisition of knowledge are the forms that correspond in some way to the patterns of psychic life prevalent at any given time.

The Ruined World According to Freud and Lacan, we begin with the awareness that something has been lost. The first thing is something missing. All attempts to make up for this loss, to find a substitute for the lost thing, intensify the sense of loss, emphasize all the more painfully that the substitute is not the object at all. There can be no replacement for something that was never there. So the search continues as a quest to replace the unsatisfactory substitute with one more satisfying, one that is perhaps not perfect but good enough for the time being. That is the now classic psychoanalytic narrative of psychic development. Melanie Klein in a controversial move that still provokes violent debate in psychoanalytic circles went back before this beginning, this Freudian beginning in loss, to its prehistory. She filled out the details with graphic imagery wrenched from the symbolism of children at play. Freud's little melancholic was not the beginning, according to Melanie Klein. For her, psychic life starts with the vivid destruction of an object, the chaotic ruin of what ought to have been a nurturing environment. Out of a nightmare of terror and outright war emerges the melancholic child fully aware of its responsibility for destroying a world and doubled up with loss and guilt. Desire, for Freud, is played out in restless attempts to complete and fulfil an emptiness that is both produced and maintained by these attempts. But for Melanie Klein desire is tinged with the guilty knowledge of responsibility. The object is not so much lost as ruined and the infant, in Freud's own phrase, becomes 'criminal from the sense of guilt'.

Two distinct patterns of phantasy can be outlined according to this basic difference between Freud and Klein. Freudian fantasy, on the model of the Fort/Da game played by his nephew during long absences of the mother, attempts to control the loss by making it good symbolically. The conservatism of fantasy is exemplified in a defence that is the equivalent of a lie: the mother is not gone (*Fort*), look! She is here (*Da*). The cotton reel is like the fetishized commodity – manifested in an endless series of objects that are each time symbolic of the one missing thing – circulating in an endless chain where each link refers metonymically only to the next link, as close as you'll get to a random process. This may seem close to the experience of the mass media, including mainstream cinema where, if you go often enough, you will be aware only of a kind of continuous series of parts never quite adding up to a single film. The plot for each film is in the most basic sense the same as the others. The narrative is reducible to two movements repeated endlessly. We begin with the awareness that something has been lost or is in danger of being lost (*Fort!*). The first thing is something missing. Then the loss is made good, the missing object replaced, the ruined world mended or replenished, or a fulfilling substitute, more fulsome than the lost or ruined original, is found (*Da!*). The variations are illimitable.

Kleinian desire, on the other hand, forces us to work a little harder. Perhaps, as violent as the phantasies are, they present a more substantial kind of promise than the hopeless Freudian ones do. But the promise, like all promises, comes with a warning. The Kleinian answer to the question 'Is that a threat or a promise?' is always 'Both, of course'. The desire to make reparation demands not only a capacity for tolerating destructive impulses, but also a willingness to return to the scariest environment imaginable, the anxious core of the self. Symbolic substitution may be necessary but it is certainly not sufficient, for to make reparation, to move forward into an ethical state, we must learn to move backwards into the state that produced the ruin in the first place. We must learn to rediscover the terrifying first months of life, to re-enter the schizoid state of the neo-natal infant. In science-fiction cinema it is possible to read an analogue of this state, represented in the ruined and hazardous landscapes in which so much of the action is played out. By what looks like a coincidence, Klein's descriptions of the ravaged world of infantile phantasy compare with some representations in contemporary science-fiction cinema. In the following sections I will provide a reading of a popular cinema genre through the theoretical matrix of psychoanalysis. I then want to use this reading to fold certain assumptions about analysis back on to psychoanalysis itself. In this way we will be able to understand better what is at stake in analysing cultural texts. The key word here is 'analysis' and the key problem concerns what remains 'unanalysed'.

Kleinian Scientificity (Klein and Bion) It is claimed that psychoanalytic theory is of a special kind. Its interest is in areas that are shared by philosophy, psychology and cultural theory, yet its purpose is always practical and clinical. Psychoanalytic hypotheses are designed for perpetual restatement by practising analysts in terms of empirically verifiable data. The violent controversy over Klein's quite radical restatement of Freud's hypotheses seems to have taken even her a little by surprise because from her own point of view she had simply maintained the ideals of the rational scientist that were Freud's own – at least some of the time. If her theories were modifications of Freud's theories, that was because they were based on what her follower Wilfred Bion would later call *negative realization*. A negative realization occurs when a preconception fails to find support in experience. The most common defence against this, which is a dreadfully frustrating experience for a vulnerable ego attempting to build itself on good preconceptions, is to counteract it with a variety of possible responses. I can ignore it, pretend that there has been no negative realization at all and stick to my preconceptions. Or I can indulge in phantasies of omniscience and omnipotence and hallucinate a world changed to conform to my preconceptions. Either way my experience is dominated by the pathological organization known to psychoanalysts as the schizoid state. If, on the other hand, I have the capacity to tolerate the anxiety caused by negative realization, the thinker in me emerges. Bion calls an event of negative realization a thought. A thought needs a container and thus the self must become a thinker in order to contain the thought – that is Bion's theory of thinking. Most of the time the thinker coexists with parts of the self that remain organized pathologically, which, in terms of thought, cling to the lie rather than the truth of the thought that is produced in negative realization. The difficulty here of course is that you don't even get negative realization without the preconceptions into which the truth comes crashing like a bad dream or your worst nightmare. The preconceptions are built on the conservatism of defensive phantasy, which is basically reactionary. Negative realization is like a tool that the infant must learn to use in order to adjust the frameworks of his internal world. It is the condition of the internal world that interests the psychoanalyst.

The first patterns of phantasy are very crude and seem to have been the consequence of extreme terror. The Kleinian ego is willed into life through an unbearable sense of persecution. Any of the frustrations of the first stages of life would, one might suppose, be enough to have you crying out for your mother. Just the failure of a finger in the mouth to maintain the hallucination of food turns the absence of the breast into some vile and ruthless monster, the notorious bad breast. But Klein insists that the violence of these early persecution phantasies originates within as an archaic negativity, not a negative realization as such – there's nothing to be realized at all yet – just negativity pure and simple. The disappearance of the satisfying breast has been prepared for, in other words, by the harassing presence from the beginning of the death instinct. When you are hungry the lie that you are not is a difficult one to maintain. So your hunger takes the shape of a monster. At the infantile stage the distinction between the self and the object is not clear but it follows the pattern of splitting and is manipulated through the two mechanisms of projection and introjection. Projection throws undesirable, monstrous parts of the self out into the object, which is either expected to contain and neutralize them or to be infected and ultimately destroyed by them. Introjection is supposed to extract good aspects of the good object and use them to build up the internal object, the rudimentary core of what will one day be the self. The trouble is, introjection can often bring in fragments of the destructive object too and by the same token the bad self can easily, in extreme hate or envy or in the glory of an omnipotent rage, just destroy the only hope of survival, the good object on the outside. The thing to stress here is that everything, parts of the object and parts of the self, are just that, parts. It is a world of part objects divided crudely into good and bad, internal and external. This is the PS position.

The next position for the infant, moving in at a speculative three months, according to Melanie Klein, is the depressive position (D), which plays two important functions. First, the force of the violent phantasies is reduced; the world is less frightening, less violent. The PS violence is considerably lessened. The key to this function is the capacity for toleration. The second function is integration. The split-off parts of the object, representing a now ruined and all but destroyed external environment, are brought together to form a single unity. All the attacks on the monstrous bad breast are now revealed to have been ruinous for the good one too, good and bad now integrated.

I'll return to the depressive position a little later. For the moment we don't need to explore it in any depth, because it plays a very small role in the first film I want to look at. The extremely popular *Armageddon* is a phantasy played out entirely on the PS level and culminates in an omnipotent destruction of the bad object, after it has been filled, literally implanted, with all the bad parts of the mythic self. A meteorite the size of Texas is hurtling towards the Earth and promises to hit it with the force equivalent to 10,000 nuclear warheads. There are four main aspects to bear in mind during my analysis. The first concerns the role of the mother, the archetypal Kleinian object, of course, and as potent as a symbol could be, but who is missing here from the beginning. This is the standard narrative where the father exchanges his daughter with a surrogate son in an ecstatic symbolic union, a classical mythic structure, on the surface at least. The second point, which is intimately related to the first, concerns the obsessive gendering of both the Earth and the rock that threatens it. The grouchy amateur astronomer who discovers it names the rock 'Dotty', after his wife, because 'she's a vicious life-sucking bitch from which there is no escape'. There are echoes of *Alien* here too of course. More important than the misogyny, which is an inescapable component of the pathological organizations at work here, is the explicit characterization of the rock, and spectacularly its cinematic realization as 'the scariest environment imaginable' with razor-sharp ice, unpredictable winds and exploding potholes. And fourth, the structural key to the whole film is coupling. The rock is attempting to couple with the earth. Ben Affleck and Liv Tyler are attempting to couple against the wishes of her father Bruce Willis. The NASA shuttles couple with the Russian refuelling space station. The drill mechanism is coupling with the Earth in order to extract oil and with the rock in order to implant a nuclear bomb. Numerous incidental couplings or attempted couplings occur along the way.

- The absent mother.
- The gender of the Earth and the rock.
- The rock as the scariest environment imaginable.
- Coupling.

At this stage I can make use of some critical methods that we have already explored. Following the method of Lévi-Strauss's structural analysis, I'll take the events of the film as if they were the terms of a system and replace them on a grid that indicates the structural relations between them.

1. A rock threatens the Earth.
2. A boy threatens the daughter.
3. The father threatens the boy.
4. The mother is absent ('She left us both').

5. Drilling strikes oil.
6. Only drilling, rather than assaulting, can save the earth.
7. Drilling team in seventeen-day training.
8. Shuttles refuel in space (destroying the Russian space station in the process).
9. Shuttles arrive on the rock (one badly damaged).
10. Drilling takes place on the rock.
11. Father sacrifices himself so the boy can return home to the daughter.
12. Earth is saved.

The grid looks something like this:

VALUED	DEVALUED	IMPLANTING	EXTRACTING
Earth	rock	rock into Earth	oil from Earth/Russia
non-military	military	boy into girl	blood into syringe
oil	bomb	bomb into rock	father into daughter

At the level of myth *Armageddon* can thus be seen as a deeply conservative and collusive text. According to the structuralist formula:

$$Fx(a): Fy(b) - Fx(b): Fa - {}_1(y)$$

The myth makes the function of extracting equivalent to the valued terms (oil, Earth, non-military personnel) but dissolves a contradiction by privileging implantation as the destruction of the non-valued terms (rock, bomb). The contradiction is solved at the level of the relation between father and boy, through the sacrifice of the father. But beneath this the film solves a series of problems. It takes the problems of technological progress – nuclear war, destruction of ecological resources and devastating pollution – and solves them by dumping them into the symbolic evil of the rock and then exploding it. All within the technological process itself.

The Kleinian terminology, which gives flesh to the abstraction of structuralist terms and functions, and which corresponds to the visual field of cinema rhetoric, can add further insights. Part objects in the unconscious take the form of greedy vaginas, monstrous breasts and pseudo-penises. This corresponds in obvious ways with the iconography of *Armageddon*.

The grid now looks something like this:

VALUED	DEVALUED	IMPLANTING	EXTRACTING
GOOD BREAST	BAD BREAST	PROJECTION	INTROJECTION
Earth	rock	rock into Earth	oil from Earth/Russia
non-military	military	boy into girl	blood into syringe
oil	bomb	bomb into rock	father into daughter

So it might be easy to argue on the basis of this grid that, far from arriving at any sense of depressive realization of responsibility, *Armageddon* simply satisfies the desire for omnipotent destruction of all that is bad in order to preserve all that is good. The ruined and destroyed object is replaced through the sacrifice of the father, which allows the fantastic replacement of the object in terms of the endless boy-gets-girl narrative of Fort/Da.

Something like the process of negative realization that produces thinking grounds Kleinian aesthetics too. The difference here is that the capacity for toleration is directed towards the inner world of phantasy as opposed to the outer world of events. The artwork, for the Kleinian, is the result of two special talents and it allows for two types of identification. Artists, according to Hannah Segal, must have an intimate knowledge of their material (clay, words, rhetoric, paint, etc.) and must also have the capacity to tolerate the internal death drive 'as fully as can be borne'. She says that the work must embody 'the terrifying experience of depression and death' (Stonebridge and Phillips 1998: 219). The artist must be able to acknowledge the death instinct, both in its aggressive and self-destructive aspects, and accept the reality of death both for the object and the self. The spectator thus identifies the artwork as a reparative re-creation of the ruined inner world and identifies with the artist as another through the medium of the work. In this case phantasy is not just the conservative force that militates against the truth. We see that it is the very principle and power of world creation. There would be no world without it. The artwork reveals the source of the world in negativity, but in a negotiated way, in a way that can be borne. These identifications allow vicarious access to the negativity of the death-drive upon which all experience is grounded. An omnipotent phantasy like *Armageddon* would not pass the test for while in terms of cinema rhetoric it is exemplary, in terms of its presentation of negativity it is just an infantile phantasy.

Soldier on the other hand provides a glimpse into something a bit deeper. *Soldier* at least takes us out of the paranoid-schizoid position. This is how Hannah Segal describes the depressive position:

> [It] is reached by the infant when he recognises his mother and other people, and among them his father, as real persons. His object relations then undergo a fundamental change. Where earlier he was aware of 'part objects' he now perceives complete persons; instead of 'split' objects, ideally good or over-whelmingly persecuting – he sees a whole object both good and bad. (Stonebridge and Phillips 1998: 205)

It is during the depressive stage that a sense of an inner reality is developed in contradistinction to a sense of outer reality. The infant now has to be able to tolerate not only the frustration of learning that its preconceptions about the object world are wrong but also the guilt in becoming aware of its own ambivalence to the object world, which includes large amounts of hate and envy previously projected into its objects. Inability to tolerate this – especially at first – results in varying degrees of regression into PS and its defences: splitting, idealization, denial, projective identification. Phantasies like *Armageddon* represent a kind of cultural version of this regression – there are many other examples. *Soldier* seems to me to present a slightly different kind of phantasy.

One of the things that critics didn't like about *Soldier* was Kurt Russell's character. One popular critic said that, if we are going to have another gun-toting kill-em-all hero, then at least he should be of the wise-cracking slick and articulate kind. But no; Kurt Russell says virtually nothing throughout and every short clipped phrase is closed off with a barked out '*sir*'. 'Yes, sir,' in response to an order at the beginning; 'I was replaced, sir,' in response to the question, 'Why did you get separated from your company?'; 'I'm going to kill them all, sir,' as an answer to the woman who asks, 'What are you going to do?' just before the bloody denouement. It is an essential part of his character once we see the film as an allegory for PS and D in the development of psychic life. (Please be aware that it is by no means necessary to see the film as an allegory for anything. What interests me, in the context of Critical Theory, is the possibility of allegory. My reading is based upon an analogy between psychoanalytic and cinematic presentations and as such any authority governing my reading rests on the accidental, on analogy itself. Later we must explore the grounds of analogy in order to tighten up the reading.)

Russell's character, Todd, is a veteran soldier of the future, a survivor of numerous galactic conflicts. The beginning of the film shows his selection at birth and consequent training. The story proceeds with the arrival of a new breed of genetically engineered soldier, one of whom fights off three of the old kind, including Todd himself, in an exercise to prove the superiority of this new breed. Todd loses the fight but not before prising an eye from his enemy's head. The unconscious Todd is then discarded on a planet that is used only for dumping waste. He becomes conscious on this wasteland littered with sharp-edged rusting metallic technological waste and is almost immediately attacked by a sudden ferocious wind that threatens to pick him up and dash him on to some jagged shard. Welcome again to the scariest environment imaginable.

However, this deserted planet of the Arcadian system, whose name turns out to be 'Arcadia 234', is not deserted after all. A community living in the protective dome of some discarded rocket has crash-landed on this planet on the way from Earth to a utopian new beginning. They gather what they can use from the wasteland around them, dodging the persecuting and unpredictable winds as well as they are able. They take Todd in on the word of their leader, a firm but fair matriarch, who says, 'We must do the decent thing and the decent thing is to help him.' The core for Todd of this community is the small oedipal family of Case, his wife and their son Nathan who has been struck dumb from a snake bite – another of the significant terrors of Arcadia 234. The crucial identification is the one between Todd and Nathan, the two near speechless, perhaps autistic children, who form the core of the film's own ego. Let's map it out. It is a terrifying and persecuting wasteland, in which a small and vulnerable yet nurturing society maintains a semblance of gentle civility. The most obvious associations of Todd's name are, first, from the colloquial 'On your todd' meaning on your own and second, probably more significantly, from the German *Tod* for death. Death comes into Arcadia. There is an irony of course here. Arcadia is at once the determined innocence and the stubborn pastoral of the new Arcadians, but this Arcadia is number 234. How many are there? They must be cropping up in the universe like shopping arcades in California. Into this Arcadia comes death. This nurturing society is built on matriarchal lines exemplified in all kinds of ways by the rhetoric, which aligns it with the quiet strength of femininity.

Despite the fact that Todd has saved someone's life from the ferocious wind the community find they cannot incorporate this efficient death-machine into their society. The crux comes not after Todd has in a pathological moment of confusion almost killed the hapless Jimmy, who has knitted him a scarf in repayment for saving his life; it comes rather when Todd fails to kill a snake in an attempt to teach young Nathan to do his own killing. For this he is cast out. Here is the classic scene. He sits outside in the dubious shelter of a huge cast-iron pipe and a tear forms on his cheek causing him some surprise. This is the beginning of two realizations. The first amounts to mourning the destroyed world, as the first sign that you realize that the external world is peopled by beings that you might not want to kill. And the second is that for the first time his inner and outer world become distinct, he is able to reflect on his own role in the ruinous destruction of his life.

When Nathan does kill a snake that is just about to bite into his sleeping father, the parents and the rest of the community realize their error. Even the most nurturing environment must find a place for Todd, the extreme vigilance of the soldier, just as the soldier must find an integrated world in order to exist. So far so good. Except the new breed make their inevitable reappearance on manoeuvres as an irrational and persecuting force more terrifying than the landscape itself. After blowing off Case's leg they proceed to disintegrate the community's matriarchal leader, followed by the community itself. All that is left now is for Todd to 'kill them all, sir'.

In classic omnipotent style Todd does indeed kill them all and joins up with the now disarmed members of his old company to steal the spaceship and take off with the survivors from Arcadia 234, just before it is blown to fragments by the bomb left on there by the evil commanders, who of course get blown to pieces as well. The film ends with young Nathan in Todd's arms, the ship on course for the original utopian planet – we might suggest it represents the idealized good breast. It is not so much the narrative, but rather the manipulation of cinema rhetoric and imagery that is interesting. The narrative mates Todd with Nathan rather than boy with girl. As such it is an allegory of the ego built on the integration between PS and D elements. As cinema rhetoric it succeeds as a vivid evocation of the inner world. The problem with D is that there is now no way of allowing access to the shocking, surprising, contingent newness of events. Whole objects tend to be what you expect them to be and the patterns of phantasy that maintain your expectations are now hidden from consciousness. The return to PS can culminate in radical defence, but it can also open experience to unpredictable changes, if the anxiety can be tolerated. Todd represents, in the combination of fear and discipline, the capacity for tolerating extreme danger, yet he has no capacity for social integration. His super-ego sets Doberman dogs on to squealing pigs and shoots you if you cannot run fast enough. Nathan on the other hand is too protected by his parents' depressive anxieties. His super-ego keeps him from reality. It is too nurturing. The film's fundamental drive is to unite Todd with Nathan, to bring PS and D together, to unite the persecuting super-ego with the satisfying one. It culminates in a satisfying way, with an all-out omnipotent phantasy that places the utopian good breast in sight through the outright destruction of the bad one, with all the bad elements of the self on it. As in *Armageddon*, there are two planets and one must be destroyed. This is a rapid retreat from mourning and perhaps represents the ultimate capitulation to pathological forces of organization. We begin with the awareness that something has been lost. The first thing is something missing. *Et in Arcadia ego.*

Problems   There is a problem with the analysis I've just provided that is a concern both for psychoanalysis and for the process of analysis generally. Analysis, as we have seen, involves the division into subject and object. As such it depends upon an unanalysed distinction between the transcendental (as theoretical matrix) and the empirical (as the passive object or example). I've just mapped a fully formed theoretical matrix derived from structuralism and psychoanalysis on to a couple of examples from contemporary mainstream cinema. What I have failed to analyse is the distinction between the analysing subject and the analysed object (the transcendental matrix and the empirical event). On what grounds can I privilege the psychoanalytic representation over the cinematic one? How can I support the implicit assumption of scientificity in psychoanalysis against the fictionality of film? It seems to me, in looking back over my analysis, that I have been using the psychoanalytic apparatus, the instruments of analysis, to probe these textual objects, drawing out of them what I need to support the argument and then demolishing what is left, exhausting the signifying potential of these films. The psychoanalytic apparatus is thus left untouched, not at all affected by the ruin it finds about itself, whereas the wretched films are shredded to nothingness by my analytic acuity. But then if that is the case, *Armageddon* could even be read as a kind of satire on psychoanalysis. Let's have another look at that grid:

VALUED	DEVALUED	IMPLANTING	EXTRACTING
GOOD BREAST	BAD BREAST	PROJECTION	INTROJECTION
PSYCHOANALYSIS	CINEMA	ANALYSIS	INTERPRETATION
SCIENCE	FICTION	INSIGHT INTO FILM	TRUTH OUT OF FICTION
Earth	rock	rock into Earth	oil from Earth/Russia
non-military	military	boy into girl	blood into syringe
oil	bomb	bomb into rock	father into daughter

It seems now that the whole analytic, interpretative enterprise (*science* approaches its object *fiction*) is thematized and contained, dramatized and satirized, within the object itself (*science fiction*). What this perhaps illustrates is the way in which the undoubtedly illuminating theoretical turns in the works of Freud, Lacan, Klein and others can too easily give rise to a kind of analytic triumphalism similar to that portrayed in *Armageddon*. Psychoanalytic interpretation tends to find *itself* in the texts it analyses. And this *finding* itself is how psychoanalysis, as an institution, *founds* itself rhetorically. According to what we should now recognize as a circular argument, its truth is an interpretation of the other. But, as Klein herself teaches, our analytic judgements of the other should rather teach us more about the phantasy of analysis itself, its projections and introjections and its positive and negative identifications.

7 The Knowledge

Concluding Remarks

The aims of this book are much more than just to introduce the ideas and arguments of a range of thinkers who have contributed to the field of Critical Theory. Rather, the book itself constitutes an argument about the need to read and re-read the key texts of the tradition as well as more contemporary works. Just as my readings of Plato and Descartes would not have been possible without recent developments, further developments in thought will also have been made possible by those re-readings. They return us all to the place of address, such that we become the new addressees of old texts and are thus transformed by the texts, which we too transform by reading in a way that addresses *our* future. In a milieu that is more than ever governed by technological thinking it will seem odd to suggest that we can develop our thought towards a still obscure future by reading ancient texts. But those texts stubbornly address us as their contemporaries, once we learn how to read them. We become more aware of the ghostly nature of our existence as historical beings. This, though, requires an effort in thinking, because there are consequences in becoming aware of the ghostly nature of our existence as historical beings. We are forced into a position of responsibility. The response must be *responsible*, that is, aware of the conditions that have constituted the texts we respond to, and responsible to those conditions. As I have suggested all along, those conditions involve something which we have no choice but to address as an absolute singularity, which means that we can neither fall back into technological methods of reading nor rely on established consensual interpretations. We must respond from the point of view of the radical alterity of the addressee. That way, Plato's address to *our* future will be assured.

Nevertheless, students of Critical Theory (within or beyond whatever school or discipline, within or beyond any university) will still ask the question: In the face of the bewildering plethora of conflicting points of view in the contemporary intellectual scene, is it possible ever to get a framework through which to understand it all? As a way of offering a qualified 'yes' in answer, I here present a simple analogy. To qualify as a taxi driver in London, England's capital city, you first have to pass a test called 'the knowledge', part of which requires you to show that you can find your way to any street in a given area and do so in the shortest possible time (showing both that you know the shortest distance and that you can avoid the known bottle-necks and so on). You must do this without the benefit of a street guide like the *A-Z*. So not only must you know where a street is but also you must be able to negotiate the hundreds of possible routes to get to it. When you first arrive, a large city is utterly bewildering, of course, but even those who have lived all their lives there keep an *A-Z* handy. Most people are comfortable with only small areas, where they live and work, to start with. And though they may know their way around beyond those areas, it is doubtful that they would know the names of many streets and likely routes to get to them without the aid of the map. Wait until a loved one or a close family member moves to an area that you don't know. Suddenly a house, the street it's in, the nearby pubs, shops and parks, the main roads on which you travel to get there, all become lodged in your consciousness for the first time with a sense of concrete and illuminated existence they could never have had just from reading the map. The London taxi driver must get to know most of the city with that sense of concrete existence.

Critical Theory challenges the newcomer with a density of areas, names and alternative routes through it, in much the same way as a city does. That is partly because it does not specify its discipline and cannot afford to ignore developments in areas that might seem foreign. You may become interested in certain aspects of the subject, certain writers even, and remain detached and aloof from others, though all that could change at a moment's notice – a chance encounter with some obscure German philosopher after picking up an intriguing reference, perhaps. The following Bibliographical Map will serve a little like a selective *A-Z* of a major city. I'll tell you how to get there but making the knowledge your own will be your responsibility.

Like all analogies, this one works only on certain levels, of course. And the notion of a map in this context is especially fraught. But my experience as an adolescent motorcycle messenger in London reminds me that I had to learn to read that *A-Z* as a musician learns the score of a symphony. As much is produced in the process of thinking – linking map to route and route to street, arriving every day at innumerable destinations and often getting lost on the way – as it is by either reading the map or acquiring knowledge of actual streets. The streets also help to illuminate the map, just as a new map, with strange emphases and inexplicable omissions, writes itself somewhere just beneath the level of consciousness. This is the map of Critical Theory, not the one I offer below in the form of a bibliography, but the one that writes itself just below consciousness as you begin to read in the bizarre cities of Critical Theory.

Bibliographical Map

The following bibliography includes each of the texts mentioned in the book and the basic works of all the writers discussed. The fields represented include all those that any curious reader in Critical Theory would want to know about. Use the following categories as a rough guide.

Continental Philosophy   Much of what is called Critical Theory in the English-speaking world involves the study of predominantly French and German thinkers. The French thinkers themselves focus to a large extent on German thinkers and each of them would acknowledge roots among the thinkers of ancient Greece. So a basic understanding of Plato and Aristotle would be useful. In addition it is worth exploring the philosophies, sometimes available only in fragments, of the pre-Socratics. Jonathan Barnes's *Early Greek Philosophy* is an indispensable source. Modern philosophy is usually understood as beginning with Descartes, and his readable *Meditations on First Philosophy* rewards detailed study. The critical tradition itself is usually regarded as beginning with Kant and his critical philosophy. Howard Caygill's *A Kant Dictionary* provides an excellent companion when reading any of Kant's works. Lewis White Beck's *Selections* contains the essential writings and has the virtue of also providing some of the early writings, which are extremely interesting. For an understanding of the tradition itself you would want to know about German Idealism and Romanticism. One of the best introductions would be G. W. F. Hegel's 'The Difference between the Systems of Fichte and Schelling', which you will find in a number of collected texts, but a particularly useful one is Allen Wood's *Selections*. Hegel's great shadow (as has often been observed) hovers over so much critical philosophy, even now, that you would probably want to know some of it first hand. The preface to *The Phenomenology of Spirit* would be a particularly useful place to start. Both Karl Marx and Friedrich Nietzsche have in different ways shaken up the tradition, both utilizing it and critiquing it, and some knowledge of these writers would be appropriate, though you will find Nietzsche in particular a challenge – albeit a provocative and entertaining one.

For the twentieth century, Husserl and Heidegger are indispensable. Husserl's *The Crisis of European Sciences* is pertinent and Heidegger's *Basic*

Writings, edited by David Farrell Krell, constitutes an excellent starting point.

No one engaging with the thought of Martin Heidegger can afford to avoid the controversy concerning his involvement with the Nazi Party in 1933 and afterwards. However, any attempt to read the philosophy with 'caution' owing to this historical association with Nazism might also represent a fall into uncritical theory. The philosophy as such – in so far as it remains philosophy in Heidegger's terms, i.e. thinking – is resolutely critical. In other words, as he maintains rather decisively in 'Letter on "Humanism"', don't look for authority in the works. The only way that a question about the legitimation of the philosophy would arise would be if it was (or anybody's thought generally was) regarded as being more or less (or in any way) authoritative. It is only on the notion of authority that you could move towards questions of qualification or disqualification. There remains little doubt, among those who read Heidegger seriously, about the importance of his work for non-dogmatic thinking. His stand (in so far as there is one) on National Socialism is a painful fact that also calls for questioning. A book edited by Thomas Sheenan called *Heidegger: The Man and the Thinker* contains texts and interviews that are helpful on this. Derrida's *Of Spirit: Heidegger and the Question* is a valuable address.

Hugh Silverman's *Continental Philosophy* collections (in Routledge) offer a wide-ranging introduction to the field as it is today. Mark C. Taylor's *Deconstruction in Context* contains a series of articles from writers after Kant that add up to a series of snapshots of the critical tradition as it relates to contemporary Critical Theory.

Critical Theory   No one working in the field today should be content without having read the work of the Frankfurt School and their associates. Theodor Adorno's writings continue to appear in translation and *The Dialectic of Enlightenment,* which he wrote with Max Horkheimer, is near enough essential reading. Martin Jay's *Adorno* is a helpful primer. The works of Walter Benjamin are also appearing in fairly thorough editions and there is a veritable industry of secondary sources. *The Essential Frankfurt School Reader* (edited by Andrew Arato and Eike Gebhardt) is a useful first step, containing selections from a wide range of authors.

Literary Theory   A large number of overviews and readers exist for anyone wanting to come to grips with twentieth-century literary theory, and there is no doubt that this field has contributed essentially to Critical Theory generally. One of the most useful introductions is by Andrew Bennett and Nicholas Royle, whose *Introduction to Literature, Criticism and Theory* offers a wide-ranging journey through literature and theory without ever falling into dogmatism or mechanical application. Peter Barry's *Beginning Theory* is another useful resource for the beginner.

Structuralism and Poststructuralism Much contemporary theory continues to refer back to the arguments and problems of structuralism and poststructuralism. The discourses in question sometimes strike us as rather old and even a little dry or abstract and there is no doubt that they have been absorbed into contemporary thought. Often, the vocabulary of poststructuralism circulates independently of the arguments it derives from so it is well worth rediscovering those arguments. One of the key writers in this respect is Roland Barthes, whose work straddles the frontier between structuralism and poststructuralism. All of his works listed in the Bibliography can be warmly recommended. Saussure's *Course in General Linguistics* remains endlessly provocative and stimulating and, like most source texts, is intrinsically interesting in itself. Jonathan Culler's *Saussure* provides a helpful overview. Terence Hawkes's *Structuralism and Semiotics* remains a quite decent commentary on early structuralism. John Sturrock's *Structuralism and Since* can also be recommended for a number of introductory articles on the key figures. Josué Harari's *Textual Strategies* and Robert Young's *Untying the Text* each collect articles that together represent a wide range of what was once regarded as 'poststructuralist' thought.

Femininst Theory An understanding of what is at stake for feminist theory is essential for understanding what is at stake in Critical Theory. Neither discourse can be subsumed in the other but both remain irreducible to any single discipline or school. In the context of Critical Theory the selections by Judith Butler, Mary Jacobus, Juliet Mitchell and Jacqueline Rose, Toril Moi, and Denise Riley can be strongly recommended.

Postmodernism For a sense of the rather indeterminate field of postmodernism you couldn't do much better than read the articles collected in Peter Brooker's *Modernism/Postmodernism*. Thomas Docherty's *Postmodernism: A Reader* will certainly help to fill out the picture. Primary texts by Fredric Jameson, Jean Baudrillard, Jean-Francois Lyotard, Gilles Deleuze and Felix Guattari would be essential.

Postcolonialism Postcolonial theory denotes a number of recent developments. To get a sense of what this implies, the reader by Patrick Williams and Laura Chrisman is the most useful. Primary texts by Edward Said, Homi Bhabha and Gayatri Spivak remain provocative and controversial, and Robert Young's *White Mythologies* and *Postcolonialism: A History* will help you to navigate.

Derrida and Deconstruction   There are a small number of fully recommendable texts on Derrida, including the following: *Deconstruction.Derrida* by Julian Wolfreys; 'Derridabase' by Geoff Bennington (in *Jacques Derrida*), and Michael Payne's *Reading Theory*. There are also three useful readers with hardly any overlap: Peggy Kamuf (ed.), *Derrida: A Reader*; Derek Attridge (ed.), *Acts of Literature*; and Julian Wolfreys (ed.), *Writing Performances: A Derrida Reader*. A collection of essays (including one by Derrida himself) about Derrida may be found in David Wood (ed.), *Derrida: A Critical Reader*. Other interesting texts about Derrida include the following: Simon Critchley, *The Ethics of Deconstruction*; Drucilla Cornell, *Philosophy of the Limit*; Rudolph Gasche, *The Tain of the Mirror*. Paul de Man's texts are both challenging and rewarding, as are those by J. Hillis Miller.

Psychoanalysis   There is such a wide range of approaches to and from within psychoanalysis that it is often difficult to know where to begin. Sue Vice's *Psychoanalytic Theory* contains a number of key essays and applications. Jacqueline Rose's *Sexuality in the Field of Vision* can be thoroughly recommended for her critical and careful readings of Lacan and Kristeva, as can her more recent *Why War?*, which includes her work on the return to Klein. To work with psychoanalysis it is, of course, essential to know the primary texts. Nearly everything by Freud is worth engaging with but *The Interpretation of Dreams* is the classic text. Penguin have produced a paperback edition in useful volumes; for Critical Theory, *On Sexuality* (Vol. 7) and *On Metapsychology* (Vol. 11) are the crucial ones. Lacan's *Seminars* are quickly becoming available in scholarly editions and his more difficult *Ecrits: A Selection* has been available for many years. There are very many useful introductions to Lacan, usually much more readable than the primary texts. Michael Payne's *Reading Theory* contains clear chapters on Lacan's *Ecrits* and Kristeva's *Revolution in Poetic Language* (as well as a commentary on Derrida's *Of Grammatology)*. Malcolm Bowie's *Lacan* and Samuel Weber's *The Return to Freud* can both be warmly recommended. Anthony Wilden's edition of Lacan's *Speech and Language in Psychoanalysis* is now quite old but it does provide an extremely clear and useful account of the (post) structuralist Lacan. Juliet Mitchell and Jacqueline Rose edit and introduce an excellent explanatory volume on the role of sexuality in Lacan's theory in their *Feminine Sexuality: Jacques Lacan and the ecole Freudienne*. The return to Klein is represented by articles collected in *Reading Melanie Klein* (edited by Lyndsey Stonebridge and John Phillips). The reference guide *par excellence* to psychoanalytic theory is J. Laplanche and J. B. Pontalis, *The Language of Psychoanalysis*.

Expository Works on Lacan   Readers of Jacques Lacan may benefit from a wide range of expository works. Lacan's texts are notoriously difficult to read but many commentaries have attempted to make them more accessible for the beginner. Elizabeth Wright's *Psychoanalytic Criticism* is a basic introduction to psychoanalysis generally and contains useful sections on Lacan. Juliet Flower-McCannell's *Figuring Lacan* is particularly useful for literature students. Elizabeth Grosz provides an introduction to Lacan in the context of the concerns of feminism. Anika Lemaire's *Jacques Lacan* is a relatively early, broadly structuralist, account. Ellie Ragland-Sullivan and Mark Bracher edit a collection of useful explanatory essays in *Lacan and the Subject of Language*. William J. Richardson's 'Lacan and Non-Philosophy' (in Hugh J. Silverman, ed.) is very good on Lacan's relation to philosophy. For a slightly more advanced introduction to Lacan via the problem of agency in a postmodern world, Slavoj Žižek's *The Sublime Object of Ideology* can be recommended.

Bibliography

Adorno, Theodor. (1973a) *The Jargon of Authenticty*. Trans. Knut Tarnowski and Frederic Will. London: Routledge.

— (1973b) *Negative Dialectics*. Trans. E. B. Ashton. New York: Seabury Press.

— (1974) *Minima Moralia: Reflections from Damaged Life*. Trans. E. F. N. Jephcott. London: New Left Books.

— (1984) *Aesthetic Theory*. Trans. C. Lenhardt. London: Routledge.

— (1989) *Kierkegaard: Construction of the Aesthetic*. Trans. and ed. Robert Hullot-Kentor. Minneapolis: University of Minnesota Press.

— (1991–92) *Notes on Literature* (2 vols). Trans. Shierry Weber Nicholsen. Ed. Rolf Tiedemann. New York: Columbia University Press.

— (1993) *Hegel: Three Studies*. Trans. Shierry Weber Nicholsen. Cambridge, MA: MIT Press.

— (1994) *The Stars Down to Earth and Other Essays on the Irrational in Culture*. Ed. Stephen Crook. London and New York: Routledge.

Aquinas, Thomas. (1952) *The Summa Theologica*. Trans. Fathers of the English Dominican Province. Chicago: William Benton

Arato, Andrew and Eike Gebhardt (eds). (1998) *The Essential Frankfurt School Reader*. New York: Continuum.

Aristotle. (1941) *The Basic Works of Aristotle*. Ed. Richard McKeon. New York: Random House.

— (1956) *De Interpretatone*. Ed. L. Minio-Paluello. Oxford: Oxford Classical Texts.

— (1994) *Nichomachean Ethics*. Ed. I. Bywater. Oxford: Oxford Classical Texts.

Attridge, Derek (ed.). (1992) *Acts of Literature*. London: Routledge.

Barnes, Jonathan. (1987) *Early Greek Philosophy*. Harmondsworth: Penguin.

Barry, Peter. (1995) *Beginning Theory*. Manchester: Manchester University Press.

Barthes, Roland. (1967) *Elements of Semiology*. Trans. Annette Lavers. London: Jonathan Cape.

— (1972) *Mythologies*. Trans. Annette Lavers. London: Jonathan Cape.

— (1977) *Image, Music, Text*. Trans. Stephen Heath. London: Fontana.

— (1990a) *The Pleasure of the Text*. Trans. Richard Miller. Oxford: Blackwell.

— (1990b) *S/Z*. Trans. Richard Miller. Oxford: Blackwell.

Baudrillard, Jean. (1988) *Selected Writings*. Ed. Mark Poster. Cambridge: Polity Press.

Beardsworth, Richard. (1996) *Derrida and the Political*. London: Routledge.

Benjamin, Andrew. (1997) *Present Hope: Philosophy, Architecture, Judaism*. London: Routledge.

Benjamin, Walter. (1969) *Illuminations*. Trans. Harry Zohn. Ed. Hannah Arendt. New York: Schocken.

— (1973a) *Charles Baudelaire: A Lyric Poet in the Era of High Capitalism*. Trans. Harry Zohn. London: Verso.

— (1973b) *Understanding Brecht*. Trans. Anne Bostack. London: Verso.

— (1977) *The Origin of German Tragic Drama*. Trans. John Osborne. London: Verso.

— (1979) *One Way Street and Other Writings*. Trans. Edmund Jephcott and Kingsley Shorter. London: Verso.

Bennett, Andrew and Nicholas Royle. (1999) *Introduction to Literature, Criticism and Theory* (2nd edn). London: Prentice Hall.

Bennington, Geoffrey and Jacques Derrida. (1993) 'Derridabase', in *Jacques Derrida*. Trans. Geoffrey Bennington. Chicago: University of Chicago Press.

Bennington, Geoffrey. (1994) *Legislations: The Politics of Deconstruction*. London: Verso.

— (1996) 'X.' *Applying: To Derrida*. Ed. John Brannigan, Ruth Robbins and Julian Wolfreys. London: Macmillan.

Bhabha, Homi. (1996) *The Location of Culture*. London: Routledge.

— (ed.). (1994) *Nation and Narration*. London: Routledge.

Blake, William. (1989) *Blake: The Complete Poems* (2nd edn). Ed. W. H. Stevenson. London: Longman.

Bowie, Malcolm. (1991) *Lacan*. London: Fontana.

Boyne, Roy. (1990) *Foucault and Derrida: The Other Side of Reason*. London: Unwin Hyman.

Brooker, Peter. (1998) *A Dictionary of Cultural Theory*. London: Macmillan.

— (ed.). (1992) *Modernism/Postmodernism*. London: Longman.

Burgin, Victor, James Donald and Cora Kaplan (eds). (1989) *Formations of Fantasy*. London: Routledge.

Butler, Judith. (1993) *Bodies That Matter: On the Discursive Limits of Sex*. New York: Routledge.

— (1997a) *Excitable Speech: A Politics of the Performative*. New York: Routledge.

— (1997b) *The Psychic Life of Power: Theories in Subjection*. Stanford, CA: Stanford University Press.

Carroll, David. (1987) *Parasthetics: Foucault, Lyotard, Derrida*. London: Methuen.

Caygill, Howard. (1995) *A Kant Dictionary*. Oxford: Blackwell.

Cornell, Drucilla. (1992) *Philosophy of the Limit*. London: Routledge.

Critchley, Simon. (1993) *The Ethics of Deconstruction*. Indiana: Indiana University Press.

Culler, Jonathan. (1974) *Structuralist Poetics*. Ithaca: Cornell University Press.

— (1975) *Ferdinand de Saussure*. Harmondsworth: Penguin.

— (1976) *Saussure*. Hassocks: Harvester Press.

— (1981) *The Pursuit of Signs*. London: Routledge.

Deleuze, Gilles. (1993) *Difference and Repetition*. Trans. Paul Patton. London: Athlone.

Deleuze, Gilles and Felix Guattari. (1984) *Anti-Oedipus: Capitalism and Schizophrenia*. Trans. Helen R. Lane and Robert Hurley. London: Athlone.

— (1987) *A Thousand Plateaus: Capitalism and Schizophrenia*. Trans. Brian Massumi. Minneapolis: University of Minnesota Press.

— (1996) *What is Philosophy?* Trans. Graham Burchell and Hugh Tomlinson. London: Routledge.

de Man, Paul. (1979) *Allegories of Reading: Figural Language in Rousseau, Nietzsche, Rilke, and Proust*. New Haven, CT: Yale University Press.

— (1983) *Blindness and Insight: Essays in the Rhetoric of Contemporary Criticism* (2nd edn). London: Methuen.

Derrida, Jacques. (1973) *Speech and Phenomena and Other Essays on Husserl's Theory of Signs*. Trans. David. B. Allison. Evanston, NJ: Northwestern University Press.

— (1974) *Of Grammatology* Trans. Gayatri Chakravorty Spivak. Baltimore: Johns Hopkins University Press.

— (1978) *Edmund Husserl's 'Origin of Geometry': An Introduction*. Trans. John P. Leavey. Ed. David B. Allison. Stoney Brook: Nicholas Hays.

— (1979a) *Spurs: Nietzsche's Styles*. Trans. Barbara Harlow. Chicago: University of Chicago Press.

— (1979b) 'Living on/Borderlines', trans. James Hulbert, in *Deconstruction and Criticism*. Ed. Harold Bloom et al. New York: Seabury Press.

— (1980) *Writing and Difference*. Trans. Alan Bass. London: Routledge.

— (1981) *Disseminations*. Trans. Barbara Johnson. Chicago: University of Chicago Press.

— (1984) 'My Chances/*Mes Chances*: A Rendezvous with some Epicurean Stereophonies', trans. Irene Harvey and Avital Ronell, in *Taking Chances: Derrida, Psychoanalysis and Literature*. Ed. Joseph Smith and William Kerrigan. Baltimore: Johns Hopkins University Press.

— (1987a) *Positions*. Trans. Alan Bass. London: Athlone.

— (1987b) *The Post Card: From Socrates to Freud and Beyond*. Trans. Alan Bass. Chicago: University of Chicago Press.

— (1987c) *The Truth in Painting*. Trans Geoff Bennington. Chicago: University of Chicago Press.

— (1988) *Margins of Philosophy*. Trans. Alan Bass. Brighton: Harvester.

— (1989) *Of Spirit: Heidegger and the Question*. Trans. Geoffrey Bennington and Rachel Bowlby. Chicago: University of Chicago Press.

— (1992) *The Other Heading: Reflections on Today's Europe*. Trans. Pascale-Anne Brault and Michael B. Naas. Bloomington: Indiana University Press.

— (1993a) *Aporias*. Trans. Thomas Dutoit. Stanford, CA: Stanford University Press.

— (1993b) *Memoirs of the Blind*. Trans. Pascale-Anne Brault and Michael Naas. Chicago: University of Chicago Press.

— (1994) *Specters of Marx: The State of the Debt, the Work of Mourning and the New International*. Trans. Peggy Kamuf. London: Routledge.

— (1995a) *The Gift of Death*. Trans. David Wills. Chicago: University of Chicago Press.

— (1995b) *On the Name*. Trans. David Wood, John P. Leavey Jr and Ian McKleod. Ed. Thomas Dutoit. Stanford, CA: Stanford University Press.

— (1996) *The Politics of Friendship*. Trans. George Collins. London: Verso.

— (1997) *Deconstruction in a Nutshell: A Conversation with Jacques Derrida*. Ed. John D. Caputo. New York: Fordham University Press.

— (1998) *Resistances*. Trans. Peggy Kamuf, Pascale-Anne Brault and Michael Naas. Stanford, CA: Stanford University Press.

Derrida, Jacques and Peter Eisenman. (1997) *Chora L Works*. New York: Monacelli Press.

Descartes, René. (1985) *The Philosophical Writings of Descartes, Vols I and II*. Trans. John Cottingham, Robert Stroothoff and Dugald Murdoch. Cambridge: Cambridge University Press.

— (1992) *Meditations metaphysiques*. Ed. Jean-Marie Beyssade and Michelle Beyssade. Paris: Flammarion.

Docherty, Thomas (ed.). (1993) *Postmodernism: A Reader*. Hemel Hempstead: Harvester.

Eagleton, Terry. (1996) *Literary Theory* (2nd edn). Oxford: Blackwell.

Flower-McCannell, Juliet. (1986) *Figuring Lacan*. London: Routledge.

Foucault, Michel. (1970) *The Order of Things: An Archeology of the Human Sciences*. New York: Random House.

— (1979) *Discipline and Punish: The Birth of the Prison*. Trans. Alan Sheridan. New York. Vintage.

Felman, Shoshana. (1988) 'On Reading Poetry: Reflections on the Limits and Possibilities of Psychoanalytic Approaches', in Muller and Richardson (eds).

Fenves, Peter (ed.) (1993) *Raising the Tone of Philosophy: Late Essays by Immanuel Kant, Transformative Critique by Jacques Derrida*. Baltimore: Johns Hopkins University Press.

Freud, Sigmund. (1953–73) *The Standard Edition of the Complete Psychological Works of Sigmund Freud* (24 vols). London: Hogarth Press.

— (1973) *Introductory Lectures on Psychoanalysis*. The Pelican Freud Vol. 1. Harmondsworth: Penguin.

— (1974) *Studies on Hysteria*. The Pelican Freud Vol. 3. Harmondsworth: Penguin.

— (1976) *The Interpretation of Dreams*. The Pelican Freud Vol. 4. Harmondsworth: Penguin.

— (1977a) *On Sexuality*. The Pelican Freud Vol. 7. Harmondsworth: Penguin.

— (1977b) *On Metapsychology*. The Pelican Freud Vol. 11. Harmondsworth: Penguin. (1978) *On Art and Literature*. The Pelican Freud Vol. 14. Harmondsworth: Penguin.

Frosh, Stephen. (1985) *The Politics of Psychoanalysis*. London: Macmillan.

Gasche, Rudolph. (1988) *The Tain of the Mirror*. Cambridge, MA: Harvard University Press.

— (1994) *Inventions of Difference: On Jacques Derrida*. Cambridge, MA: Harvard University Press.

Green, Henry. (1978) *Loving. Living. Party Going*. Harmondsworth: Penguin.

Grosz, Elizabeth. (1990) *Jacques Lacan: A Feminist Introduction*. London: Routledge.

Hamilton, Paul. (1996) *Historicism*. London: Routledge.

Harari, Josué V. (ed.). (1979) *Textual Strategies: Perspectives in Poststructuralist Criticism*. London: Methuen.

Hawkes, Terence. (1977) *Structuralism and Semiotics*. London: Methuen.

Hegel, G. W. F. (1969) *Science of Logic*. Trans. A. V. Miller. London: Allen and Unwin.

— (1975) *Hegel's Aesthetics: Lectures on Fine Art*. Trans. T. M. Knox. Oxford: Oxford University Press.

— (1978) *Phenomenology of Spirit* [1807]. Trans. A. V. Miller. Oxford: Oxford University Press.

— (1989) *Selections*. Ed. Allen Wood. London: Macmillan.

— (1991) *Elements of the Philosophy of Right*. Trans. H. B. Nisbet. Ed. Allen Wood. Cambridge: Cambridge University Press.

— (1994) *Introductory Lectures on Aesthetics*. Trans. Bernard Bosanquet. Harmondsworth: Penguin.

Heidegger, Martin. (1962a) *Being and Time*. Trans. J. Macquarrie and E. Robinson. New York: Harper and Row.

— (1962b) *Kant and the Problem of Metaphysics*. Trans. James Churchill. Bloomington: Indiana University Press.

— (1968) *What is Called Thinking?* Trans. J. G. Gray. New York: Harper and Row.

— (1971) *Poetry, Language, Thought*. Trans. Albert Hofstadter. New York: Harper and Row.

— (1972) *On Time and Being*. Trans. J. Stambaugh. New York: Harper and Row.

— (1975) *Early Greek thinking*. Trans. D. F. Krell and F. A. Capuzzi. New York: Harper and Row.

— (1977a) *The Question Concerning Technology and Other Essays*. Trans. W. Lovitt. New York: Harper and Row.

— (1977b) *Basic Writings*. Ed. David Farrell Krell. London: Routledge.

— (1993) *Basic Concepts*. Trans. Gary Aylesworth. Bloomington: Indiana University Press.

— (1996) *Basic Writings* (2nd edn). Ed. D. F. Krell. London: Routledge.

— (1998) *Pathmarks*. Ed. William McNeill. Cambridge: Cambridge University Press.

Horkheimer, Max and Theodor Adorno. (1979) *Dialectic of Enlightenment*. Trans. John Cumming. London: Verso.

Husserl, Edmund. (1954) *The Crisis of European Sciences and Transcendental Phenomenology*. Trans. David Carr. Evanston, NJ: Northwestern University Press.

— (1962) *Ideas: General Introduction to Pure Phenomenology*. Trans. W. R. Boyce Gibson. New York: Collier Books.

— (1988) *Cartesian Meditations: An Introduction to Phenomenology*. Trans. Dorion Cairns. Dordrecht. Martinus Nijhoff.

Jacobus, Mary. (1986) *Reading Woman: Essays in Feminist Criticism*. London: Methuen.

Jakobson, Roman. (1960) 'Closing Statement: Linguistics and Poetics', in *Style in Language*. Ed. Thomas A. Sebeok. Cambridge: MIT.

— (1987) 'Two Aspects of Language and Two Types of Aphasic Disturbances', in *Language in Literature*. Ed. Krystyna Pomorska and Stephan Rudy. Cambridge, MA: Belknap Press.

Jameson, Fredric. (1992) *Postmodernism, Or, the Cultural Logic of Late Capitalism*. Durham, NC: Duke University Press.

Jay, Martin. (1984) *Adorno*. Cambridge, MA: Harvard University Press.

Joyce, James. (1955) *A Portrait of the Artist as a Young Man*. Harmondsworth: Penguin.

Judovitz, Dalia. (1988) *Subjectivity and Representation in Descartes: The Origin of Modernity*. Cambridge: Cambridge University Press.

Kamuf, Peggy. (1988) *Signature Pieces: On the Institution of Authority*. Ithaca, NY: Cornell University Press.

— (ed.). (1992) *Derrida: A Reader*. Hemel Hempstead: Harvester.

Kant, Immanuel. (1987) *Critique of Judgement*. Trans. Werner S. Pluhar. Indianapolis: Hackett.

— (1988) *Selections*. Ed. Lewis White Beck. London: Macmillan.

— (1995) *Political Writings*. Ed. Trans. H. B. Nisbet. Ed. Hans Reiss. Cambridge: Cambridge University Press.

— (1996) *Practical Philosophy*. Trans. Mary J. Gregor. Cambridge: Cambridge University Press.

— (1998) *The Critique of Pure Reason*. Trans. Mary J. Gregor. Cambridge: Cambridge University Press.

Klein, Melanie. (1986) *The Selected Melanie Klein*. Ed. Juliet Mitchell. Harmondsworth: Penguin.

Klein, Melanie. (1988a) *Envy and Gratitude*. London: Virago.

— (1988b) *Love, Guilt and Reparation and Other Works*. London:Virago.

Kofman, Sarah. (1990) *Freud and Fiction*. Oxford: Blackwell.

Krafft-Ebing, Richard von. (1965) *Psychopathia Sexualis*. Trans. Harry E. Wedeck. New York: Putnam.

Kristeva, Julia. (1985) *The Kristeva Reader*. Ed. Toril Moi. Oxford: Blackwell.

— (1991) *Strangers to Ourselves*. Trans. Leon Roudiez. Hemel Hempstead: Harvester.

Lacan, Jacques. (1968) *Speech and Language in Psychoanalysis*. Trans. with Notes and Commentary by Anthony Wilden. Baltimore: Johns Hopkins University Press.

— (1977a) 'The Mirror Stage as Formative of the Function of the I as revealed in Psychoanalytic Experience' and 'The Agency of the Letter in the Unconscious: or Reason Since Freud', in *Ecrits*.

— (1977b) *Ecrits: A Selection*. Trans. Alan Sheridan. London: Tavistock.

— (1986) *Seminar XI: Four Fundamental Concepts of Psychoanalysis*. Trans. Alan Sheridan. Harmondsworth: Penguin.

— (1987a) *Seminar I. Freud's Papers on Technique*. Cambridge: Cambridge University Press.

— (1987b) *Seminar VII: Ethics*. Cambridge: Cambridge University Press.

Lane, Christopher. (1995) *The Ruling Passion: British Colonial Allegory and the Paradox of British Homosexual Desire*. Durham, NC: Duke University Press.

Laplanche, J. and J.-B. Pontalis. (1973) *The Language of Psychoanalysis*. London: Hogarth Press.

Leach, Edmund. (1989) *Lévi-Strauss*. Chicago: University of Chicago Press.

Lechte, John. (1994) *Fifty Key Contemporary Thinkers: From Structuralism to Postmodernity*. London: Routledge.

Lemaire, Anika. (1979) *Jacques Lacan*. London: Routledge.

Lévi-Strauss, Claude. (1966) *The Savage Mind*. Chicago: University of Chicago Press.

— (1968) *Structural Anthropology Vols I and II*. Trans. Claire Jacobson and Brooke Grundfest Schoepf. London: Allen Lane.

Loomba, Ania. (1998) *Colonialism/Postcolonialism*. London: Routledge.

Lyotard, Jean-Francois. (1984) *The Postmodern Condition: A Report on Knowledge*. Trans. Geoff Bennington and Brian Massumi. Manchester: Manchester University Press.

— (1985a) *Just Gaming*. Trans. Vlad Godzich. Manchester: Manchester University Press.

— (1985b) *The Postmodern Condition: A Report on Knowledge*. Trans. Brian Massumi. Minneapolis: University of Minnesota Press.

— (1988) *The Differend: Phrases in Dispute*. Trans. Georges Van Den Abbeele. Manchester: Manchester University Press.

The Lyotard Reader. (1989) Ed. Andrew Benjamin. Oxford: Blackwell.

Marks, Elaine and Isabelle de Courtirvon (eds). (1990) *New French Feminisms: An Anthology*. Amherst: University of Massachusetts Press.

Marx, Karl. (1967) *Capital*. Vol. 1. Trans. Samuel Moore and Edvard Aveling. Ed. Frederick Engels. New York: International.

— (1970) *The German Ideology*. Trans. W. Lough, C. Dutt and C. P. Magill. Ed. C. J. Arthur. London: Lawrence and Wishart.

— (1973) *Surveys From Exile: Political Writings*. Ed. David Fernbach. Harmondsworth: Penguin.

Marx, Karl and Frederick Engels. (1969) *Selected Works Vol. 1*. Trans. W. Lough. Moscow: Progress Publishers.

Mehlman, Jeffrey. (1981) 'Trimethylamin: Notes of Freud's Specimen Dream', in *Untying the Text*. Ed. Robert Young. London: Routledge.

Meltzer, Donald. (1978) *The Kleinian Development*. Perthshire: Clunie Press.

Miller, J Hillis. (1987) *The Ethics of Reading: Kant, de Man, Eliot, Trollope, James and Benjamin*. New York: Columbia University Press.

— (1995) *Topographies*. Stanford, CA: Stanford University Press.

Mitchell, Juliet and Jacqueline Rose (eds). (1982) *Feminine Sexuality: Jacques Lacan and the ecole Freudienne*. London: Macmillan.

Moi, Toril. (1985) *Sexual/Textual Politics: Feminist Literary Theory*. London: Routledge.

Muller, John and William J. Richardson (eds). (1988) *The Purloined Poe: Lacan, Derrida and Psychoanalytic Reading*. Baltimore: Johns Hopkins University Press.

Nietzsche, Friedrich. (1968) *The Will to Power*. Trans. Walter Kaufmann. New York: Random House.

— (1986) 'On Truth and Lie in an Extra-Moral Sense', in Taylor (ed.).

— (1995) *On the Genealogy of Morality*. Ed. Kieth Ansell-Pearson. Cambridge: Cambridge University Press.

Payne, Michael. (1993) *Reading Theory*. Oxford: Blackwell.

— (1996) *Reading Knowledge: Barthes, Foucault and Althusser*. Oxford: Blackwell.

— (ed.) (1995) *Encyclopaedia of Critical and Cultural Theory*. Oxford: Blackwell.

Plato. (1961) *The Collected Dialogues of Plato*. Ed. Edith Hamilton and Huntingdon Cairnes. Princeton, NJ: Princeton University Press.

Ragland-Sullivan, Ellie and Mark Bracher (eds). (1991) *Lacan and the Subject of Language*. London: Routledge.

Richardson, William J. (1988) 'Lacan and Non-Philosophy', in *Philosophy and Non-Philosophy Since Merleau-Ponty*. Ed. Hugh J. Silverman. London: Routledge.

Riley, Denise. (1988) *'Am I that Name?': Feminism and the Category of 'Women' in History*. London: Macmillan.

Rose, Jacqueline. (1979) *Sexuality in the Field of Vision*. London: Verso.

— (1993) *Why War?* Oxford: Blackwell.

Rousseau, Jean-Jacques. (1997) *The Social Contract and Other Later Political Writings*. Trans. and ed. Victor Gourevitch. Cambridge: Cambridge University Press.

Said, Edward. (1978) *Orientalism*. London: Routledge.

— (1993) *Culture and Imperialism*. London: Chatto and Windus.

Saussure, Ferdinand de. (1978) *Course in General Linguistics*. Ed. Charles Bally and Albert Sechehaye in collaboration with Albert Reidlinger. Trans. Wade Baskin. London: Collins.

Sheenan, Thomas. (1981) *Heidegger: The Man and the Thinker*. Chicago: Precedent.

Silverman Hugh. (1987) *Continental Philosophy*. London. Routledge.

Skura, Meredith Anne. (1981) *The Literary Use of the Psychoanalytic Process*. New Haven: Yale University Press.

Spivak, Gayatri. (1987) *In Other Worlds: Essays in Cultural Politics*. London: Methuen.

— (1991) *The Postcolonial Critic: Interviews, Strategies Dialogues*. Ed. Sarah Harasym. London: Routledge.

— (1996) *The Spivac Reader: Selected Works of Gayatri Chakravorty Spivak*. Ed. Donna Landry. London: Routledge.

Stonebridge, Lyndsey and John Phillips (eds). (1998) *Reading Melanie Klein*. London: Routledge.

Sturrock, John (ed.). (1980) *Structuralism and Since*. Oxford: Oxford University Press.

Taylor, Mark C. (ed.). (1986) *Deconstruction in Context: Literature and Philosophy*. Chicago: University of Chicago Press.

Vice, Sue. (1994) *Psychoanalytic Theory*. Cambridge: Polity Press.

Weber, Samuel. (1982) *The Legend of Freud*. Minneapolis: University of Minnesota Press.

— (1992) *The Return to Freud: Jacques Lacan and the Dislocations of Psychoanalysis*. Cambridge: Cambridge University Press.

Williams, Patrick and Laura Chrisman. (1993) *Colonial Discourse and Postcolonial Theory: A Reader*. Hemel Hempstead: Harvester, .

Williams, Raymond. (1976) *Keywords: A Vocabulary of Culture and Society*. London: Fontana.

Wittgenstein, Ludwig. (1958) *Philosophical Investigations*. Trans. G. E. M. Anscombe. New York: Macmillan.

— (1961) *Tractatus Logico-Philosophicus*. Trans. D. F. Pears and B. F. McGuiness. New York: Humanities Press.

Wolfreys, Julian. (1998) *Deconstruction. Derrida*. London: Macmillan.

— (ed.). (1998) *Writing Performances: A Derrida Reader*. Bloomington: Indiana University Press.

Wood, David (ed.). (1992) *Derrida: A Critical Reader*. Oxford: Blackwell.

Wright, Elizabeth. (1998) *Psychoanalytic Criticism: A Reappraisal* (3rd edn). Cambridge: Polity Press.

Young, Robert. (1990) *White Mythologies: Writing History and the West*. London: Routledge.

— (1995) *Colonial Desire: Hybridity in Theory, Culture and Race*. London: Routledge.

— (1999) *Postcolonialism: A History*. Oxford: Blackwell.

— (1981) (ed.) *Untying the Text: A Poststructuralist Reader*. London: Routledge.

Žižek, Slavoj. (1989) *The Sublime Object of Ideology*. London: Verso.

Index

Un/Settled Multiculturalisms: Diasporas, Entanglements, Transruptions

Edited by Barnor Hesse

This anthology reconsiders the meanings of multiculturalism in the West. In introducing a new conceptual language, the volume stresses the importance of distinguishing between the multicultural as a signifier of the unsettled meanings of cultural differences, and multiculturalism as the signfied of attempts to 'fix' their meaning in national imaginaries. The book also casts the debates about multiculturalism in the contexts of globalization, post-colonialism and what Barnor Hesse calls 'multicultural transruptions' – which he sees as resurgent, irrepressible multicultural issues.

This book is divided into two parts. The first considers a variety of diaspora formations, examines their impact on how cultural differences are lived and poses questions about Western societies. The second part focuses on media constructions of the 'Asian Gang' in Britain, gender and sexuality in 'ragga music', and the ambivalences of Black/White identities in post-Apartheid South Africa. The contributors explore the consequences of understanding cultural identities as cross-cut by other identities and entangled with wider social issues.

The conclusion by Professor Stuart Hall makes a timely reassessment of the multicultural question for the social cohesiveness and political future of liberal democracies.

'A provocative collection that unsettles precisely those issues too readily taken for granted, renewing the vigor of multicultural debates in genuinely original and productive ways. Thinking through the multicultural at this juncture cannot avoid taking up this text.' *Professor David Theo Goldberg*

November 2000
Cultural Studies
Hb 1 85649 559 0 £49.95 $69.95
Pb 1 85649 560 4 £15.95 $25.00
288 Notes Bibliography Index

Arguing with the Phallus: Feminist, Queer and Postcolonial Theory: A Psychoanalytic Contribution

Jan Campbell, School of Cultural and Community Studies,
University of Sussex

'A subtle, well-informed and lucid bringing-together of strands of psycho-analysis that have been kept apart for too long.' *Professor Andrew Samuels, University of Essex*

'A remarkable achievement, as much for its engagement with an astonishing range of debates within and beyond psychoanalysis, as for its impassioned commitment to feminist, queer and postcolonial politics ...' *Steve Pile, senior lecturer, Faculty of Social Sciences, Open University*

'Jan Campbell has made a bold intervention in a rich and complex area of debate. *Arguing with the Phallus* is argumentative in the best sense, scrupulous in its dealings with the work of other theorists while making its own powerful case ...' *Professor Pete Nicholls, University of Sussex*

What can psychoanalysis offer contemporary arguments in the fields of femin-ism, queer theory and postcolonialism? Jan Campbell introduces and analyses the way that psychoanalysis has developed and made problematic models of subjectivivy linked to issues or sexuality, ethnicity, gender and history. Via discussions of such influential and diverse figures as Lacan, Irigaray, Kristeva, Dollimore, Bhabha, Toni Morrison and Alice Walker, Campbell uses psycho-analysis as a mediatory tool in a range of debates across the human sciences, whilst also arguing for a transformation of psychoanalytic theory itself. Alert to the issues at stake in either a wholesale acceptance or rejection of psycho-analysis, Campbell offers the possibility of a renegotiated interpretation of the symbolic system as a necessary and valuable intervention in cultural theory.

Women's Studies/Cultural Studies/Literary Theory/Psychoanalysis
Hb 1 85649 443 8 £45.00 / $65.00
Pb 1 85649 444 6 £14.95 / $22.50
256pp

Travel Writing and Empire: Postcolonial Theory in Transit

Edited by Steve Clark, Visiting Fellow, School of Advanced Study, University of London

Travel writing has become central to postcolonial studies; this book provides a comprehensive introduction to the genre. It combines detailed evaluations of major contemporary models of analysis – new historicism, travelling theory, and post-colonial studies – with a series of specific studies detailing the complicity of the genre with a history of violent incursion. These explore:

- 'othering' discourses – of cannibalism and infanticide
- the production of colonial knowledge – geographic, medicinal, zoological
- the role of sexual anxiety in the construction of the gendered, travelling body
- the interplay between imperial and domestic spheres
- reappropriation of alien discourse by indigenous cultures

The book resists the temptation to think in terms of a simple monolithic Eurocentrism and offers a more complex reading of texts produced before, during and after periods of imperial ascendency. In doing so, it provides a more nuanced account of the hegemonic functions of travel-writing.

Hb 1 85649 627 9 £45.00 / $65.00
Pb 1 85649 628 7 £14.95 / $23.50
224pp
Index Notes Bibliography

Writing the Environment: Ecocriticsm and Literature

Edited by Richard Kerridge and Neil Sammells, Bath College
of Higher Education

The contemporary environmental crisis asks fundamental questions about culture. Like other radical critiques, environmentalism cuts across academic boundaries and offers a major challenge to existing cultural and political divisions. This is the first book to draw together the rich variety of environmentalist positions – from ecofeminism to deep ecology – and theorize their contribution to critical theory, literature and popular culture.

The first part of the book examines theoretical controversies in environmentalist literary criticism. Contributors explore a wide variety of issues including sexual politics and nature, the link between environmental and cultural degradation, the influence of Heidegger on environmentalism, and the degree of continuity between poststructuralist theory and ecological perspectives. Part two presents a green rereading of literary history, including chapters on the manipulation of natural phenomena as a vehicle of social control, 'nature poetry' as political intervention, and *fin de siècle* exotic fiction as an expression of the colonialist's conception of 'jungle country' and Otherness in general. The book concludes by looking at contemporary culture: from poetry to children's books, including an analysis of television nature programmes.

Cultural Studies/Environment/Literary Theory
Hb 1 85649 429 2 £45.00 $65.00
Pb 1 85649 430 6 £14.95 $25.00
256pp Index Metric demy